GURKHALI MANUAL

GURKHALI MANUAL

G. W. P. MONEY

THIRD EDITION

GYAN

Published by

Gyan Publishing House
5, Ansari Road
Daryaganj, New Delhi-110002
Phone: 011-47034999, 9811692060
E-mail: books@gyanbooks.com

Distribution Network
gyanbooks.com
India, USA, Canada, UK, Australia, France

ISBN : 978-81-212-4411-4 (PB)
First Published, 1917

2nd Impression 2020

Printed at: Gyan Press, Delhi.

Gurkhali Manual
Author: G. W. P. Money

FOREWORD TO THE FIRST EDITION

SINCE joining a Gurkha Regiment, I in common with others have found the scarcity of books on Khaskura a great disadvantage to the study of the language. For some years I have been collecting notes for myself and I have now embodied these notes in a small book at the instigation of some of my friends, in the hope that they may be of use to officers joining Gurkha regiments.

I have not touched on Limbu or Raikura, and men from Eastern Nepal will probably use different Khaskura words to those which are shown here. The words in this vocabulary are all used by men of Central Nepal, from where the bulk of Gurkhas in our army are recruited.

I fear mistakes will be found, especially in the Gurungkura, because this dialect is difficult to write, as the pronunciation is intricate and many words appear identical.

Further, the dialect differs in different parts of the country. For instance, certain Gurungs from Lamjung call a bone "nogri," while a Gurung from Kaski speaks of it as "riba," and in all probability will have no clearer idea of what a "nogri" is than the Sultan of Turkey or Henry the VIII.

I do not think intricacies of grammar and syntax are necessary for officers talking to Gurkha ranks, and so I have not included them in this book.

In every cantonment there is a "line bāt," or local argot, which does not come into the province of these notes, and every regiment has its own translation for such words as "plain clothes," "night duties," etc.

In conclusion, I should like to express my thanks to many Gurkha ranks whose patience has enabled me to draw up these notes, and I would also like to thank in anticipation many officers, with a better knowledge of the language than myself, for the corrections and criticisms which I hope they will send, to enable me to improve this small book which I now place with diffidence in the hands of the printers.

April, 1917.

CONTENTS

THE ALPHABET

This is just the same as the Deva Nagri:—

VOWELS.

(*a*) Initial or after a vowel.

अ	आ	इ	ई	उ	ऊ	ऋ	ॠ	ऌ	ॡ	ए	ऐ	ओ	औ	अं	अः
a	ā	i	ī	u	ū	ri	rī	liri	liri	e	*ai*	o	au	ang	aha

(ri, rī, liri, liri: these do not often occur.)

(*b*) Medial or final forms.

ा ि ी ो ौ ं ः

as in

का	कि	की	कु	कू	के	कै	को	कौ	कं	कः
kā	ki	kī	ku	kū	ke	kai	ko	kau	kang	kaha

(also क — ka)

Note.—The vowel i (ि) is written *before* the letter it comes after. In English Gurkhali Vocabulary long *a* and long *i* are marked, short *a* and *i* are unmarked, short *a* being pronounced as the *u* in b*u*n b*u*t, etc , and long *a* as the *a* in f*a*ther.

CONSONANTS.

क	ख	ग	घ	ङ	च	छ	ज	झ	ञ
k	kh	g	gh	ñ	ch	chh	j or z	jh	ṅ
ट	ठ	ड	ढ	ण	त	थ	द	ध	न
ṭ	th	ḍ	ḍh	ṇ	t	th	d	dh	n

प	फ	ब	भ	म	य	र	ल	व	श	ष	ह	क्ष	त्र	ज्ञ
p	ph	b	bh	m	y	r	l	w	sh	kh or sh	h	chhe	tra	gna

Note—b is written व not ब often in Nepal and *w* if written ब्व.

Compound letters are made by joining singles together, omitting part of one (usually the first one) or both:—

क्ख	क्य	क्त	ख्व	ग्ध	ग्न	ग्व	त्व	प्प	ट्ट	श्ल	व्य
kkh	ky	kt	khw	gdh	gn	gw	tw	pp	ṭṭ	shl	wy

ष्ठ	प्ल	प्य	न्त	न्ध	ब्ब	ब्ज	द्म	द्य	द्व	द्ग
shṭh	pl	py	nt	ndh	bb	bj	dma	dya	dwa	dga

Dative.—This is only used as a dative. To a place is the locative case.

Agent.—This is used as the Urdu *ne.* It is also used in the Instrumental sense : With a pen, Kalam le.

Locative.—Other meanings besides " in " are—into, on, among; at or to (a place).

Other postpositions can be used, *e.g.*, Chhoro sita, with a son.

Article.—There is no article such as the English " a " or "the.' When the sense requires an article the following are used :—

Yotā, one ; koi, some ; yo, this ; tyo, that.

Gender.—Only feminine objects are feminine. They are declined exactly the same as above. The feminine is formed from the masculine as follows :—

(1) If the masculine ends in a consonant, add ī.

(2) If ,, ,, ,, vowel, add nī.

This is the general rule. There are several exceptions, notably :—

Chhoro, son ; chhori, daughter. Rājā king ; rāni, queen. Ghorā, horse ; ghorī, mare. Kukur, dog ; kukurni, bitch.

THE ADJECTIVE AND NUMERALS.

The adjective precedes the noun it qualifies. It is declined precisely as the noun above. A few general rules as to the change of an adjective for the feminine may be noted ; there are many exceptions to them though, and they are often incorrectly used in conversation.

Adjectives ending in a consonant do not change at all.

Adjectives ending in *a* or *o* change this vowel into *i* for the feminine, and those ending in *o* change the *o* into *a* for the masc. plural.

Adjectives ending in other vowels add *ni* for the feminine.

Comparison.—This is formed by the word " bhandā," than ; " dekhi " is also sometimes used instead of " bhandā." The adjective does not change at all.

Comparative.—Simply "bhandā" (or "dekhi") used: Ranbir is better than Narbir," "Ranbīr Narbīr bhandā rāmro chha."

Superlative.—"Sabai bhandā" ("sabai dekhi") used: "Ranbir is best" "Ranbīr sabai bhandā rāmro chha."

NUMERALS.

(1) Cardinal.

Except as mentioned below, these are exactly the same as the Urdu ones. Another form though is very frequently used by adding "otā." Thus the word tin, three, would be tīnotā; chār, four, would be chārotā, etc.

The differences from Urdu are: Sun, O; Yotā, 1; duita or dui, 2.

Note.—(1) When speaking of a number of a class of people the word "janā," which means persons, is often inserted:—Five goldsmiths, pānch janā sunār. Six women, chha janā shwāshni.

(2) In speaking of numbers above 40, etc., multiples of 20 (bis) are often used:—Eighty would be "chār bīsi," 85, "char bisi pānch."

Numerals behave like adjectives, preceding the noun they qualify.

(2) Ordinal.

These, with the below mentioned exceptions, are formed from the short form (Urdu form without "otā") of the Cardinals by adding "wan." In some cases they are slightly contracted.

Pānch, 5; Pānchwan, 5th, etc.

Exceptions.—First, pahilo; Second, dusro; Third, tīsro; Fourth, chautho; Sixth, chhatto.

(3) Collective.

Add *a* to the Cardinal: "bisa, a twenty," etc.

The following are special: Jor (or jora), a pair; panjā, a five; kori, a score. Saikara, per cent.

(4) Fractions.

The ordinary Urdu words are used.

(5) Multiplicative.

Add guna, fold. Duguna, two-fold, double. Tiguna, three-fold, treble. Sātguna, seven-fold, etc.

Another word for double is " dohoro " and for treble " teharo."

(6) Distributive.

One at a time—ek ek karera ; two at a time—dui dui karera, etc.

(7) Adverbial.

Once, yotā, palta ; twice—dui palta, etc. (lit., one time, two times, etc.). Firstly, pahilo palta ; secondly, dusro palta, etc. (lit. first time, etc.).

For dates, days, months, weights, etc., see vocabularies.

PRONOUNS.

(1) Personal.

Singular.

	1st Person.	2nd Person.	3rd Person.
Nom. ..	M, (म), I	T, (त) thou	U, (ऊ) he, she, it
Acc. and Dat.	M lāi	T lāi	Uslāi
Gen. ..	Mero	Tero	Usko
Abl. ..	M bāta	T bāta	Usbāta
Agent ..	Maile	Tainle	Usle or Ule
Loc. ..	M mā	T mā	Usmā

Plural.

Nom. ..	Hamiharu	Timiharu	Uniharu
Acc. and Dat.	Hamiharulāi	Timiharulāi	Uniharulāi
Gen. ..	Hamiharuko or hamro, etc.	Timiharuko or timro, etc.	Uniharuko, etc

In the plural the " haru " can be dropped.

(2) Possessive.

These are the Genitive of the personal pronoun above. They are declined like adjectives ending in " o."

(3) DEMONSTRATIVE.

This one

	Singular.	Plural
Nom.	.. yo	iniharu
Acc. and Dat.	yeslāi	iniharulāi
Gen.	.. yesko	iniharuko
Agent	.. yesle	iniharule
Loc.	.. yesmā	iniharumā
Abl.	.. yesbāta	iniharubātā

That one.

	Singular.	Plural.	
Nom.	.. tyo or u	tiniharu	(uniharu)
Acc. and Dat.	tislāi or ulāi	,,	lāi (uniharu lāi)
Gen.	.. tisko or usko	,,	ko (,, ko)
Agent	.. tisle or usle	,,	le (,, le)
Loc.	.. tismā or usmā	,,	mā (,, mā)
Abl.	.. tisbāta or usbāta	,,	bāta(,, bāta)

The genitive termination " ko " changes to kī and kā as in the genitive of a noun. The haru in the plural can be dropped throughout. Tyo is also used as the third personal pronoun and as the definite article. " The same " is formed by the emphatic form of tyo or u : tyeī, uī.

(4) RELATIVE. Who, which, that.

	Singular.	Plural.
Nom.	.. jo	jun or jo jo
Acc. and Dat.	jaslāi	junlāi or jas jaslāi
Gen.	.. jasko	junko or jas jasko
Abl.	.. jasbāta	junbāta or jas jasbāta
Agent	.. jasle (or jole)	junle or jas jasle
Loc.	.. jasmā	junmā or jas jasmā

The " ko " of the genitive changes into kā or kī as usual (see previous paras). For the plural, junharu can be used instead of jun. The form jo jo, etc., is not so common as the first one.

What *Relative.*

This is translated by " jye " (nom. sing.). It does not alter, the acc. being jyelai, etc., etc. The plural can be shown by doubling as jo jo above: jye jye (nom. plural), jye jyekāi (acc. plural), etc.

(5) INTERROGATIVE. Who?

This is ko. It is declined in singular and plural, both forms, exactly like the relative jo ; ko, kaslāi, kasko, etc. Plural: kun or ko ko, kunlāi or kas kaslāi, etc.

What? *Interrogative.*

This is kye and is exactly similar to the relative jye, the *k* being substituted for the *j*.

(6) INDEFINITE Someone, anyone.

	Singular.	*Plural.*
Nom. ..	koi	koi koi
Acc. and Dat.	kasailāi	kasai kasailāi
Gen. ..	kasaiko,	kasai kasaiko,
	etc.	etc.

Something, anything (Indefinite).

	Singular.	*Plural.*
Nom. ..	kei	kei kei
Acc. and Dat.	keilāi	kei keilāi
Gen. ..	keiko,	kei keiko,
	etc.	etc.

Another, the other (Indefinite).

	Singular.	*Plural.*
Nom. ..	aru or ārko (i, a,)	aru aru or ārka
Acc. and Dat.	arulāi or ārkolāi	aru arulāi or arkalāi.
Agent ..	arule or ārkole,	aruarule or ārkale,
	etc.	etc.

Other forms :—

1. Nobody—koi and the verb in the negative, koi ne.
2. Nothing—kei and the verb in the negative.

3. A few—ali.
4. No one (nothing) at all. As 1 and 2, but with "pani," "even," added.
5. This one—yei.
6. That one—ui or tyei. These two words also mean "the same": see under Demonstrative Pronouns (para 3).

(7) HONORIFIC.

(1) The plural of the personal pronoun is used for the singular. Thus "hami" comes to mean "I." "Timī" means "thou," and "unī," he. The verb is conjugated ordinarily, being of course in the plural. The word "timī" is preferable to "t" for thou, the latter being only used to greatly inferiors or among familiars (French—tu).

(2) There are two still more respectful forms for the second person: "āphu" and "tapāin," the latter being most respectful of all. These are declined in the ordinary way.

	Singular.	*Plural.*
Nom. ..	āphu or tapāin	āphuharu or tapāinharu
Acc. and Dat.	āphulāi or tapāinlāi	āphuharulāi or tapāinharulāi
Agent ..	āphule or tapāinle, etc.	āphuharule or tapāinharule, etc.

Āphuharu is often shortened to āphharu. These words may be translated like the Urdu "āp" by "your honour." For the form of verb they take see Conjugation of the Verb, Honorific tenses, page 11.

(8) REFLEXIVE. Self.

	Singular	*Plural.*
Nom. ..	āphu	āphu āphu
Acc. and Dat.	āphulāi	āphu āphulāi
Agent ..	āphule	āphu āphule
Gen. ..	āphnu	āphnu āphnu
Loc. ..	āphumā, etc.	āphu āphumā, etc.

The emphatic form is very often used (āphai): I myself, m aphai.

The genitive, âphnu, of course means "own." For the locative when it means "among selves" "āpāstmā" is used:—"They spoke among themselves" "Uniharule āpaṣtmā bāt garyā."

ADVERBS.

Only the formation of relative, correlative, etc., is shown here. adverbs are indeclinable.

FORMATIONS.

	Time.	*Place*	*Direction.*	*Manner.*	*Quantity.*
Near Demonstrative	aile (*c*) now	yahān here	yetā hither	isto (*a*) like this	iti as much as this
Remote Demonstrative	tab (*b*) then	wahān there	utā thither	usto like that	utti as much as that
Interrogative	kaile (*d*) when ?	kahān where ?	katā whither ?	kasto (*e*) how ?	kati how many? how much?
Relative	jab when	jahān where	jaṭā whither	jasto (*f*) as	jati as much as
Correlative	tab then	tahān there	teṭā thither	tisto such	teti so much

Notes.—(*a*) iseri also used.
(*b*) us belā mā occasionally used.
(*c*) ab used ; also is bela ma.
(*d*) kab ? also used.
(*e*) kasari also used.
(*f*) jasari also used.

It will be noted that the near demonstratives are more or less commenced with an *i* vowel; the remote with a *u*. The interrogative with *k*; the relative with *j* and the correlative with *t*.

Other adverbs and forms such as "whatever," etc., see Vocabularies. In a sentence the adverb precedes the word it modifies as closely as possible.

CONJUGATION OF THE VERB.

The verb is very regular with a few exceptions, of which the most common is Jānu, to go.

The postposition le (ले) is used as a sign of the agent just as the Urdu *ne* is used; the verb, though, always agrees with the nominative.

The root of a verb is formed by dropping the Infinitive termination, *nu* : Garnu, to do ; root, gar.

CONJUGATION OF A TRANSITIVE ACTIVE VERB (positive).

I.—Verbs with root ending in a consonant.

Garnu, to do. Root, gar.

(*a*) PRESENT INDICATIVE. I am doing ; I do.

1. M garchhu	1. Hamī garchhanu
2. T garchhas	2. Timī garchhau
3. U garchha	3. Unī garchhan

This is the most common form, but it is really a contraction of two forms with slightly different meanings. The common form is therefore used with both meanings. The full forms are :—

(1) M garne chhu—I am a man who does, I am a doer, I do.

(2) M gardai chhu—I am doing (at the present moment), I do.

Another form of (2) is—M garna lagya ko chhu, etc. This is frequently used.

(*b*) IMPERFECT INDICATIVE. I was doing.

1. M	gardā	thyan	1. Hamī	gardā	thyanu
2. T	,,	this	2. Timī	,,	thyau
3. U	,,	thyo	3. Uni	,,	thya

This tense is occasionally abbreviated to—M garthyan, etc.

Another form, as in the Present Tense, is :—M garnā lagya ko thyan, etc.

(c) Past Indicative. I did.

1. Maile garyan	1. Hamīle garyaun
2. Taile garis	2. Timīle garyau
3. Ule garyo	3. Unīle garva

(d) Present Perfect Indicative. I have done.

1. Maile garyā ko chhu	1. Hamīle garyā kā chhaun
2. Taile ,, ,, chhas	2. Timīle ,, ,, chhau
3. Ule ,, ,, chha	3. Unīle ,, ,, chhan

Another form of this tense, with the sense—I have finished doing—is Maile gari sakya or Maile gari halya. See Completive verbs, page 16.

(e) Past Perfect Indicative. I had done.

1. Maile garyā ko thyan	1. Hamīle garyā ka thyaun
2. Taile ,, ,, this	2. Timīle ,, ,, thyau
3. Ule ,, ,, thyo	3. Unīle ,, ,, thyan

This is often contracted into—Maile garī thyan, etc.

Another form (I had finished doing) is Maile garī saki (or hali) thyan, etc. See Completive verbs, page 16.

(f) Future. I will do.

1. M garunlā (or garlā)	1. Hamī garaunla
2. T garlas	2. Timī garaulā (or garlau)
3. U garlā	3. Unī garnan (or garlan)

The present tense, M garchhu, etc., is often used loosely for the future.

(g) Future Perfect. I will have done.

1. Maile garyā ko hunla	1. Hamīle garyā ko hunla
2. Tainle garyā ko holas	2. Timīle garyā ko houla
3. Ule garyā ko holā	3. Unīle garyā ko hunan

Haru can be added in the plural. The " ko " is often left out.

(*h*) IMPERATIVE MOOD. Let me do.

1. M garun	1. Hamī garun
2. T gar	2. Timī gar
3. U garos	3. Unī garun

The 2nd person singular is the ordinary imperative :—" gar," " do ! "

(*i*) AORIST. I may do.

This is exactly the same as the Imperative above.

(*j*) CONDITIONAL MOOD. I should (would) have done.

1. Maile garne thyan	1. Hamile garne thiyun
2. Tainle garne this	2. Timile garna thyau
3. Ule garne thyo	3. Unile garna thya

This is also used in the sense—Ought to have done.

(*k*) SUBJUNCTIVE. If I do, etc.

As these tenses are the same as the Indicative with " bhane " or " bhane dekhi " suffixed, they are not given.

(*l*) HONORIFIC.

Past.—Formed by the present Infinitive with " bhāyo " : " garnu bhāyo."

There is no change.

Imperative.—Add "hawas" to the present Infinitive:—"garnu hawas," " please do." This is sometimes contracted to "garnous."

These are the tenses taken by the pronouns " āphu " and " tapāin " (page 7).

(*m*) INFINITIVE MOOD. To do, etc.

Present.—Garnu, to do. This is used as an Imperative too sometimes. Perhaps a contraction for garnu hawas.

Other tenses are formed by using the participle of the tense with the Infinitive " hunnu," to be.

(*n*) PARTICIPLES.

Present.—Gardā, gardakherī meaning doing, while doing, etc.

Past.—Garyā ko. Done. This is practically an adjective.

Past Conjunctive.—Garera ; garikana. Having done.

II—Verb with root ending in a vowel.

Pathauna, to send ; root, pathau.

The following tenses only are differently formed, the auxiliary and other tenses being formed as for "garnu," using of course the participles etc. of "pathaunu."

(*a*) PRESENT INDICATIVE. I am sending.

1. M pathaunchhu	1. Hami pathaunchhaun
2. T pathaunchhas	2. Timi pathaunchhan
3. U pathaunchha	3. Uni pathaunchhan

(*c*) PAST INDICATIVE. I sent.

1. Maile pathāyan	1. Hamile pathāyaun
2. Taile pathāyis	2. Timile pathāyau
3. Ule pathāyo	3. Unile pathāyan

(*f*) FUTURE. I will send.

1. M pathāla	1. Hami pathaunla
2. T pathālas	2. Timi pathaula
3. U pathāla	3. Uni pathaula n

(*n*) PARTICIPLES.

Present.—Pathaundā, pathaundā kheri, while sending.
Past.—Pathāyā ko, sent (adjectival).
Past Conjunctive.—Pathāyera, pathāikana, having sent.

CONJUGATION OF THE AUXILIARY VERB. Hunnu, to be.

The pronouns which are the same as for garnu are omitted. Pos. means positive and Neg. negative.

(*a*) PRESENT INDICATIVE. I am, etc.

Pos. : Chhu, chhas, chha, chhaun, chhan, chhan.
Neg. : Chhaina, chhainas, chhaina, chhainaun, chhainau, chhainan.

Alternative Form :—

Pos. : Hun, hos, ho, haun, hau, hun.

Neg. : Hoina, hoinas, hoina, hoinaun, hoinau, ho inan.

(*b*) Past Indicative.. I was.

Pos. : Thyan, this, thye, thyaun, thyau, thya.

Neg. : Thyina, thyinas, thyina, thyinaun, thyinau, thyinan.

Alternative Form :—

Pos. : Bhāyan, bhāis, bhāyo, bhāyaun, bhāyau, bhāya.

Neg. : Bhāina, bhāinas, bhāina, bhainaun, bhāinau, bhainan.

(*c*) Present Perfect. I have been.

Pos. : Bhāyāko chhu, bhāyākochhas, bhāyākochha, bhāyākachhaun, bhāyākachhau, etc.

Neg. : Bhāyāko chhaina, chhainas, etc.

(*d*) Past Perfect. I had been.

Pos. : Bhāyāko thyan, bhāyāko this, bhāyāko thyo, bhāyāka thyaun, etc.

Neg. : Bhāyāko thyina, bhāyāko thyinas, etc.

The bhāyāko is sometimes contracted to bhaye.

(*e*) Future. I will be.

Pos. : Hunla, holas, hola, hounla, houla, hunan.

Neg. : Howaina, howainas, howaina, howainaun, howinau, howainan.

The present is sometimes used loosely for this tense.

(*f*) Future Perfect. I will have been.

Pos. : Bhāyāko hunla, bhāyāko holas, bhāyāko hola, bhāyāka hounla, etc.

Neg. : Bhāyāko howaina, bhāyāko howainas, etc.

(*g*) Imperative Mood. Let me be, etc.

Pos. : Houn, ho, hawas, houn, hawa, hun.

Neg. : Na houn, na ho, na hawas, etc.

(*h*) Aorist. I may be.

Same as imperative.

(*i*) Conditional Mood. I would (should) have been.

Pos.: Hunne thyan, hunne this, etc.

Neg.: Hunne thyina, hunne thyinas, etc.

(*j*) Subjunctive Mood. If I am, etc.

This is the same as the Indicative with "bhane" or "bhane ḍekhi" "if" added.

(*k*) Infinitive Mood. To be, etc.

Present.—Pos.: Hunnu, to be. Neg.: Na hunnu, not to be.

Other tenses formed by using the participle of the tense with Hunnu.

(*l*) Participles.

Present.—Hundo, hundakheri, hundai (emphatic) meaning being, while being, etc.

The Neg. of hundai is hundaina. For the others prefix "na."

Past.—Bhāyeko, been. Neg. na bhāyeko.

Past Conjunctive.—Bhāyera, having been. Neg. na bhāyera.

NEGATIVE VERBS.

In all tenses of all verbs, which are formed with the auxiliary verb, the negative of the auxiliary verb is used, *e.g.*:—

Imperfect Indicative. Pos. M garda thyan; Neg. M garda thyina, etc.

The other tenses are as below, and are in two forms, one for verbs whose root ends in a consonant, the other for those whose root ends in a vowel.

The pronouns are omitted.

Verbs whose root ends in a consonant, *e.g.* Garnu, to do' Root, gar.	Verbs whose root ends in a vowel, *e.g.* Pathāuṇu, to send. Root, pathāu.

TENSE : (*a*) PRESENT INDICATIVE.

Singular.	*Plural.*	*Singular.*	*Plural.*
1. Gardena	1. Gardenaun	1. Pathāunna	1. Pathāunaun
2. Gardenas	2. Gardenau	2. Pathāunas	2. Pathāunau
3. Gardena	3. Gardenan	3. Pathāuna	3. Pathāunan

(*c*) PAST INDICATIVE.

1. Garinna	1. Garyunna	1. Pathāyena	1. Pathāyenaun
2. Garinas	2. Garyauna	2. Pathāyenas	2. Pathāyenau
3. Garina	3. Garinan	3. Pathāyena	3. Pathayenan

(*f*) FUTURE.

Singular.	*Plural.*
1. Garne bhaina	1. Pathaune bhaina
2. ,, bhainas	2. ,, bhainas
3. ,, bhaina	3. ,, bhaina
1. Garna bhainaun	1. Pathauna bhainaun
2. ,, bhainan	2. ,, bhainan
3. ,, bhainan	3. ,, bhainan

The Negative Present Indicative is also used loosely.

IMPERATIVE, INFINITIVE, AORIST. PARTICIPLES.

Both verbs prefix " na " " not " before the verb.

E.g. Imperative.—Na garun, na gar, na garos, etc.

Na gar means " don't do." The honorific imperative also takes " na."

PASSIVE VOICE.

The verb " jānu " to go is used as in Urdu.

I was being placed—M rākhi goyo ko thyan, etc.

CAUSAL VERBS.

These are formed (1) by adding " āu " to the root :

uthnu, to rise ; uthāunu, to raise. Boknu, to carry ; bokāunu, to cause to carry.

(2) by lengthening the root vowel:
mārnu, to die; mārnu, to kill; nikalnu, to come out; nikālnu, to take out.

(3) by the verb pathāunu, to send:
"Make him keep step." Tis lāi kadam rākhne pathāu.

COMPLETIVES.

These are formed with the verb saknu. Sometimes hālnu is used:—

To have finished doing, gari saknu or gari hālnu.

INCEPTIVES.

These are formed with either lagnu (as a rule) or thālnu.

To begin to do—garnu lagnu or garnu thalnu (the latter chiefly used when restarting a work after an interval.)

POTENTIAL.

These are formed with the verb saknu, to be able: garnu saknu, to be able to do.

PERMISSIVE.

These are formed with the verb dinu, to give: garnu (or garne) dinu, to let do.

FREQUENTATIVE.

These are formed with garnu: gardai garnu, to be in the habit of doing.

DESIDERATIVES.

Formed with māngnu, to want: garne māngnu, to want to do.

CONTINUATIVES.

Formed with rahnu, to remain: gardai rahnu, to continue doing.

(b) MAGARKURA GRAMMAR

This language is really colloquial, and there is hardly any strict grammar. Many of the words defy spelling.

DECLENSION OF THE NOUN. Mija, a son.

Singular.

Nom. ..	.. Mījā, a son
Voc. ..	.. E ! Mījā, O ! son
Acc. ..	.. Mīje ki (mījāki or mījā), son
Gen. ..	.. Mījā-o (mījā ki), of son
Dat. ..	.. Mījā ke (mījā kenang), to son
Ag. ..	.. Mījā-e (mījāi), by son
Loc. ..	.. Mījā-ang, at son
Ab. ..	.. Mījā-ing, from son

Plural.—No change. If very necessary to show the number, the Khaskura word "haru" may be suffixed; or the Magar adjective "pata" "all" used :—

Mījāharu, sons ; pata mījā, all sons, all the sons.

Other postpositions may be used, *e.g.* "Mījā khata" "(in company) with a son."

Article.—None. If the sense requires one, "kāt," one ; "sui," some ; "issa," this ; "hossa," that ; may be used.

Feminine.—No special form.

THE ADJECTIVE AND NUMERALS.

Adjectives precede the word they qualify. They do not change. A characteristic termination for an adjective is "chu" or che ; white, bochu ; heavy (not light), lischu ; good, sieche. This is usually dropped with the form "mole" of the auxiliary verb (q.v.). "This is heavy" may either be—"issa lischu le" or "issa lismole."

Comparison.—This is formed by the word "denang," than. The adjective does not change at all.

Comparative.—Simply denang used : "This man is better than that"—"Issa bhurmi hossa denang siamole."

Superlative.—"pata denang" ("than all") used : "This man is best"—"Issa bhurmi pata denang siamole."

NUMERALS.

(1) CARDINAL.

Except for the first five these are exactly the same as Khaskura (q.v.). The first five are : one, kāt ; two, nis ; three, sum ; four, buli ; five, banga.

They precede the word they qualify.

(2) ORDINALS. Same as Khaskura.

(3) COLLECTIVE. No separate form. Cardinal used.

(4) and (5) MULTIPLICATIVE AND FRACTIONS. Khaskura used.

(6) DISTRIBUTIVE.

One at a time—Kāt kāt zātniking ; seven at a time—sāt sāt zātniking.

(7) ADVERBIAL.

Once, kāt phera ; twice, ni phera ; seven times, sāt phera.

These can also mean "first time," etc., loosely ; pahīlo phera, etc., also used.

PRONOUNS.

(1) PERSONAL.

Singular.

	1st Person.	2nd Person.	3rd Person.
Nom.	.. gnā	nang	hos, hosya
Acc.	.. gnā ki (or gnā)	nang, nang ki	,,
Gen.	.. gno	nango, ngo	hoche
Dat.	.. gnā ki, gnā	nang ki	hoski
Agent	.. gne	nge	hose

Plural.

	1st Person.	2nd Person.	3rd Person.
Nom. ..	kānko	nāku	hosa, hosruk
Acc. ..	kānko	nāku, nāku ki	,, ,,
Gen. ..	kāuung	nākung	hoskung, hosruking
Dat. ..	kanke	naku-e	hosruke
Agent	kāne	nākoi	hose, hosrūke

(2) POSSESSIVE.

The genitives of the personal pronouns are used.

(3) DEMONSTRATIVE.

"This" is "issa," "that" is "hossa." These do not change

(4) RELATIVE.

There is no relative "who." "The man who goes will return" (Khaskura: jo manchhā jālā, pharki ālā) is paraphrased in Magar to; This man will go (and) will return—Issa bhurmi ānunge āleise.

Similarly for the relative "what," the ordinary interrogative form "hi" is used: "What you say, is true"—"Hi nāku dele, sāncho le."

(5) INTERROGATIVE. Who?

One form of this is "su" indeclinable. The other form is:-
Nom.: kos; Acc. and Dat.: koski (or kos); Agent: kose; Genitive: kuche. Plural the same: Who are these?—"Issa kos ale" or "Issā su ale?"

What? *Interrogative.*

This is "hi?" and is indeclinable.

(6) INDEFINITE.

Someone is "sui," indeclinable. No one is "sui" with the verb in the negative. Something is "hira" or "sura." Nothing is the same with the verb in the Negative. Another, the other is "phoko," which is an adjective.

(7) Honorific.

If required Khaskura form used. " Nāku " is usually good enough.

(8) Reflexive.

This is not often used; if extra emphasis is required the following may be used :—

(1) Mino. means "own," and corresponds to the Khas., " āphnu."

(2) " I myself did "—" Gnā milikāt zātā " (lit., I alone did).

ADVERBS.

See Vocabulary for a special word.

Formations.

	Time.	*Place.*	*Direction.*	*Manner.*	*Quantity.*
ear Demon-strative	chāhan, inang now	ilang here	ilak hither	incho like this	irik as much as this
Remote Demon-strative	tab then	holang there	holak thither	horancho like that	hotna as much as that
Interro-gative	sien ? when ?	kulang? where ?	kulak ? whither ?	kuncho ? how ?	kurik ? how many, much ?
Relative	jab when	jahān where	jata whither	jasto as	jati as much

Correlative—same as remote form.

CONJUGATION OF THE VERB.

Verbs are very regular. They do not alter at all for person or number which are determined by the pronoun or context. In the vocabulary the root of the verbs is given.

(1) An ordinary Verb.

To do. Root, zāt.

Present tense.—Add " le " or " mole " to root :—

I am doing—" Gnā zātle " or " gna zātmole."

Past tense.—Add " a" or " moliā " to root :—

I did—" Gnā zātā " or " gnā zātmoliā."

Future tense.—Add " e " to root, and prefix " a " :—
You will do—" Nāku āzāte."

Imperative.—Add " o " to root. Roots ending in " a " change the " a " to " o " :—

Do !—" zāto." Sometimes shorter : " zāta." Give ! (root, " yā ")—" yo ! "

Honorific Imperative.—Add " ni " to root :—
Please do—" zātni."

Infinitive or verb noun.—Add " ki " to root :—

" To do " or " the deed," " zātki." This form is used in the compound verbs.

" You began to do "—" Naku zātki lesa."

PARTICIPLES.

Present.—Add " nang " to root :—
" While doing "—" zātnang."

Relative.—Add " chiu " to root :—

(the) doing (man)—" zatchiu " ; the running man—" kherchiu bhurmi."

Past.—Add " niking " to root :—

" Having done "—" zātniking."

(2) AUXILIARY VERB. To be.

Root, chhan.	*Other form.*
Present tense.—" le " or " mole " sometimes " ale " :—	" chhanle " " naku chhanle "
You are—" Nāku le " or " nāku mole."	
Past tense.—" lia " or " molia " :—	" chhana "[1]
You were—" nāku lia " or " nāku molia."	"naku channa"
Future tense.—" ale " :—	" achhane "
You will be—" nāku ale."	" naku achhane "

[1] This form is used when " bhayo " is used in Khas. If "thio" is used in Khas. the Magar is " lia " or " molia. "

Imperative.—" chhana "—Be !

Infinitive or verb noun, used as above :—

" chhanki."

Participles.—As above :—

" chhannang," " chhanchiu " and " chhanniking."

NEGATIVE.

The negative " mā " (not) is used before verb in all tenses except the imperative :—

I am not doing—" gnā mā zātle." This is not—" Issa māle."

You did not begin to do—" nāku zātki mā lesa."

Imperative.—In this tense " nā " is used instead of " mā " :—

Do !—" zāto." Don't do—" nā zāto." Please don't do—" nā zātni."

CAUSAL VERBS.

These are usually formed by adding " ak " to the root. If the root ends in a vowel a suitable consonant is often inserted :—

To learn, root " pāh " ; to teach, root " pahāk " ; to wake, rise, root " so " ; to awake, rouse, root " sotak."

COMPLETIVES.

These are formed with the verb " biat," to finish :—

" Have you finished doing ? "—" Nāku zātki biata ? " " You have not finished cooking "—" Nāku pinki mā biata."

INCEPTIVES.

These are formed with the verb " les," to begin, which corresponds to the Khaskura " lagnu." This verb must not be confused with " Leis " which means to return, and which has a slightly longer vowel sound.

" I began to go "—" Gnā nungki lesā."

POTENTIAL.

These are formed with the verb " heg," to be able :—

" I can do "—" Gnā zatki hegle." " He could not do "—Hossa zātki mā hegā."

PERMISSIVES.

These are formed as in Khaskura by the verb "ya," to give :—

"Please let him go"—"Hossa lāi nungki yāni."

DESIDERATIVES.

These are formed with the verb "pa"—Gnī which means to demand is also used but not so good :—

"I want to eat"—"Gnā jeki pāle (gnīle)."

CONTINUATIVES.

These are formed like Khaskura with the verb "mu," to sit :—

"I kept on eating" (continued to eat)—"Gnā jeki mụa."

(c) GURUNGKURA GRAMMAR.

This language is essentially a colloquial one, and there is practically no grammar at all. In Magarkura many of the words defy spelling, in Gurungkura they nearly all do.

DECLENSION OF THE NOUN. Kolo, a son.

		Singular.	*Plural.*
Nom.	..	Kolo, son	Kolme, sons
Voc.	..	E ! Kolo, O ! son	E ! Kolme, O ! sons
Acc.	..	Kolo lāi, son	Kolme lāi, sons
Gen.	..	Kole (kole-e), son's	Kolme-e, sons'
Dat.	..	Kolo lāi, to son	Kolme lāi, to sons

Plural.—If required " me " can be added as above. It need not be used. Most words do not contract in the plural as " kolo " does :—

" mhi," man ; " mhime," men.

Other prepositions may be used, *e.g.* " Kolo-ni " " (in company) with a son."

Article.—None. If the sense requires one," " ghri," one.

Feminine.—No special form.

THE ADJECTIVE AND THE NUMERALS.

Adjectives, as a rule, come after the word they qualify. They occasionally precede it, more especially in the genitive case.

A characteristic termination for adjectives is " ba " : " chiaba," good ; this however is often dropped in a sentence : It is good—" Chiaba mo " or " chiammo." Adjectives do not alter.

Comparison.—This is formed as in Khas. by the Khaskura word " bhanda "—" than."

Comparative.—Simply " bhandā " used : " This man is better than that "—" Chu mhi cha bhandā chiām mo."

Superlative.—Use " tāye bhandā," " than all " : " This man is best "—" Chu mhi taye bhandā chiām mo."

NUMERALS.

(1) CARDINAL.

These come after the word they qualify, like adjectives. They do not change.

The first ten are : 1, ghri; 2, gni,; 3, som ; 4, pli ; 5, gnā ; 6, tu ; 7, nī ; 8, pre ; 9, ku ; 10, chu. Above this the Khaskura words are used, except for multiples of ten : 20, gnichu ; 30, somchu (or sonju) ; 40, plichu ; 70, nichu, etc.

There is another form of these first 10 numerals and that is by adding " ola" or " la " to the short form : 2, *gni or gniolā* ; 3, *som* or *somla*, etc.

ORDINALS, COLLECTIVE, FRACTIONS, MULTIPLICATIVE, DISTRIBUTIVE.

These are all the same as in Khaskura, which see.

(7) ADVERBIAL.

Once, ghri ple ; twice, gni ple ; etc. These also mean first time, second time, etc.

PRONOUNS.

(1) PERSONAL.

Singular.

	1st Person	2nd Person.	3rd Person.
Nom. ..	gnā	ki	chu, cha
Acc. ..	gnā lāi	ki lāi	,, ,,
Gen. ..	gny	kei	cheyi
Dat. ..	gnā lāi	ki lai	chulai
Agent ..	gnei	kei	cheie

The nom. can apparently be loosely used for any case.

Plural.

Nom. ..	gnī	ki	kiama or chama
Acc. ..	gnī lāi	ki lai	,, or ,,
Gen. ..	gnīla	kei	kiema or chame
Dat. ..	gnilai	keilai	kiama or chame lai
Agent ..	gnīe	kei	kiame or chame

(2) Possessive.

The genitive of the Personal pronouns are used.

(3) Demonstrative.

"This" is "chu," "that" is "cha." Indeclinable, and usually precede their word.

(4) Relative.

There is no relative "who." "The man who goes, will return" (Khaskura: jo manchha jāla, pharki ala) is paraphrased in Gurung to: "This man will go (and) will return": "Chu mhi yale yekale."

Similarly for the relative "what," the interrogative form "to" is used:—

What you say is true—To ki bimo, sãncho mo.

(5) Interrogative. Who?

This is "kāb."

What? *Interrogative.*

This is "to" and is indeclinable.

(6) Indefinite.

Someone or something is "kāwa."
No one or nothing is "kāwa" with the verb in the negative.
Another, the other is same as in Khaskura.

(7) Honorific.

If required the Khaskura forms are used.

(8) Reflexive.

Not often used except when great emphasis is required.
"I did (it) myself"—"Gnā ghrī le" (lit. I one did).

ADVERBS.

Formation only given ; for any word see Vocabularies.

	Time.	*Place.*	*Direction.*	*Manner*	*Quantity.*
Near	tokan	chura	chui	chaima	chage
Demon-strative	now	here	hither	like this	as much as this
Remote	tab	kir	keyai	chima	uti
Demon-strative	then	there	thither	like that	as much as that
Interro-gative	kaiyan ? when ?	kana ? where ?	kana ? whither ?	kagle? kaida? how ?	kati ? how much, many ?

Relative—same as in Khaskura.

CONJUGATION OF THE VERB.

Verbs do not alter at all for person or number, which are determined by the pronoun or context. In the vocabulary the root of the verb is given.

(1) An Ordinary Verb.

To say. Root " bī."

Present Tense.—Add " mo " to root :—

I am saying—" Gnā bīmo."

Past Tense.—Add " i " to root. Roots in " i " don't change. Roots in " a " may be regular as " ai " or contract to "e," if the " a " is short :—

I said—" Gnā bī." You did—" Ki le " (root " la ").

Future Tense.—Add " lai " or " sio " to root :—

You will say—" Ki bilai " or " Ki bisio."

Imperative.—Add " d " to root. :—

' Say ! "—" Bid ! " There is no Honorific form.

Infinitive or Verb Noun.—Add " l " to root :—

" Gnā bīl kai "—" I finished saying."

Participles.—Present.—Add " mai " to root : " While saying "—" Bimai."

Relative.—Add "Bai" to root :—
"The running man"—"Bhagdibai mhi" (root bhagdi).
Past.—Add "moro" to root : "Having said"—"Bimoro."

(2) AUXILIARY VERB. To be.

	Positive.	*Negative.*
Present Tense.—	"mo" ; "you are"—"ki mo."	"are."
Past Tense.—	"mule" ; "you were"—"ki mula."	"arelo."
Future.—	"tolai" ; "You will be"—"ki tolo."	
Participles.—	As above : "mai, being." "moro, been."	

NEGATIVES.

For the negative of the Auxiliary Verb see above. In all tenses of an ordinary verb, the negative sign "ā" is used before the verb :—

"I am going"—"Gnā yāmi." "I am not going"—"Gnā ā yāmo."

The past tense often shortens the vowel : "Did"—"le." 'Did not"—"a la."

In conversation when asking a question, the "ki" between the positive and negative is often omitted :—

"Have you married or not ?"—"Ki biah le ā la."

COMPLETIVES.

These are formed with the verb "kā" (corresponds to the Khas. saknu).

"Have you finished work or not ?" "ki ke kāi ā kā"

POTENTIALS.

These are formed with the verb "kā" "to be able."

"Can you sing or not ?"—"Ki kwi prīl kām ā kām."

PERMISSIVES.

These are formed with the verb "pi," to give.

"Let him go"—"Cha lāi yāl pid."

GURUNG BURGA.

English	*Khas.*	*Burga-kura.*	*Gurung-kura.*	*Years.* (Start 15th April).			
Mouse	Musa	Chulo	Namu	1876	1888	1900	1912
Cow	Gai	Lonlu	Mhe	1877	1889	1901	1913
Tiger	Bāgh	Tolo	Chien	1878	1890	1902	1914
Cat	Birālu	Hilo	Nawa	1879	1891	1903	1915
Eagle	Garud	Maleru	Jure	1880	1892	1904	1916
Snake	Nāg	Saleri	Pokri	1881	1893	1905	1917
Horse	Ghorā	Talo	Ghorā	1882	1894	1906	1918
Sheep	Bherā	Lulo	Kui	1883	1895	1907	1919
Monkey	Bandar	Pralo	Yogā or timu	1884	1896	1908	1920
Bird	Chara	Chalo	Name	1885	1897	1909	1921
Dog	Kukur	Khilo	Nagu	1886	1898	1910	1922
Deer	Mirga	Pho	Pho	1887	1899	1911	1923

These Burga years start on 15th April of the corresponding English year. Nearly all Gurungs know which Burga they were born in, even if they don't know their age. The age can be then worked out. For instance, if in 1916 a young recruit says he is Kukur Burga, he would have been born in 1898, making him 18; the other years of the Kukur Burga being 1886 and 1910 which would make him far too old or too young.

CHAPTER II.

VOCABULARIES.

(a) ENGLISH-GURKHALI VOCABULARY.

Where no Magar or Gurung word is given the Khas word should be used in Magar or Gurungkura, using however the proper verb terminations. In such cases the root of the Magar verb is usually formed by adding " di " to the Khas verb root, the Gurung root by adding " i."

In Khaskura the infinitive of the Verb is given, but in Magar and Gurung the root is given. For formations of other tenses see the Grammar.

The Gurkhali-English Vocabulary which follows this often contains a fuller explanation of a word than is possible when translating from English.

" g " at the end of a verb means garnu, *e.g.*, shwang g. =shwang garnu (M. shwang zat. G. shwang la) ; (*t*) = transitive ; (i) intransive.

ENGLISH	KHAS	MAGAR	GURUNG
A	yotā योटा	kāt	ghrī
Abcess	pilo (f) पिलो	juma	ṛu
Above [1]	māthi, ūnbho मांथी, ऊंभो	dhênām	kwera
Abrazed	chitriako चीथरेको	rusa	toi
Absent	gairhazir, gail गैरहाजिर, गैल		
Abuse [2]	gāli गाली	dia	cha (verb)
Accident [3]	achānchak अचानचक		
Accord[4]	ichchha इच्छा		
Account	hisāb हिसाब		

[1] Mathi is best word. Over and above (*i.e.* in excess) is ubryako.

[2] " He swore " is ordinarily " U le gali dio."

[3] " He did it by accident " is " U le na janera gario " (he did it, not knowing about it). An accident in the street, etc. ; no word used, the particular nature of the accident would have to be specified.

[4] " He did it of his own accord "—" U le aphnu ichchha le gario."

ENGLISH	KHAS	MAGAR	GURUNG
Accoutrements	tostān, asbāb तोस्तान, असबाब		
Accusation	dosh दोष		
Ache, to	dukhnu दुख्नु	big	nā
Ace	ekkā एक्का		
Acid	khatto खट्टो	bīr	kiu
Acorn	bānj ko gerho बांज को गेड़ो		
Acquaintance	chinā jāni चीना जानी	chinesa barmi	gnoshe mhi
Across	pāri पारी	pārlak	kianja
Act, to [1]	shwāng g. स्वांग ग:	utengia z.	utengia l.
Add, to	jornu जोड्नु	jordi	
Address, an	patā पता		
Adhere, to	tāsnu टास्नु	lāk	ngaya
Adornment	gahanā गहना		
Advice	ārthi, salāh अर्थी, सल्लाला		
Adze	bānsula बान्सुला		
Afraid, to be	darnu डरनु	biri	gni
	jhasang hunnu झसंग हुनु	gān	loy
After	pachhi पछी	nūnlak	li
Afternoon[2]	sānjh सांझ	nabélak chum	gnesa
Again	pheri फेरी		
Age	umar उमर		
Agreed	rāji राजी	mān	saiñ
Ague	jaro जरो		

[1] *i.e.* to play the fool.

[2] TIME. For months see footnote 5 of p. 33.

MISCELLANEOUS. To-day—Aja (M. chining ; G. tinya). To-morrow—Bholi (M. pihin ; G. pana). Day after to-morrow—Parsi (M. aprin ; G. nogni). Next two days Naparsi and kani parsi respectively.

Yesterday—hiju (M. tisini ; G. tela). Day before that—asti (M. kaiakin; G. wingi).

Days ago—jhan asti ; years ago—uile uile.

This year—Aja ko sal (M. chilez ; G. tidi). Last year—pur ko sal (M milez ; G. tiambesal). Year before that—Pral ko sal (M. kalez : G. nodi sal).

Next year—Agun sal (M. Nāmlez ; G. Koringba sal).
Dawn—ujialo. Sunrise—Surajuday. Sunset—Surajast.
Last-night—Ajko rat ; To-night—bholi rat.

ENGLISH	KHAS	MAGAR	GURUNG
Aim, to	tāknu ताकनु	tākdi	·cha
Air (wind)	bâtās बतास	nàmshu	namru
Alert	chanākho चनाखो		
Alike	eknāse एकनासे		
Alligator	guhi, sus गुहि, सुस		
Alive	jiundai जिऊंदै		soke
All	sabai सबै	pàttâ	tai
Almond	badām बदाम		
Alms	dān दान		
Aloe	râmbāns रामबांस		
Alone	êkelài एकलै	milikāt	ghri
Along[1]	see footnote 1		
Aloud	chărko चरको		
Alphabet	kakhara कखरा		
Already	paile पैले		noso
Also	panī पनी		
Alter (t)	badalanu वदलनु		
(i)	ārko hunnu अरको हुनु		
Always	sâdhain सधैं		
Ambush	lukne thaun लुकने ठाउं	kopile tu	lobe loh
Amidst	mājh mā माझ मा		
Amuse, to	ramāunu रमाउनु	marāng	toya
Ancestor	jiju bāje (great-grandfather, grandfather) जिजूबाज्ये		

TIME. I have no time (Leisure)—m lai kehi phursat chhena.
What is the time ?—Kati baje chha ? or kati bajio ?
At such a time, don't cough.—Testo bela ma, na khans.
How many times did he go ? U kati palta gayo ?

YEAR. Sāl or săn mean year in the sense of "which year."
Bărās means the length of time of a year.

NEPALESE ERAS :—

Nepal Sambat	1 is A.D. 880.	Our 1910	is therefore	N. S. 1030.
Vikram Sambat 1	1 is B.C. 57.	Our 1910	,, ,,	Vik. S. 1967.
Saka	1 is A.D. 78.	Our 1910	,, ,,	Saka 1832.

[1] "Come along with me"—"Mero sangma au."
"He went along the road"—"U bato bato goyo."

ENGLISH	KHAS	MAGAR	GURUNG
And	aru, ra अरु, र	ra	
Anger[1]	rīs रीस	jamso	ris
Angle	kunā कुना		
Animal	jantu, pashu जन्तु, पशु		
Ankle	golī gānthā गोली गांठा		
Annoy, to	khijānu खिजानु	kuw	gni
Anoint[2]	ghasnu घसनु	mol	pho
Another[3]	ārko आरको	phoko	kiangu
Answer, an	utàrā उतरा		
,, back, to	mukh jornu मुख जोड्नु		
Ant	kamilo कमिलो	māhar	nabro
,, , white	dhumiro धुमीरो		
Antelope	mirg मिर्ग		pho, tonsi
Anxiety	shok, surtā शोक, सुरता		
Any	koi कोई	sui	khābe
Ape, an	dheruwā ढेड़वा		
Apology[4]	māph माफ		
Appearance (of a person)	rup रुप		
Apple	sew सेव		
Appoint	khatāunu खठाउनु	khatdi	kate
Approach	pugnu làgnu पुगनु लगनु	tākke lês	phe
Apricot	khumāni खुमानी		
April[5]	baisākh बैसाख		

[1] This is the noun. To get angry is Rishaunu (M. jamso kew ; G. ris tai).

[2] The slave-making ceremony by anointing with oil is Telia Chakur.

[3] Bring another (different) man—nola (arko) manchha lau ;
Bring another (one more) ,, —yota aru manchha lau ;
It belongs to another—arko ko ho ;
They hit one another—uni harnu āpāstma hanna han bhayo.

[4] " Please excuse me "—" m lai maph garnu hawas."

[5] MONTHS. These start on the 15th of the English months. The Khaskura of a month in the vocabulary therefore means the 15th of that month to the 15th of the next, *e.g.* April—Baisakh. Baisakh is 15th April to 15th May.

ENGLISH	KHAS	MAGAR	GURUNG
Archer[1]	dhanudhāri धनुधारी		tale kleom mhi
	guleli khelne गुलेलोखेलने	koreli geschiu	
Arise	uthnu उठनु	so	re
Arm, fore	hāth हाथ	hūt	yo
,, upper	pākhurā पाखुड़ा		
Armourer	kāmi कामी		
Armpit	kākhī काखी		gneongle
Army	laskar लसकर		
Around	chārtīra चारतीर		
Arouse	uthāunu उठाउनु	sotāk	tā
Arrange	sajāunu सजाउनु	sajādi	
Arrive	pugnu पुगनु	tāk	phe
Arrow[1]	kār काउ	surr	me
	matengrā मटेंग्रा	khurli	uli
As	jasto, jhai जस्तो, झै	dinche	beo
As many as	itī यतो	irik	chaki
Ascend	charnu चढ़नु	kāl	kre
	ukalnu उकलनु		
Ascent	ukālo उकालो		
Ashes	kharāni खरानी	barap	nebro
Ashamed	laz lāgiāko लाज लाग्याको	kora lesa	pië
	,, manniako ,, मान्नयाको ,,	heoa	,,
Ask	sodhnu सोधनु	gīn	nui
(demand)	māngnu मांगनु	nīm	ri
Ass[2]	gadāh गदाह		
Assault	jhaptanu झपतनु		
Assemble (i)	thuprinu थुपरिनु		
(t)	thupriāunu थुपरिआउनु		
Assistance[3]	gohār गोहार		
Astride	ghunrā dāsera घुंड़ादासेरा	gunra tos-niking	chikra turemoro

[1] Dhanu is a bow that throws an arrow kar ; guleli is a small bow for projecting earthen balls (matengra) or small stones, etc.

[2] The word of rebuke—" You ass " is " jainrya " or " murkha."

[3] Gohar is also " Call for help " and also for shelter.

English	Khas	Magar	Gurung
Astronomer	jotishi जोतिशी		
At	mā मा		
Attack	dhāwā धावा		
,, ,, to	chhopnu छापनु	gu	kā
Attempt	mihniṭ g. मिहनत गः		
Auction	lilām लिलाम		
August[1]	bhādao भादौ		
Aunt [2]	jethi āmā or phupu जेटी श्रामा फुपु	mizar mai	mate, āmate phāne
	kānchhi āmā कान्छी श्राम्मा[2]	kanchhi mai	āmchu

[1] See footnote 5, p. 33.

[2]

Relations.	Khaskura	Magar.	Gurung.
Aunt (paternal), elder than father.	Phupu		phāne
Aunt (paternal), younger than father	Kānchhi āma	kanchhi mai	āmchu
Aunt (maternal), elder than mother.	Jethi āma	mizar mai	mate, āmate
Aunt (maternal), younger than mother.	Siāni āma		āmchu
Brother, elder	Dāju ; dāl		āge
,, younger	bhāi	boy	
Brother's wife	bowāri		
Brother-in-law, elder (wife of ditto)	Jethān (Jethāni jethu)		
Brother-in-law, younger	Sāla		shiombo
Brother's son	Bhatija	batja	
,, daughter	Bhatiji	batji	
Cousin (from maternal uncle).	Sāla, sāli or solti (marriageable).		shiombo, gnolosyo.
Cousin (from other sources).	dāju, bhāi, didi, bhāini (not marriageable).		
Daughter	chhori	jā	chame
,, in-law	bowāri		
Granddaughter	natini		kweme
Grandfather	Bāje		
Grandmother	Bāje		
Grandson	Nāti		kwe
Great-grandfather	Jiju		
Father	Bābu	bua	aba

ENGLISH	KHAS	MAGAR	GURUNG
Avenge	badalā linu बदला लिनु	badala lā	
Awake (t)	jagāunu जगाउनु	ju	ti
(i)	jāgnu जागनु		
Away	tārā टाड़ा	los	rego
Awkward (clumsy)	lothro लोथरो		
Axe	bāncharo बनचरो	āruwa	tā
Axle	dandā डन्डा		
BABY	nāni नानी		kolo
Bachelor	kane कने		
Back	kando कन्डो	jang	ko
Bad	narāmro नरामरो	māsieche	achhab
Badge (distinctive)	chino चीनो		
,, (of rank)	billā बिलला		
Bag	thailo थैलो	sāna	nedo

RELATIONS.	KHASKURA.	MAGAR.	GURUNG.
Father-in-law	Sasura	kuba	keñ
Mother	āma	mai	
,, in-law	Sāshu, māiju, māit moma		angi, shiame
Sister, elder	didi	dai	nāni
,, ,, husband of	Bina		agmo
Sister, younger	bhāini		
Sister-in-law	Sāli		
,, law's husband	Sārhu		
Sister's daughter	bhānji		
,, son	bhānich		
Son	chhoro	jā	cha mo
Son-in-law	Jawain		
,, law's son	bhānich		
Uncle (paternal) older than father.	Jetha bā		bāte
Uncle (paternal) younger than father.	Kānchha bā		bācheo
Uncle (maternal)	māma	kuba	
Father's sister's husband	phupaju	pusain	

Second marriage make no difference, step-son is still chhoro.

" What relation is he to you ? "

" U timi lai kya {bhanchha / parchha ? "}

ENGLISH	KHAS	MAGAR	GURUNG
Bait	chāro चारो		
Bake, to	seknu सेकनु	arim	rom
Balance	tulo, tarāju तुलो, तराजू	pāra	pāra
Balcony	pidi पीड़ि		pata
Bald	khuilo खुइलो		
Bale	kumlo कुमलो	bucha	noi
Ball	gin गीन		
Balloon	gobāra गोबारा		
Bamboo	bāns बांस	hok	ri
Banana	kerā केरा	mocha	maja
Bandage	patti पट्टी		
Bank (river)	pākhā, chheo पाखा, छेव		
Banker	sāu साव		
Bar (rod)	ghārā घारा		
(wood bolt)	āglo अागलो		
(gate)	tagāro तगारो		
Barbed	kānre काणे	ju	
Barber	nāi नाइ		
Bare-headed	murilo मुड़िलो		
Bark, to	bhuknu भुकनु	nu	chi
(tree)	bokrā बोकरा		pi
Barren			
(woman)	bānji बांजी	tāri	tāra tari
(ground)	rukho रूखो		
Basement (floor)	bhuintalla भुइँ तल्ली		
Basket [1]	doko, korkā डोको, कोरका	dhakar, korkā	peh, korka
	thunsē, dālo ठुंसो, दालो	thunse, giring	
	petaro पेटारो	birin	piring
Bat (bird)	chamerā चमेड़ा	gīchin	pāpa
Batch	toli टोली		
Bathe, go	nohānu नोहानु	resh	kri

[1] Korka is a large basket, doko a small one. Tunse is one with no mouth. Petaro, a tapered one.

English	Khas	Magar	Gurung
Bathing	asnān अस्नान		
Be, to	hunnu हुनु	chhan	
Beak	thond ठोंड	methar	thor
Beam (big)	dalin दलीन		
(small)	bolo बोलो		
Bean	simi सिमी		
Bear	bhālu भालू		bhalu, tama
Beard	dāri दाड़ी		
Beat, to[1]	hānnu, mārnu हान्नु, मार्नु hirkāunu हिर्काउनु	gnap sāt, dung, dāthuk	li, sia
Beautiful	rāmro रामरो	sieche	chhiaba
Beauty	rup रूप		
Because	kinakī किनकी	hikinungki	tole
Become	hunnu हुनु	chhan	mo
Bed	kāth काठ		
,, , to make	bichhāunu बिछाउनु	tāng	'ti
Bedding	ochchhyān ओच्छ्यान		klo
Bee	māuri मौरो	gôns	kue
Beetle	gobāre kirā गोबारा कोरा	bendu	gobar pulu
Before[2]	aghine अघिने aghāri अघाडो	mining	gnoso
Begin, to	lāgnu, thālnu लाग्नु, थाल्नु	les	che
Behind	pachhī पछी	nuning	li
Behaviour	chalan चलन		
Believe, to	pattyāunu पत्याउनु	jāk	kwe
Bellows	bhānti, khalāti भांति खलाती		
Belly	bhunri भूंड़ि	tuk	pho
Below	tala, undho तल, ऊंधो	māklak	nwai, piri

---

1 Mārnu literally means to kill.

U le kukur lai { lorole / bahduk le } { hanio / hirkayo } He { beat the dog with a stick / shot the dog (lit., hit the god with a gun).

2 "I told you before"—"Māi le timi lāi aghinai bhanyo."
"Before my house"—"Mero ghar ko sāmne."
"Before eating your food, do this"—"Roti na khāyera, isto gar."

ENGLISH	KHAS	MAGAR	GURUNG
Beggar	bhikhāri भिखारी	niechi	riba mhi
	māngne मागने	barmi	
Belch, a (used with ānutocome)	dakkar दक्कर		
Belt	peti पेटी		
Bend, to	mornu मोरनु	mordi	
	khunchāunu खुंचाउनु		kuti
Bend over, to	niuranu न्यूड़नु	nuwāk	
Bent, stooping	ghobto घाबटो		
Between	bhittra भित्र		
	mājhmā माझ मा		
Beyond	pallo patti पल्लोपट्टी	āla patti	kiali
Big	thulo ठुलो	karāncho, sum	tebe
Bind, to[1]	bāndhnu, kasnu बांधनु, कसनु	chak	phu
Bird[2]	chara, panchhī चरा, पंछी	gua	name
Biscobra	gohara गोहरा		
Bite, to	toknu टोकनु	jik	chiy
Bitter	tito तीतो	kha	kai
Black	kālo कालो	chichu	mlônkia
Blacksmith	kāmi कामी		
Blade (knife)	dhār धार		
(grass)	biruwā बिरुवा		
Blame	dos दोस		
Blanket	kāmlo, pākhi कामलो, पांखी	pākhi	rari
Blessing	āsik आसिक		

[1] Kasnu literally means to tighten.

[2] Male birds are bhālya, female are Pothi.

Kinds :—Dhukur (Dove). Parewa (tame pigeon). Malewa (wild pigeon). Halesa (green pigeon). Daphe (mihal). Bhangera (Sparrow). Titra (Partridge). Kag (Crow). Kalij (College pheasant). Majur (Peacock). Bater (Quail). Hans (Duck, goose). Gida (Vulture). Baj (Hawk). Chil (Kite). Harphori (Lamagaya). Bagula (Heron). Neole (Black bird with distinctive cry). Chakhura (Chikor). Dhobini (small black and white bird. Tāwa (Jay.) Bajewa (Large wild pigeon). Saru, dāngre (mina). Dhanes (horn bill). Kurāng kurung (a lark).

ENGLISH	KHAS	MAGAR	GURUNG
Blind			
(one-eyed)	kānā काना		
,, (can't see)	andho अन्धो		
Blink	chimchim g. चिमचिम ग:		
Blister	phoko फोको		
Blockhead	latheprā लठेपरा		
Blood	ragat रगत	hiu	ko
Blotting-paper	sosnyā kāgaj सोसन्या कागज		
Blow, to	phuknu फुक्नु	mut	phu
out, to	nibhānu निभानु	sāt	si
Blue	nilo निलो	picha	pingio
Blunt	bodo बोदो		
Blush, to	lāj ānu लाज आनू		
Boar	banel बनेल		to
Board	phalyāk फल्याक		
Boat	dungā डुङ्गा		
Bodice	cholo चोलो		
Body	āng, jyu आँग, ज्यू		ju
,, (figure)	sarīr सरोर		
Bog	dhāp, simsar धाप, सीमसार		
Boil, to (t)	umālnu उमाल्नु	hatāk	plo
(i)	unglnu उंगल्नु	hāt	ploiya
	usīnnu[1] उसीन्नु	mung	
, a	khatīra खटीरा	mā	pora
Bold	āntilo आंतिलो		
	karāntilo क्रांतिलो		
Bolt (door)	āglo आगलो		jagla
Bomb	bamgolā बमगोला		
Bone	hār हाड़	mirus	rība (in Kaski), nogri (below Lamjung)
Book	postak पोस्तक		
Bootmaker	sārki सारकी		
Border (country)	dosān दोसान		

[1] Usinnu is not generally used as regards water.

ENGLISH	KHAS	MAGAR	GURUNG
Bore, to	ghochnu घोचनु	dajhīk	
Borrow, to	rin linu रिण लिनु		
Both	duita दुइटा	nīs	niola
Boundary	sān, latthā सान, लट्ठा dosan दोसान		
Bow, to	dhok g. ढोक	jor	pheo
a (for arrows)	dhanu धनु		urta
(small)	guleli गुलेली		
Bowl (n)	batuko बटुको	bela	bela
Box	kandī कन्दी		
Boy[1]	chhoro, ketā छोरो, केटा	mija	cha, pasi, kolo
Bracelet	churā bālā चुरा बाला	gel	
Bracelet-seller	churāti चुराती		
Braces	gālich गालीच		
Brain	gidi गिदि		karasia
Bran	chokar चोकर		
Branch (tree)	hāngo हांगो.	dāla	
Brave	bīr āntilo बीर, आंतिलो		
Bread	rotī रोटी	bishkān	kei
Break, to (t)	tornu टोड़नु	giāk	cho
(i)	bhānchnu भांचनु	gi	,,
Breast	chhāti छाती		ku
Breasts	thun, dudh थुन, दूध kachonā कचोना		gnie
Breath	sāns सांस		so
Bribe	ghus घुस		
Brick	int ईन्ट		
Bride	dulhāni दुलहानी	dulhi	prensio
Bridegroom	dulhā दुलहा		
Bridge	sānghu सांघु	sānghu	cha (lamjung)
Bridle	Kareli करेलो		
Brim	nimtho निमठो		mian

[1] Chhoro is a larger boy than keta.

ENGLISH	KHAS	MAGAR	GURUNG
Bring, to	liāunu ल्याउनु	rāk	pau
Brittle	jhuro झूरो	marāngche	
Broad	chāklo चाकलो		
	gajīlo गजीलो		
Broom	kucho कुच्चो	bareni	
Brother	dāju, bhāi दाजु, भाई	daju boy	āgi, bhai
Brown	khairo खैरो		
Bucket	dotho, dālo, डोठो, डालो	dākre, giring	
Buckwheat	phāpar फापर		pre
Bud	kopīlā कोपीला	mibrung	
Buffalo (male)	rāngo रांगो		mayeranga
,, (female)	bhainsi भैंसी		maye
Bug[1]	urus उड़ुस		kobe
Build, to	banāunu बनाउनु	khās	
Bulb	dallā डल्ला	gera	
Bull[2]	goru, bāchhā गोरू, बाछा	thor	klia
Bumblebee	baunrā भौंरा		
Bunch, a	jhuppā झुप्पा		
Bundle	bharī bito भारी, बिटो		te
	gattha गत्था		
Burn, to (t)	polnu पोलनु	juāk	kru
(i)	bālnu, jalnu बालनु, जलनु	ju, jos	mara
Burst, to	phutnu फुटनु	būt	ti
Bury, to[3]	purnu, gārnu पुरनु, गाड़नु	jantāk	
Bush	jhār, pothrā झाड़, पोथ्रा		gno
But	tara तर		
Butcher	kasāi कसाई		
Butt (rifle)	kundā कुन्दा		
Butter	nauni नोनी		
,, milk	mahi मही		kol
Butterfly	putli पुतली		tamlo

[1] "A bug" e.g. "what sort of a bug is that ?"—"Kasto kira chha?" A "B flat" is Urus or Chepti (G. Kobe). A flea is Upinya (M. Bachum; G. Tomi). A louse is junra (M. Sit; G. Shie).

[2] Goru is a bullock. A non-ploughing bull is bachha.

[3] Gārnu is not so polite.

ENGLISH	KHAS	MAGAR	GURUNG
Buttock	chāk चाक	puta	maisi
Button	tānk टांक		
Butts	gumti गुमटी		
Buy, to	kinnu किननु	loh	ki
By	le ले		
By-way	gorentho bāto गोंरेठो		yoi kya
	chorbāto चौर बाटो		
CABBAGE	gobi गोबी		
Cactus	sionri स्यूएाी		
	nagphimī नागफिमी		
Cage	pinjaro पिंजरो		
Calf (cattle)	bahar, bāchho बहड़, बाछो		
,, (leg)	tikhra तीखड़ा	paregia	
Call	dāknu डाकनु	et	whī
	jhikāunu झिकाउनु		twī
Calm (n)	sunsān सुन्सान		
Camel	unt ऊंट		
Camp	parau पाड़ाउ		
,, (stage for night)	bās बास		
Can (be able)	saknu सकनु	heg	kā
Canal	kulo कुलो		
Cane	lauro, bet लौरो, बेत	dānga	pahre
Cap	topi टोपी		kuile
Capsize, to (t)	ghoptāunu घोपटाउनु	korāk	koreya
	lotāunu लोटाउनु		
(i)	ghoptnu घापठनु	kor	kuri
	lotnu लोटनु		
Carcass (human)	murdā मुर्दा		
(animal)	sīno सीनो		
Card	tās तास		
Cardamons	alāinchi अलाइंची		
Careful	jatan garne जतन गरने		
Caress	musārnu मुसारनु		
Careless	bearthai बेअर्थै		

ENGLISH	KHAS	MAGAR	GURUNG
Carpenter	karmi कर्मी		
Carriage	gāri गाड़ी		
Carrot	gājar गाजर		
Carry, to	boknu बोकनु	bu	noh
Cascade	chhārā छारा		
Cask	pīpā पीपा		
Caste	jāt जात		
Cat	birālu बिरालु	suttu	nawa
Catch, to	samātnu समातनु	jīm	khā
Cauliflower	phulgopi फुलगोबी		
Cause	kāran कारण		
Cave	orār ओद्यार		
Cellar	bhatti भट्टी		
Centipede	khajuro खजुरो	nantraman	
Ceiling	chhānā छाना		chachan
Cemetery	chihān चिहान		chokou
Ceremony[1]	tewār तेव्हार		
Certainly	kāchh काछ		
Chaff	bhuso भुसो		
(laughter)	hānsi thatā हांसी ठटा		
Chain	sānglo सांगलो		
Chalk	khari खडी		
Chancre	tānki तांकी		
Change, to	sāntnu सांटनु	yes	te
Charcoal	gol, angār गोल अंगार	migrig	karapho
Charge (care)	sonpī सौंपी		
Charity	dān दान		
Charm	mantra मन्त्र		
,, (personal)	mohāni मोहनी		
,, (on wrist at Rikhi Tarpan)	rākhi राखी		

[1] Slave making (oil anointing) is Telia Chakur. Feet washing (marriage) is Gorha dhoie. Pleasing show is Mangal Jatra. Giving daughter to son-in law is Kanya Dan. A "show" is tamasha. Bridegroom at Bride's house is Janti. Walking round the sacred fire is Phera. Marriage tie is Anchal Ghata. Divorce is Sinko Dago or Sinko Pangra.

ENGLISH	KHAS	MAGAR	GURUNG
Chatter-box	kachkachia कचकचे		
	gangania गनगने		
Cheap	sahango, sasto सहंगो सस्तो		
Cheat, to	dhāntnu ढांटनु		lui
	thagnu ठगनु	thagdi	,,
	chhalnu छलनु		
Cheek	gālā गाला		kāmbo
,, , to	gijāunu गिजाउनु	gijdi	gne
Cherry	payān पईयां		
Chess	satrang सतरंज		
Chest	chhāti छाती		ku
Chestnut	pāngrā पाङ्गरा	surka	
Chew, to	chabāunu चबानु	tay	gniy
Chicken (small)	challā चल्ला	gumja	nakai pasi
Chicken-pox	kānkarā कांकड़ा		
Chikor	chākhura चाखुरा		
Chief[1]	mukhiā मुखिया		
Chil (kite)	chīl चील	mollo	timu
Child	bālakha, ketā, बालख, केटा	lenza maja	kolo
Childless	aputā अपुता		
Children	chhorā, chhori छोरा, छोरी	jujāko	pasipasia
	nāntinā नानतीना		kolmai
Chilli	khursāni खुरसानी		
Chimney	angethī अंगेठी		kota
Chin	chiunro च्युंड़ो		ka
China (country)	chīn चीन		
(substance)	chinī चिनी		
Chips	lobrā लोबरा		
Chisel	chhinā छीना		
Choke, to	asāltnu असाल्टनु		koya
	gānthi thuninu घांटी थुनिनु		
Cholera	haizā हैजा		

[1] Mukhia is a headman. Below him comes the jimwal. The chief (main) road is (Mul bato).

ENGLISH	KHAS	MAGAR	GURUNG
Choose, to	chhāntnu छांटनु		
Chum	jori, sangī जोड़ी, संगी	lapha	āgu, tume
Cinnamon	sinkaula सिनकौला		
	dālchini दालचिनी		
Cinder	kharāni खरानी	barap	nebro
Circle	gherā घेरा		
,, , to (as a hawk)	măndăl mārnu मन्दल मारनु		
Circumstance	hāl, hālat हाल, हालत		
Civilian (not in army)	dhākre ढाकरे		
Claim	dāwā दावा		
Clan	pad, tar पद, टर		
Clap, to	thapri mārna थपड़ी मारनु		yoglatu
Clasp, medal	dandi डंडी		
Clatter	khatrāng khutrung खतरांग खुतरुंग		
Claw	nangrā नंगरा	ārgin	
,, (crab)	sanāsu सुनासु		
Clay	chhiphlo māto छिपलो माटो	ārmetche jāh	pleba sa
Clean	saphā, chokho सफा, चोखो		
	sugghar सुग्घर		
Clear	sāngulo सांगुलो		
Clench, to	pārnu पारनु		la
Clever	chanākho चनाखो		
Cliff	chuli चुली		
Climate (cool)	shital शीतल		
(hot)	aul औल		
,, (of a place)	hāwā pāni हावा पानी		
Close, to	thunnu थुननु		
	dhāknu ढाकनु	hup	u
Cloth[1]	lugā लुगा	barin	khway

[1] Indian and English clothes with Urdu names are not given. Clothes is Luga (M. Barin; G. Khway). To put on clothes or to wear them is Luga, etc., Launu or Lagaunu (M. Bil; G. ka). To take them off is jhignu.

English	Khas	Magar	Gurung
Cloud	bādal, dhunri बादल, धुंरी		machea
Clove	luwang लवङ्ग		
Clue	thāha थाह		
Clumsy	lothro लोथरो		
Coal	koilā कोइला	migrig	
Coax, to	phakāunu फकाउनु	hum	wha
Cobweb	jālo जालो		
Cock	bhālyā भाल्या		
Cocoanut	golā, naruwal गोला, नरुवल		
Coffin	kaphan कफन		
Coin[1]	shikkā शिक्का		
Cold (adj.)	jāro, chiso जाड़ो, चिसो	jum	ku, niu
(noun)	rugā रुगा		sorma
Collide, to (t)	thokar lagāunu ठोकर लगाउनु		
(i)	thokar lagnu ठोकर लगनु		
Colour	rang रंग		
Comb	kāngiyo कांगियो	sath	prese
Come, to	ānu आनु	rā	kha
Comet	puchhāri tārā पुछड़ी तारा		
Comic	shwāng, tattā शवांग, टटा	utengia	
Compulsion	kar कर		
Complaint	phirāt फिरात		
Concerning	bāra mā बारा मा		
Condition	hāl, hālat हाल हालत		
Confess, to	kael g. कायल ग:		
Confuse, to	ghabrāunu घबराउनु		
	ātinu आंतीनु	atidi	
Contractor	thekidār ठेकादार		
Conquer, to	jitnu जितनु	ju, jitdi	to

(M. do. G. pli). Loincloth (small) is Langoti (or Doti). Loincloth down to knees is Patoka (M. Lapeta ; G. paki). Cloth over shoulder is Galek. Nepalese shirt is Bhoto. Ordinary one is Kurta. Bodice is Cholo. Skirt is Gunio. Blanket worn is Khadi (N. Garbuna). Woman's head cloth, Majetro (M. lurupu). Woman's breast cloth, rumal. Nepalese cloth (material)—ainthaya bhāngro. Nepalese raiment (knotted in front) ghādo.

[1] British Rupee is Kampani (G. Mhoi). Nepalese one (not common) Shikka. Nepalese 8-anna piece is Mohar (old name—Mundra Mole).

ENGLISH	KHAS	MAGAR	GURUNG
Convict, to	aprādhi thahranu अपराधी ठहरनु		
Cook, a	bhānsi भानसे		
,, to	pakāunu पकाउनु	pin	mi
Cook-house	bhānsagher भानसघर		
	chulo चुलो		
Cooking pots[1]	bhānrā भांड़ा		
Cool	chiso चिसो		nu
Coolie	bharyā भरिया		
Copper	tāmā तामो		kioro
Copy, to	sārnu सारनु	sarīsh	
(imitate)	nakal pārnu नकल पारनु		
a	nakal नकल		
Cork	birko बिरको		ka
Corn	anāj अनाज	ana	ana
Corner	kunā कुना		
Corns	khīlī खीली		
Corpse	murdā मुर्दा		
Cotton	kapās कपास		
Cough, a	khokī खोकी		piu
Count[2]	gannu गननु	hil	choi
Country	desh देश		
Courage	sāhas, dhiraj साहस, धिरज		
Court-yard	āgan आंगन	ārba	yu
Cousin[3]			
Cover (lid)	dakhan ढकन		

[1] Thāli is a brass round dish. Kadhai is a cauldron. Panio is a large flat spoon ; daru an ordinary spoon. Tauli is a cooking sauce-pan ; batuko or katora, a cup. Bhădu is millet. Tāwa, a flat dish for cooking chipaties on. (M. Kasai).

[2] Numerals are :—Khas. Yota, duita, etc., as Urdu. Magar. Kạt, nis, sum, buli, banga, etc., as Urdu, Gurung (written after noun). Ghri, gni som, pli, nga, tu, ni, pre, ku, chu. Twenty is gnichu, 30 is sonju. Also "ola" is added—2, gniola, etc. Men often speak of large numbers in multiples of 20, *e.g.* 85 would be char bisi panch.

[3] See footnote 2, pp. 35-36.

English	Khas	Magar	Gurung
Cover, to	chhopnu छोपनु dhāknu ढाकनु	hup	u
Cow	gāi गाई	het	mhe
Cow-shed	goth गोठ		prôn
Coward	kāphar काफर		
Cowrie	kaurhī कौड़ी		
Crab	gangathā गंगठा	re	kore
Crack, to	phutnu फुटनु		ti
Cramp, to get	akrinu अकड़ीनु		
Cream	kuṛāni कुरानी		
Crease, to	dobriānu दोबराआनु		ta
Creep, to	gasari gasari गसरी गसरीं jānu जानु		
Creeper, a	laharā लहरा		nori
Crime	pāp पाप		
Criminal	aprādhi अपराधी		
Cringe	nidre garnu निद्रे गरनु		
Cripple	lulo लुलो		
Crocodile	guhi, sus गुहि, सुस		
Crooked	bāngo बांगो	goche	kudu
Cross[1]	terchho टेरछो	phennām	peto
Cross-legged	paleti mārera पलेटी मारेर		
Cross-examine	sawāl kātnu सवल काटन		
Crow	kāg काग		kawa
Crowbar	sabbal सब्बल		
Crowd, a	jātra जात्रा		
Crown	mukut मुकुट		
Cruel	nithur निथुर		
Crush, to	kuchnu कुचनु	puchi	ple
Cry, to (weep)	runu रुनु	rāp	kro
(call out)	karāunu कराउनु	chiāk	
Cuckoo	kuku कुकु		
Cucumber	kānkro कांकड़ो	gniey	lakai

[1] This means horizontally, at the same level.

ENGLISH	KHAS	MAGAR	GURUNG
Cultivate	kamāunu कमाउनु		
Cultivator	kisāni किसानी		
Cup	batuko बटुको katorā कतोरा	bela	bela
Curl, to	ghumāunu घुमाउनु		
Curly	ghumāyāko घुमायाको ghungari घुंगरी		
Curry	tyun तयुन	met	ta
Curtain	pardā पर्दा		
Custom	rītī, bhāni रीति, भानौ		
Cut, to	kātnu काटनु	chi	tho
Cymbals	manjuri मंजुरी		
DACOIT	dāku डाकु	kusche barmi	yomo mhi
Dagger	sangīn, chepsa संगीन, चेपसी		
Dam	bănd वन्द		
Damage	nās नास	dasha	
Dance, to	nāchnu नाचनु	sie	shia
Dancing place	rodi रोदी		
Danger	dăr डर		ṅi
Darkness	andhyāro अनधयारो	chum	michu
Dasehra	dasyen दस्येन		
Date	bār, tithī बार, तिथी		
Daughter	chhori छोरी	jā	chami
Dawn	ujelo, rāmi ऊजेलो, रामी rumi रुमी	gorak, liha	nāga
Day	din दिन		tai
Daytime	diuso दिउंसो	ṇamsin	teba
Dead	mario ko मरयोको	siā	siba
Deaf	bairo बैरो		
Dear (fond)	piyāro प्यारो		
(expensive)	mahngo महंगो		
Death (fig)	kāl काल		
Debt	rin रिण		chake
Debtor	asāmi असामि		
Deceive, to	dantnu, thagnu ढांटनु, टगनु		

ENGLISH	KHAS	MAGAR	GURUNG
December [1]	pus पूस		
Decrease, to			
(t)	ghatāunu घटाउनु		
(i)	ghatnu घटनु		
Deep	gairo गैरा	lup	
Deer	mirga मिर्ग		pho
Defile, a	bhanjyāng भनजयांग		
Deformed	kubro कुबड़ी		
Delay, a	abelā अबेला		
Delight	ānand, bhog आनन्द, भोग		
Dented	kuchio कुचियो		
Descend, to (from train, etc.)	utranu उतरनु	jhal	toi
(come down)	tala ānu तल आनु	maklak ra	
Descent	orālo ओरालो	litim	kioro
Desert, to	bhāgnu भागनु	jo	
, a	retilo thaun रेतिलो ठाऊं	balua sa	tamle klo
Deserter	bhagaura भगौड़ा		
Despise, to	hela g. हेला ग:		
Destiny	bhāg भाग		
Destitute	hari kangāl हरी कंगाल		
Devil	bhut भूत		
Devotee	bhagat भगत		
Dew	os, sit ओस, सीत		
Dhal	dhāl धाल	techo	paitu
Dhan (growing rice)	dhān धान	chosān	milāh
Diagonally	chhatkvā छटक्या		
Diamond	hirā हिरा		
(jewel)			
(cards)	inta ईंट		
Diarrhoea	chherauti छरौटी pakhāla पखाला		
Dice	pānsā पांसा		

[1] See footnote 5, p. 33.

English	Khas	Magar	Gurung
Die, to	marnu, bitnu मरनु, बितनु	si	si
Different	beglai, bhinno वेगलाइ, भीन्नो		
	nolā नोला		
Difficult	asajilo असजिलो		
Difficulty	kathin कठिन		
Dig, to	khannu खननु	ko	ta
Dip, to	chobnu चोबनु	tàk	
Dirt	kasingar कसीगंर		
Dirty	phori, mailo फोहरी, मैलो		
Discharge, to take	nām kātnu नाम काटनु	nām chi	mhi ta
Discover, to	pāunu पाउनु	din	yo
Disease	rog रोग		
Disgrace	helā हेला		
Disguise, in	bhes badalera भेस बदलेरा		
Dish	thāli थाली		
Dishonest	chhali, kapti छली, कप्टी		
Dismiss, to (i)	chhutnu छुटनु		
	chhornu छाड़नु	dās	wāti
(t)	chhutāunu छुटाउनु	chhutedi	
Disperse, to (i)	phijāunu फिजाउनु		
(t)	phailānu फैलानु		
Dispute, a	jhagrā झगड़ा		
Distant	tārā ठाड़ा	los	rega
Disturbance	hul, danga हूल, दंगा		pañ
	hāhu हाहु		
Ditch (drain)	kulo कुलो		
(pit)	khālto खालटो		
Divorce, to	chhutāunu छुटाउनु	chhutedi	wāti
	tyāgnu त्यागनु		
Dizziness	ringato रिंगटो		
Dizzy	jiring jiring जिरिङ्ग जिरिङ्ग		
to be	ringāunu रिंगाउनी		
Do, to	garnu गरनु	zāt	la
Doctor	baidhi बैदी		
Doe	murlī मुर्ली		

English	Khas	Magar	Gurung
Dog	kukur कुकुर	chui	nagu
Dog (wild)	boānso बोआंसो		
Donkey	gadāh गदाह्		
Door	dailo, dhoka दैलो, ढोका	galam	mara ngia
Double	dohoro दोहोरो		
Doubt	sankā संका		
Dove	dhukur ढुकुर		
Down	tala, muntira तल, मुनतिर undho ऊंधो	māklak	noi
Downhill	orālo ओरालो	litim	
Dowry	dāijo दाइजो		
Drain	kulo कुलो		
Draw, to (pull)	tānnu तातनु	tāndi	tāni
Drawer	khopi खोपी		
Drawers	jāngia जांग्या		
,, long (trousers)	suruwāl सुरूवाल		
Dream	sapanā सपना		mohra
Dress	luga, poshāg लुगा, पोशाग	barin	khway
Drink	khānu खानु	ga	to
Drive away, to	dhapāunu धपाउनु	dhabdī	dhabdi
Drizzle	jhimjhime झिमझिमे		
Drop, a	thopo थोपो		
Drought	obāno ओबानो।		
Drown, to (t)	dubāunu डुबाउनु	thāk	plun
(i)	dubnu, burnu डुबनु	thā	plu buri yā
Drum	tambar तम्बर		
(tomtom)	mādal मादल		mādā
Drunk	mātya ko मात्या को	mora	gne
Drunkard	matwālā मतवाला		
Dry (adj.)	sukyako सुक्याको	chhokche	kāre
, to	sukāunu सुकाउनु	chhok	swon
Duck	hāns हांस		
Dumb	lātā लाटा		
Dung	mal मल		
(human)	gu गू	beṇ	kli

ENGLISH	KHAS	MAGAR	GURUNG
Dung (cattle)	gobar गोबर		
Dust	dhulo धुलो		
Dwarf	bāuniā बावन्या		
Dwell, to	rahnu रहनु	mu	ti
Dye, to	rangāunu रङ्गाउनु		
Dysentery	ragatmāsi रगतमासी		sekuntar
EAGLE	hārphori हारफारी		jure
	garul गरूल		
Ear	kān कान	kep	nave
Early	bhyāna भ्यान	gorak	nāga
Earring	mundro मुंद्रो		māra
Earth (world)	dunyā दुनिया		
(substance)	māto माटो	jāh	sā
Earthquake	bhuinchāl भुईचाल		
East	purab पूरब		
Easy	sajilo सजीलो		
Eat	khānu खानु	je	cha
Eaves	balenī बलेनी		
Edge (ground)	cheo छेव		
(knife)	dhār धार		
Edgeways	dhārilo धारीलो		
Eel[1]	bām, rājbām बाम, राजबाम	bulanga	
	chuchubām चुचुबाम		
Effort	mihnat मिंहनत		
	jatan जतन		
Egg	phul फुल	miru	nake phu
Either, or	yāt yāt यात यात		
Eject, to	phirnu फिरनु	kā	go to
Elbow	kuinā कुईना		kurdung
Elder	jetho जेठे	mizar	tauku
Elephant	hāthi हाथी		
Ember	bhubro भुबरो		
Embrace, to	angāl hālnu अङगल हालनु	angal kā	angal chom
Emerge, to	niklnu निकलनु	kew	toi

[1] Rajbam is a large eel, chuchubam a pointed one.

ENGLISH	KHAS	MAGAR	GURUNG
Empty	khāli खाली	murlang	
End, the	khatam, anta खतम, अंत		
	ānkhari आंखरी		
to (i)	saknu सकनु	beg	ka
Endure, to (to suffer)	sahanu सहनु		
Enemy	bairi, satur बैरी, सतुर		
Energy	bal बल		po
Enlist (t)	lāhur mā lāunu लाहुर मा	laur ang rāk	
(i)	lāhur mā āunu ,, ,,	laur ang rā	
Enough !	bhayo भयो	chana	tai
Entangle	aljhnu अलझनु		
Enter, to	pasnu पसनु	paidi	hoi
Entire	sārai सारै		
Entrails	āndrā आन्द्रा	mekhe	karou
Entreat, to	binti garnu बिन्ती गरनु		
Envelope, an	liphāpa लिफापा		
Envy	dāha डाह		
Epidemic	sarnya rog सरन्या रोग		
Erase, to (i)	metnu मेटनु	metdis	miti
(t)	metaunu मेटाउनु		
Erect	thāro ठाड़ो		
Error	bhul भूल		
Escape, to	bachnu बचनु	ji	soi
	umkanu उमकनु	bis	
Escort	paharā पहरा		
Especially	khāsgari खास गरी		
Estate	māl matta मालमत्ता		
Eunuch	khassi खस्सी		singare
Et cetera	ityādi इत्यादि		
Even (conj.)	pani पनी		
Even (adj).	samma सम्म		
Evening	sānjh, beluka सांझ, बेलुका	chhum	gnesa, nāri
Ever	kaile कैले		
Evidence	gawai गवाई		

English	Khas	Magar	Gurung
Evil	pāp पाप		
Ewe	bheri भेड़ी		ku
Exact (emphatic denom.)	twāk टवाक		
Exactly	chain चैं		
Examination	intihān इनतिहान		
Examine, to	jāchnu जाचनु		
Except	sewai सेवाइ		
Exchange, to	sāntnu सांटनु	yes	te
Excited	antiyā अंतिया		
Excitement	garbar गरवर		
Excuse	bahānā बहाना		
Executioner	pore पोरै		
Expensive	mahngo महंगो		
Explode	phutnu फुटनु	but	ti
Extinguish	mārnu मारनु	sāt	sa
Eye[1]	ānkhā आंखा	mik	mi
Eye-brow	ānkhi-bhaun आंखीभौं	mik pug	michcha
Eye-lash	parela परेला	michcha	michcha
FACE	anhwār अनव्हार		li
Faeces	jhārā झाड़ा	ben	kli
Faint, to (adj.)	murchhā hunnu मुरच्छा ऊनु		
Fair (just)	sidho, sāncho सीधो सांचो		
(light)	goro गोरो	bahu	tarkya
Fairy	parī परी		
Fall (on ground)	lotnu लोटनु	kor	kura
,, (precipice)	khasnu खसनु	jāl	tay
,, down (as wall)	bhatkanu भतकनु		
False	jhuthā झुठा		
Family	kulkutumb कुलकुटम्ब		

[1] The black round the eye is Gajul.

English	Khas	Magar	Gurung
Famine	anīkāl अनीकाल		
Famous	jasīlo जसीलो		
Far	tārā टाड़ा	los	rego
Fashion	rīti रीति		
(custom)			
(habit)	bānī बानी		
Fasting	upās उपास		
Fat (adj.)	moto मोटो	desu	choi
(noun)	boso बोसो	mesos	chhi
Fatal (place)	marm मर्म		
Fate	bhāg भाग		
Father	bābu बाबु	bua	āba
Fault	birāun बिराउनु		
,, to make, spoil a show	birāunu चाउनु	biradi	biradi
Favour, to	ruchāunu रुचाउनु	jāk	kho
Fear, to	darnu डरनु	biri	gni
(noun)	trās, dar त्रास, डर		
Feather	pwānkh प्वांख	mikar	piha
February	phāgun फागुन		
Feel, to	chhāmnu छामनु		
,, (as earth-quake)	chal pāunu चाल पाउनु	chāl dīn	
Female[1]	murli मुर्ली		
Fence	bār बाड़		
Ferry	ghāt घाट		
Festival	tewār त्येवार		
Fetter	nel नेल		
Fever	jaru, tāp जरो, ताप		
Few	kamti, thorai कमती, थोड़ै		
Fiddle	sārangi सारंगी		
Fife	murali मुरली		
Field	khet खेत	gāra	moro

[1] Of humans, shwashni; of birds, pothi; of goats, pathi. Of other animals, murli.

English	Khas	Magar	Gurung
Fig	beru बेड़ू		
Fight, to	larnu लड़नु	pun	ne
,, (war)[1]	larāi, lām लड़ाई, लाम		
Figure (numeral)	ankha अंख		
Figure (body)	āng, sarīr आङ्ग, सरीर		
Fill, to	bharnu भरनु	ping	pluya
Fin	pakhetā पखेटा		
Find, to	pāunu पाउनु	din	yo
Fine, a	dand डण्ड		
(adj.)	rāmro रामरो	sieche	chiaba
Finger[2]	angulo, aunto अंगुलो, औंठो		uri
Finger-nail	nang नङ्ग	argin	yoshi
Finish, to	saknu सकनु	biat	kha
	bhyāunu भ्याउनू		
, the	khatam खतम		
Fire	āgo आगो	men	mhe
Fire-fly	junkiri जुनकिड़ी	bamlidu	mitala
Fire-place	chulā चुला		
Fire-wood	dauro दौरो	sing	si
Fish, a[3]	māchhā माछा	dissi	tānga
Fist	mutthi मुट्ठी		
Fit, to	milnu मीलनु	kat	kriya
	atāunu अताउनु	sin	kaiya
(adj.)	tagro, sansa तगड़ो, संसा		
(able)	lāik लाइक		
Flag[4]	jhandi, dhajā झन्डी, धजा		
Flame	jwālā, swālā जवाला, स्वाला		

[1] Lam is really the road to the war.

[2] Thumb, Fore, Middle, Fourth, Little are Buro, Jetho or Kalmi or Chor, Mailo, Sainlo, Kanchho Aunlo respectively.

[3] Kinds : Asla, long white. Pakheta (lit., fin.), a small fish with a large dorsal fin, which enables it to move very fast. Bhoti (like a rock fish). Budina (large headed). Junge (with whiskers). Godeta (striped). Bagi (has two small horns like thorns). Kuranga ; Shahar (Mahseer).

[4] Dhaja is a small flag on a temple.

ENGLISH	KHAS	MAGAR	GURUNG
Flank	cheo छेव		
Flat	chepto चेपटो	peso	plenze
Flaw	khot खोट		
Flea	upīyā ऊंपया	burchum	tomi
Flesh	shikār, māsu शिकार, मासु	sia	sia
Float, to	bahnu, bagnu बाहनु, बगनु		
Flock, a	bagāl बगाल		
Flood	jalthal, bel जलथल, बेल		
Floor	bhui भुइँ	ja	sa
Flour	pītho पीठो		pro
Flow, to	bahanu, bagnu बहानु, बगनु		
Flower	phul फ़ूल	sārr	tā
Flute	bānsuli बांसुली		
Fly, to			
(as bird)	urnu उड़नु	bur	piriya
(escape)	bhāgnu भागनु	ju, jo	bhāgdi
(insect)	mākha माखा	jima	chiomi
(,, small)	jhinga भिङ्गा		
(horse)	dāns डांस		
Foam	gāj, phen गाज, फेन		
Fog	kuhiro कुहिरो	dambu	maseo
Fold, to	dobriānu दोबरयानु		ta
Follow	pachhi 2 jānu पछी २ जानु		
Food	khānā खाना	jeki	chabise
Fool	anāri, murkha अनाड़ी, मुर्ख		
Foot (human)	khuttā खुट्टा	hīl	pahle
(animal)	lāt लात		
Foot-mark or step	pāielo पाइलो		mai
For	lāi, ko lāgi लाई, को लागी		
Force	bal बल		
Ford, to	tarnu तरनु		
, a	janghār जांघार		
Fore-arm	hāth हाथ	hut	yo
Fore-head	kapāl कपाल	tār	kara
	nidhār निधार		

ENGLISH	KHAS	MAGAR	GURUNG
Foreign	pardesh परदेश anyadesh अन्यदेश		
Forest	ban बन		
Forget, to	birsnu बिरसनु	miag	siomle ya
Forgive, to	chhimā, māph क्षमा, माफ garnu गरनु		
Forsake, to	chhornu छोड़नु tyāgnu त्यागनु	dās	wāti
Foundation	jag जग		
Fox	lomri लोमड़ी		
,, (blackpine Martin)	molsāpri मोलसाप्री		heku
,, small	phyāunro फ्याउरो		
Freckle	chhoyā छोया		
Frequently	gharī ghari घड़ी, घडी		
Free (gratis)	muphtai, tisi मुफते, तिसी	hotane	chalen
Fresh	ālo आलो		
Friday	shukrbār शुक्रबार		
Friend	sangi, jorī संगी, जोड़ी	lapha	āgu-tume
Frighten, to	darāunu डराउनु tarsāunu तरसाउनु	biri	gnig
Frog	bhiāgutā भ्यागुता	rogate	atkou
From	bāta बाट	ing	
Front (adj.)	aghilo अघिलो		
Frost	tusāro तुसारो		
Frown, to	mukh nichornu मूख निचोड़नु	nir ru	sung nichikla
Fruit	phalphul फलफूल		
Full	bhariāko भऱ्याको	pinga	ple
Fun	thattā ठट्टा		
,, , to poke at	thattāunu ठटाउनु	datuph	toy
Funeral	malāmi मलामी		
Fungus (mildew)	dhumsi धुमसी		
Furlough	razā रजा		
Future	āune आउने	rachiu	kowri
Fy	chhi chhi छी छी		

English	Khas	Magar	Gurung
GAIN	naphā नफा		
Gale	ādhi, bhaunri आधि, भौंरी		namur
Gambling	juwā जुवा		
Gaol	jhelkhānā झेलखाना		
Garden	bāri बाड़ी		
Garlic	lasun लसुन	arek	gno
Gate	dhokā ढोका	galam	marangia
Gather, to	batolnu बटोलनु		tun
Gem	lāl, manhi लाल, मणी		
Generous	dātā दाता		
Gentle	bistari बिस्तरि		
Get, to	linu, pāunu लिनु, पाउनु	lā, dīn	ki, yo
Ghee	ghiu घ्यू		chhiku
Ghost	bhut, pret भूत, प्रेत		
Giant	rāshes राशेस		
Giddiness	ringāto रिङ्गाटो		
Giddy, to be	tauko ringāunu ; टाउको रिङ्गाउनु		
	bhāuanau charnu भाउनौ चड़नु		
Gift	dān दान		
Giggle	khitkhiti खितखितौ	khitkhiti	khitkhiti
	hansnu हँसनु	ret	nishoo
Ginger	suto, aduwā सुटो, अदुवा		
Girl [1]	chhori, taruni छोरी, तरुनी	lenze māja, ārnām	chame, rime
Give	dinu दिनु	yā	pi
Glad	khushi, ramāyā खुशी, रमाया	maranga	sain
Glass	shisā शिसा		
Glow worm	junkiri जुनकिड़ी	bamlidu	mitala
Glue	gun गून		
Go, to	jānu जानु	an, nung	ya
Goat [2]	bākrā बाकरा	rā	ra
God	prameshwar प्रमेश्वर	bhagwān	bhagwan

[1] The various words are chhori, taruni, chelli, cherana, kanya, kuwari

[2] Mother, big female, ram, young, castrated are mau, patekri, bohkia, patha, kassia respectively.

English	Khas	Magar	Gurung
Goitre	gānrā गांड़ा		
Gold	sun सून	gel	māra
Gong	ghantā घण्टा		
Gonorrhoea	sujāk सूजाक		
Good	rāmro, jāti रामरो, जाती	sieche	chhiaba
,, (moral)	bhalo भलो		yobe
Good-bye	bidā बिदा		
Governor	mukhiā मूख्या jimwāl जिमवाल		
Grain (as corn)	dānā दाना	gera	ro
(weight)	rati रति		
Grand	thulo ठुलो	karāncho	tebe
Grandson, etc.[1]			
Grape	angur अंगुर		
Grass	ghās, jhār घास, झाड़		chhi
,, (spear)	kuro कुरो	ātungia	tinyu
Grateful	guni गुनी		
Grave (noun)	chihān चिहान		chokou
(adj.)	gambhīr गम्भीर		
Graze, to	charāunu चराउनु	archega	cha
Grease	boso बोसो	mesoṣ	chi
Great	thulo ठुलो	karāncho, sum	tebe
Greedy	lobhi लोभी		
Green	hario हरियो	phicho	pingya
Grey	phusro फुसरो	poncho	
Grief	dukha दुख		
Grievance	dukhsukh दुखसुख		
Grind	pinnu पिननु	nug	prc
Ground	bhui, jimi भुइँ, जिमी	ja	sa
Grow	barhnu बड़नु umranu उमरनु	lung, git	
Grumble	gangan garnu गनगन गरनु		
Guess, to	andāz garnu अन्दाज गरनु		
Guest	pahuno पाहुनो		preme

[1] See footnote 2, pp. 35-36.

ENGLISH	KHAS	MAGAR	GURUNG
Guide, a	aguwā अगुवा		
, to	bāto batāunu बाटो बताउनु		
Guitar	hārmoni, bin हारमोनी, बीन		
Gulp, to	nilnu निलनु	mel	klo
Gutter	kulo कुलो		
(ground)			
(roof)	donrā डोंड़ा		
HABIT	bāni, rītī बानी, रीती		
Hag	boksi बोकसी		
Hail	asīnā असीना	jhirlung	tiseo
Hair	raun रौं	chhām	mui (legs, etc.) karra (head)
(moustache)	jungā जुंगा	mur	mora
(Hindu topknot)	tupi टुपि		tamu
Halt	ubhīnu, arinu उभीनु, अड़ीनु	tong	rā
Hammer (big)	ghan घन		
(small)	hatoṛo हतोड़ो		
(of gun)	ghora घोरा		
Hand	hāth हाथ	hūt	yo
Handcuff	hāthkari हाथकड़ी		
Handful	hāthbhari हाथभरी	hutbhari	yotiko
Handwriting	likh, achhar लिख, अछर	rīk	prī
Handle, a	benr बेंड़	mimu	u
Hang (t)	jhundāunu झुंडाउनु	chelok	chiu
(i)	jhundnu फुन्डनु		chiuya
(execute)	phansī dunu फांसी दिनु		
Happy	khushi खुशी ramāyo रमायो	marānga	sain
Hard	sāro सारो	jāra	
,, (irksome)	gāro गारो		
Hare	kharāh खराह chaugarah चौगड़ा		
Harlot	pātar, besyā पातर, बेसिया		
Harm	bāni, nās हानी नास	dasha	

ENGLISH	KHAS	MAGAR	GURUNG
Harvest	bālī बाली		
Hat	topī टोपी		kule
Hate	dāha डाह		
Hatchet	bancharo बनचरो	aruwa	ta
Hatless	murilo मड़िलो		
Haversack	jholi झोली		
,, band on cooly	nāmlo नामलो	biri	tobi
Havoc	nās, hānī नास, हानी	dasha	
Hawk	bāj बाज		
Hay	sukio ghās सुकथो घास	chokche-ghas	karaba chhi
Haze ; heat	tuyānlo तुयांलो		
Head	tāuko, munto टाउको, मुन्टो	tālu	kara
Heap	thupro थुपड़ो		
Hear, to	sunnu सुनन्	she	the
Heart	muto मुटो	gin	thi
Hearts (cards)	pān पान		
Heat	ghām घाम		
Heat-rash	ghamārā घमाड़ा		
Heaven	akās, sarga अकास, सरग		mu
Heavy	garungo गरुंगो	līs	liko
Hedge	bār बाड़		
Heel	kurkuchā कुरकुचा		pale ti
Hell	narka नरक		
Help [1]	gohār गोहार		
Hemp	patuwā पटवा		pāta
Hen	pothi पोथि		yoma
Here	yahān यहाँ	ilang	chui
Herb	jāributi जाड़ी बुटी		moi
Herd	bagāl, bathān बगाल, बथान		
Herdsman	gothālā गोठाला		pronde
Hermit, m.f.	māta माता		
Hero	surbīr शूरबीर		
Heron	bagulā बगुला		

[1] See footnote 3, p. 34.

ENGLISH	KHAS	MAGAR	GURUNG
Hiccough	baruki बारुकी		
Hide, to (t)	lukāunu लुकाउनु	archik	loh
(i)	luknu लुकनु	archi	lo
(noun)	chhālā छाला		tīpi, tipli
High	alko अलको	lung	nuba
Highlands [1]	lekh लेख		
Hill	pahār, daurā, पहाड़, डांडा		
(medium)	lekh लेख		ye
(big)	parbat परवत		
(foot of)	kachhār कछार		
Hillside	cheo, pākho चेव, पाखो		
Hind	murli मुड़ली		
Hinder, to	chheknu छेकनु	tun	tundi
Hinge	kabjā कबजा		
Hint	sān सान		
Hip	phirpātā फिरपाटा		
History	sawāi सवाई		
Hit, to	hānnu हाननु	dung dāthuk	li
	hirkānu हिरकानु	sāt, gnāp	
Hither	yeta येटा	ilak	chiu
Hockey	bhukundo भुकुन्डो		
Hoe (1 finger broad)	tikho kuto तिखो कुटो		
(2 fingers)	kuto कुटो		
(4 ,,)	kodālo कोदालो		
(8 ,,)	kodālī कोदाली		
(10 ,,)	pharuwā फड़ुवा		
Hold, to	thāmnu थामनु		
(keep)	rākhnu राखनु		
	samātnu समातनु		
Hole (nature)	dulo दुलो		kuh
,, (made)	chhenr छेंड़		
Holi	hori होरी		

[1] Highlander (man who lives in snow) sheshi.
,, (Scotch) Ghāgra, which really means a skirt.

ENGLISH	KHAS	MAGAR	GURUNG
Holiday	chhutti छुट्टी		
Hollow (noun)	khālto खालटो		
(adj.)	dungrā डुंगरा		
	khokaro खोकरो		
Holy	pabitra पवित्र		
Home	ghar घर	im	thi
Honey	mah मह		kway
,, juice	raś रस	mor	kudu
Honour	mān मान		sain
,, your	tapāin तपाईं		gnio
Hoof	khur खुर		
Hook	angkusyā अङ्गकुस्या		
,, fish	balsi बलसी		
Hookah (wood)	bānse बांसे		
Hop, to	uphārnu उफारनु	phorju	uphridi
Hope	āsrā āshā आसरा, आशा		
Horn	sing सिङ	mirang	ru
Hornbill (bird)	dhanês धनेस		
Hornet			
(small)	aringāl अरीङगल	aregun	chikru
(big)	bachhiu बच्यू		
Horse	ghorā घोड़ा		
Horsefly	dāns डांस		
Host	niuto dine निउतो दिन्य		
Hot (water)	tāto तातो	khānche	tāwe
(day)	niāno, ghām न्यानो, घाम	jāl	toi
Hour	ghantā घन्टा		
House	ghar घर	im	thi
Hover, to	nāchnu नाचनु	shi	shie
	thirnu थिरनु		
How	kasto, kasari कस्तो कसरी	kuncho	khai, kada
,, much	kati कती	kurik	kati
Howl [1]			

[1] To howl as an animal is kāraunu. To weep is runu.

English	Khas	Magar	Gurung
Huddled up	khutruka खुतरुक		
Hug, to	chhāti mā lagāunu छाती मा लगाउनु		
Huldi (turmeric)	besār बेसार		
Hunchback	kubro कुबड़ो		
Hungry	bhukh lāgiā ko भुख लागया को	tukresia rangsia	phokre
Hurricane	ādhi bhaunri आधि भौंरी		
Husband	lognia लोगने	linja	piu
Husbandman	kisāni किसानी kheti garne खेती गरने		
Hut	jhupro झुपड़ो		
Hyaena	bhāpsilā भापसीला		plousiala
I	m म	ngā	ngā
Ice	hiun हिऊं		
Idea	bichār बिचार		
Idiot	murhka मुर्ख		
Idleness	alchhi अलछि		ple
Idol	murti मुर्ती		
If	bhanedekhin भनेदेखिन	pranta	
Ignorant	ghāmar, murkha घामड़, मूर्ख		
Ill	birāmi बिरामी	chāh (to be)	nā
Immoral	pāpi, dust पापी, दुस्ट kapāsi कपासी		
Impertinence	gustāki गुसताकी		
In	mā मा	ang	ra
Including	samet समेत		
Increase, to (t) (i)	barhāunu बड़ाउनु barhnu बड़नु	karānk lung	
Indian (adj.)	desi देसी		
Infant	nāni, bālak नानी, बालक		kolo
Inject, to	khopāunu खोपाउनु bhed g. भेद गः	khopdi	khopdi
Ink	masi मसी		
Inn	powā, bhatti पोवा, भट्टी		

ENGLISH	KHAS	MAGAR	GURUNG
Inoculate, to	khopāunu खोपाउनु	khopdi	khopdi
Insect	kirā किड़ा	du	māja
Inside	bhitra भित्र		
Insolent	shekhi शेखी		
	abhimāni अभीमानी		
Instead of	badlā mā बदला मा		
Intelligent	chalāk चलाक		
Intentionally	jānībujhera जानीबुझेर		
Interest (money)	biāz ब्याज		
In vain	suddai सुदैइ	hotane	chalan
Iron	phalām फलाम		pwa
Island	tāpu टापू		
Itch, to	chilāunu चिलाउनु	oso	kiye
, the	luto लुतो		
Ivory	hāthi ko dānt हाथीकोदान्त	hathi sia	hathi sa
JACKAL	siāl स्याल	sila	
January [1]	māgh माघ		
Jar	bhāro, gharā भाड़ो, घड़ा		
"Janr" [2]	jānr जांड़	hān	pāh
,, (strained	janr ko jol जाड़ को जोल	hana midi	pāh kiku
Javelin	bhālā भाला		
Jaw	bāngaro बांगरो		
Jay	tewa chara तेवा चड़ो		
Jealous	dāhi डाही		
Jewel	gahanā गहना		
Jew's harp	māchungi माचुंगी		
Join, to	jornu जोड़नु		
Joke	hansi thattā हांसी ठट्टा		
Joy	ānand, bhog आनन्द, भोग		
Judge, to	nisāphi g. निसाफी ग:		
, a	nisāph निसाफ		
Juice	ras, jol रस, जोल		kudu

[1] See footnote 5, p. 33.

[2] A drink made out of rice.

ENGLISH	KHAS	MAGAR	GURUNG
July [1]	sāwan सावन		
Jump, up	uphrinu उफड़ीन	uphridi	
, over	phāl kātnu फालकाटनु	phāl chi	phal tho
, down		phal kā	
June [1]	asār असाड़		
Jungle	ban बन		
Just (adj.)	sidho,sancho सीधो,सांचो		
(adv.)	bharkar, aile भरकर, अइले	chahān inang	toka
KALASI	pīpā पीपा		
Keen	tez तेज		
Keep, to	rākhnu राखनु	dā	the
(maintain)	pālnu पालनु	kok	wai
Kernel	gudi गुदी		
Kerosine	matti ko tel मट्टीको तेल		
Kettle	bhaddu, ketli भड्डू, केतली		
Key	chābi चाबी		
Kick, to	khuttā le hānnu खुट्टा ले हानु	hil e dathuk	
	lāt le hirkāunu लात ले हिरकाउनु		
Kid	pāthi पाठी		
Kidney	mirgula मिरगुला		
Kind (noun)	kisam किसम		
(adj.)	dayā दया		
King	rājā राजा		muru
Kiss, to	moai khānu मोआइ खानु	moai je	moai cha
Kitchen	bhānse ghar भानसे घर		
Kite	chil चील	mollo	
Knave	thag, kapti ठग, कप्टी		
(cards)	gulām गुलाम		
Knead, to	muchhnu मुछनु	jhaumki	
Knee	ghunrā घुंड़ा	chīga	
Kneecap	pāngrā पांगरा		

[1] See footnote 5, p. 33.

ENGLISH	KHAS	MAGAR	GURUNG
Knife (pen)	chāku चाकु		
,, (on kukri)	karda कर्द	dung, sāt	
Knock, to	hānnu हान्नु	dāthuk	
,, down	lotāunu लोटाउनु	korak	koreya
,, ,, (house, etc.)	bhatkāunu भत्काउनु		
Knot	gāntho गांठो		
Know, to	jānnu जान्नु	war	rā
,, how to	dornu दोरनु		
Knowledge	thāha, sanka थाह, संक bidhyā बिद्या		
Knuckle	gāntho गांठा		
LABOUR	kāj, kām काज, काम	zātke	ke
Laces	tanā तना		
Ladder [1]	lisnu, sīrhī लिसनु, सीढ़ी		
Lake	talāu, tāl तलाउ, ताल		
Lame	dunro डुंड़ो		
Lamentation	bilāp बिलाप		
Lamp	bati बती		
,, (small) earthenware)	diwo दिवो		
Lance Naick	piut पिउट		
Land(not sea)	jamin जमिन	ja	sa
(country)	desh देश		
Landslip	pairo पैरो		tui
Language	kurā कुरा		ta
Languor	dheruwā ढेड़ुवा		
Lap	kākh काख	ku	kona
Large	thulo ठुलो	karāncho, sum	tebe
Lark (bird)	kurang kurang कुरङ्ग कुरङ्ग chara चरा		
Last	ākhiri आखिरी pachhillo पछिल्लो	nunlak	lilili

[1] Lisno is wooden ladder. Bharyang are stone steps.

English	Khas	Magar	Gurung
Last, to	rahnu रहनु		
Late	dhilo ढिलो		liyai
Lately	hālko हालको		
	āja bholī आज भोली	chining pihin	tinya pana
Laugh, to	hānsnu हांसनु	ret	nisheo
,, at	gijāunu गिजाउनु		
	khishāunu खिशाउनु		
Law	ain ऐन		
Laziness	alchhi अलछि		ple
Lead,[1] to	doryāunu डोरयाउन		
(noun)	sīsā सीसा		
Leaf	pāt पात	lā	lā
Leak, to	chunu चुनु	jur	chai
Lean, to	ārish lagaunu अडीश लगाउनु	ārish ledi	
over, to	dhalkanu धकलनु		
	jhuknu झुकनु		
(adj.)	dublo दुबलो	rut	che
Learn, to	siknu सिकनु	pāh	lo
Leather	chhālā छाला		tīpi
Leech	juko जुको	lawat	tipy
Left (adj.)	debro देवरो		
Leg	khuttā खुट्टा	hīl	pale
Legend	sawāi सवाई		
Leisure	phursat फुरसत		
Lemon	amilo अमिलो	bīr	kiu
Lend, to	rin dinu रिण दिनु	rin yā	chake pi
Leopard	chituwa चितुवा		cheto
Leper	kori कोडी		
Less[2]			

[1] *i.e.*, to lead along by the hand, etc.

[2] Hindustani kamti can be used. To become less is ghătnn (घटनु) M Tun. To make less is ghătaunu ; The Battalion less one company—Battaion yota Kumpani chorira.

English	Khas	Magar	Gurung
Lesson	arthi अर्थी		
Let, to	dinu दिनु	ya	pi
Letter (post)	chittī चिठ्ठी		
(writing)	achchar अच्चर		
Level	samma, chepto सम्म, चेपटो		
Lick, to	chātnu चाटनु	lāk	le
Lid	dhakkan ढक्कन		ka
Lie, a	dhāntkurā ढांटकूरा		
, to	dhāntnu ढांटनु		lu
down, to	sutnu सुतनु	mis	ro
Life	jyān ज्यान		
Light, to (t)	bālnu बालनु	mot	mara
(i)	jalnu जलनु	jur	lui
,, (not dark)	ujyālo उज्यालो	tianche	
" (not heavy)	halungo हलुंगो	kiāngche	yoi
Lightning	bijlī बिजली		
Like (adj.)	jasto जस्तो	dinchu	miôn
, to	ruchāunu रुचाउनु	jāk	ko
Lily	kamal to phul कमल को फुल	kamali sarr	kamala ta
Lime	kamero कमेरो		
Limp, to	khuchyāng (2) खच्यांग(२) garnu रगनु		
Lion	sher शेर		
Linseed	alsi अलसी		
Link	sikrī सिकरी		
Lip	onth ओंठ	burlin	mode
Litter	kasingar कसींगर		
Little	siāno स्यानो	mārchu	cheoba
Live, to			
(dwell)	basnu, rahnu बसनु, रहनु	mu	ti
(alive)	jiunu जिउनु		so
Liver	kalejo कलेजो	mīgin	nāno
Lizard	chhepāro छेपाड़ा		
Load	bhār, kumlo भार, कुमलो		te
Loan	rin रिण		

ENGLISH	KHAS	MAGAR	GURUNG
Lock	tālā ताला		
Locust	salau सलौ		tiri
Log	muro मुड़ो		
Loin-cloth	langothī, dhotī लंगोठी, धोती		phāsu
Loins	chutar चूतड़		maisi
Lonely	ekelai एकलै	millikāt	ghri
Long	lāmo लामो	lotsa	ringi
Look, to	hernu हेर्नु	dāng, ons	neo
for, to	khojnu खोजनु	pā	māya
Loop	ghero घेरो		
Loose (adj.)	khokalo खोकलो		kholekhole
to (unravel)	phuskāunu फुसकाउनु	phorsāk	pla
(let go)	chhornu छोड़नु	dās	wāti
Lose, to	harāunu हराउनु	māt	mā
Loss	hāni, nās हानी, नास	dasha	
Lost, to get [1]	metnu मेटनु		
Loud	charko चरको		
Louse	jumrā जुमड़ा	sik (of head) geres (of body)	shie
Love	priti, māyā, प्रीति, माया prem, tith प्रेम, तीथ		
Low (adv.)	tala, undho तल, उन्धो	māklāk	maye kiro
(adj.)	hocho होचो	tunche	mawale
Luck	bhāg भाग		
Lucky	bhāgemān भाग्यमान		
Luke-warm	mantāto मनतातो		
Lump	dallo डल्लो		
Lung	phokso फोकसो		kloba
MAD	jhallā झल्ला		
Maiden	taruni तरुनी	ārnām	rīme

[1] This is in the sense of disappearing, e. g. as the wake of a ship disappears.

To get lost (lose one's way) is bāto biraunu.

ENGLISH	KHAS	MAGAR	GURUNG
Maimed	khurundo खुरुन्डो ghāyal bhāyāko घायल भायाको		
Main (adj.)	mul मूल		
Maize	makāi मकाई		
Make, to	banaunu garnu बनाउनु गरनु	khās, zāt	la
bed	bichhāunu बिछाउनु	tāng	ti
noise	hallā garnu हल्ला गरनु		
Male [1]	jhānk झांक		
Mallet	mungro मुंगरो		
Man	mānchha, jana मानछ, जना mānis मानिस	bhurmi	mhi
Mango	ām आम	satak	
Mangy	khuilyā खुइल्या		
Manhood	ādhabāins आधाबाइसं		
Manner	parkār, rītī परकार, रीति		
Manure	mal मल	ben	
Many	dheri, sasti धेरै, सस्ती		ley
March, to	hitnu हिटनु	wān	yā
(month)[2]	chait चैत		
Mare	ghorī घोड़ी		
Mark	chino चिनो		
Market	bazār बजार		
Marmot	pia प्या		
Marry, to	biāh garnu ब्याह गरनु	biah zāt	biah la
Mars (planet)	mangal मङ्गल		
Marsh	dhāp, shimshār धाप, शिमशार		
Marvelous	gajab गजब		
Master	guru गुरु		
Mat	māndro मान्द्रो		peho
Match	diyāsalāi दियासलाई		
Matter (pus)	pip पिप	mā	noho

[1] Of birds, Bhalya. Goats, Bhokya and Khassia. Human, Lognia Chhoro. Of others, Jhank.

[2] See footnote 5, p. 33.

ENGLISH	KHAS	MAGAR	GURUNG
Mattress	tosak, gadda तोसक,गद्दा		
May [1]	jeth जेठ		
Measles	dādura दादुरा		
Meaning	artha अर्थ		
Meat	shikār, māsu शिकार, मासु	sia	se
Medicine	okhadi ओषदी	usah	moi
Meek	sudu सुदो		
Meet, to	bhetnu भेटनु	dūp	to
	phela pārnu फेला पारनु		
Melon	kharbhujā खरभुजा		
Melt, to	galnu गलनु	galish	galiy
Mend (patch)	tālnu टालनु		
Mercy	chhimā छीमा		
Metal	dhātu धातु		
Meteor	phutne tārā फुतने तारा		
Micturate, to	mutnu मुतनु	rosh ka	ku toy
Midday [2]	madhyān मध्यान	numshin	
	dopahar दोपहार		
Midnight	ādhārāt आधारात		adhamisa
Middle	mājh माझ		
Mildew	sinduri rog सिन्दुरी रोग		
	dhumsi धुमसी		
Milk, butter	mahi मही		
Milk	dudh दुध	gnie	
,, sour, curd	dahi दही		
Mill (water)	ghatta घट्ट		
Millet	bhadu भदु	kasāunri	
Mina (bird)	dangre, sāru दाङगरे सारु		
Minal	dāphe डाफे		
Mind, the	man मन		
, to	dhanda mānnu डन्डा माननु		
Mine, a	khāni खानी		
,, (explosive)	surung सुरुंग		

[1] See footnote 5, p. 33.

[2] See footnote 2, pp. 31-32.

English	Khas	Magar	Gurung
Miscarry, to	tuhinu तुह्निु	lo	
Miser	sum सुम		
Mist	kuhiro कुहिरो		machoo
Mistake	bhul भूल		
Mistress (chief)	mukhiāni मुखयानी		
Mole (animal)	chhuchundro छुचुन्दरो		
(body)	kothi कोठी		
Moment	chhin छिन		
Monday	sombār सोम्बार		
Mongoose	niolo musā न्योलो मुसा		
Monkey	bānar, lāku बानर, लाकु		timu
,, (large)	dheruwā ढेड़्वा		sobargi
Month	mahinā महिना		
Moon [1]	jun जून	geaut	lăngi
Moral (adj.)	tapāsi तपासी		
Morning [2]	bhiyāna भ्यान	gorak	nāka
Mortar	bajralep बजरलेप		
Mosque	masjid मसजिद		
Mosquito	lāmkhutyā लामखुया		
Moss	jhyāu झ्याऊ		
Moth	putli पुतली		tāmlo
Mother [3]	āmā आमा	boya, me	ama
Mould, a	sāncho सांचो		
Mountain	parbat, lekh परबत, लेख		
Mouse	musā मुसा	biu	namu
Moustache	jungā जुंगा	mur	mora
Mouth	mukh मुख	nir	sun
Move, to (t)	sārnu सारनु		sare
(i)	hitnu हिटनु	wān	prā
Much	dhere धेरै		ley
Mud	hilo हिलो		

[1] In high-flown language Chandra ; New Moon is Aunsi jun. Full Moon is Purănio jun.

[2] See footnote 2, pp. 31-32. [3] See footnote 2, pp. 35-36.

ENGLISH	KHAS	MAGAR	GURUNG
Mulberry	kimu किमू		
Mule	khachchar खच्चर		
Multiply, to	gunnā gunnu गुन्ना गुन्नु		
	gunnu गुन्नू		
Mumps	hānre हांड़े		
Murmur	gangan गनगन		
Muscle	nasā नसा		cha
Mushroom	chyāu च्याऊ	mugan	chyapo
Music [1]	gīt, rāg गीत, राग	ling	kwī
Musk	kasturī कस्तूरी		
,, deer	kasturā कस्तूरा		
,, pod	binā बिना		
Mustard	rāi राई		
Mutiny	balwā, gadr बल्वा, गदर		
Muzzle	mohri मोहरी		
NAICK	amaldār अमलदार		
Nail (finger)	nang नङ्ग	ārgin	yoshi
(iron)	preg, kil प्रेग, कील		
Naked	nāngo नांगो		
Name	nām, nāun नाम, नाऊं	ārmin	mi
Nape	ghichrā घिचरा		kare
Narrow	sānguro सांगुड़ो		
Navel	nāito नाइटो	pere	pade
Near	nir, najīk निर, नजीक	kherap	gnār
Necessary, to be	chāinnu चाहिन्नु	chaidis	chaidi
Neck	ghānti घांटी	dunga	orko
,, back of	ghuchuk घुचुक		kare
Necklace	mālā माला		
Needle	siyo सियो	ārcha	ta
Neighbour	chhimeki छिमेकी		

[1] Tune is bhākhā or rāg. A song is git. First line phet, second line tuppa.

Instruments. Mādel—a tomtom; dhol—big drum. Manjun—cymbals. Bansuli—flute. Machungi—Jew's harp. Morali—pipe (made from hookah bowl). Sarangi—fiddle. Harmoni—guitar.

English	Khas	Magar	Gurung
Nephew [1]	bhatijā भतीजा	bhānza	
Nerve	nasā नसा		
Nervous	harbar, ātine हड़बड़, आतीने		
Nest	gunr गूंड़	min	chôn
Net	jāl जाल		
Nettle	sisno सिसनो	gio	polo
Never	kaile ne कैले ने	ma sien	
New	nayā, naulā नया, नौला (different)	minam	
Next [2]	ārko आरको		
Nice	nakali नकुलो		
Niece [1]			
Night	rāt रात	nabi	mīsa
Nip, to	chimātnu चिमाटनु	chilik	
off, to	chunrnu चुंड़नु		
Nod (in sleep)	jhulnu झुलनु		
Noise	sabd, hallā सब्द, हल्ला	ot	
N. C. O.	hudedār हुदेदार		
North	utar उत्तर		
Nose	nāk नाक	nā	nā
Nose-ring (centre)	bulāki, mundro बुलाकी, मुन्द्रो		
,, (outside	phulī फूली		
Nostril	nāk ko dulo नाक को दुलो		
November [3]	mangsīr मङ्गसीर		
Now	aile, bharkar ऐले, भरकर	inang, chahān	toka
Numb, to be	kakrinu ककरीनु		
(adj.)	kakrio ककरीयो		
Nut	badām बदाम		
(betel)	pān पान		
(chewing)	supāri सुपारी		
Nutmeg	jāiphul जाइफुल		

[1] See footnote 2, pp. 35-36.
[2] "The man next Ranbir"—"Ranbir ko chheo ko manchha."
[3] See footnote 2, p. 33.

English	Khas	Magar	Gurung
OAK	bānj ko rukh बांज को रुख		
Oar	gabana गबना		
Oat	jau जौ		
Oath	kiriā किरिया		
Obey, to	mānnu माननु		
Obligation	kar कर		
Oblique	chhatkyā छटक्या		
Obscene	phohri फोहरी		
,, (of talk) used by women	nanāuli नानउली		
Obstinate	magro मगरो		
October [1]	kārtik कार्तिक		
Odd	amel अमेल		
Odour (good)	bāsin बसिन		thāh
(bad)	gandha गन्ध		
Often	ghari ghari घड़ी घड़ी		
Oil	tel तेल	siri	chhiku
Ointment	mallam मल्लम		
Old	buro (people) बुढो		
	purāno (things) पुरानो		
,, (worn out, of people)	thotro थोतरो		
Omen	sagun सगुन		
On	mā, māthī मा, माथी	ang	
Once	ekpaltā एकपल्टा	katpalta	palta ghri
Onion	piāz पियाज		
One-eyed	kānā काना		
Only	mātrai मात्रै		
Open, to	ugharnu उघड्नु	pho	to, phai
Opinion	mato मतो		
Opium	aphīm अफीम		
Opportunity	maukā मौका		
	belā बेला		
Opposite	pāri, sāmne पारी, सामने	parlag	kyanja

[1] See footnote 5, p. 33.

ENGLISH	KHAS	MAGAR	GURUNG
Or	yā या		
Orange	santalā सुनतला		
,, pig	kesara केसरा		
Order, to	arhānu अढ़ानु		
, an	agyan, āin आज्ञा, आन्ग		
, to put in	thankiāunu थनक्याउनु		
Ornament	gahanā गहना		
Orphan	tuhura, dāto टुहुरा, दातो		
Other	ārko अरको	phoko	
Outstrip, to	uchhinu उछिनु	rit	tô
Oval	lāmchhe लामछे		
Oven	agenā अगेना		koda
Over (prep.)	māthi माथी	dhenām	taye
(finished)	bhaisakio भाइसक्यो bhyāyo भयायो	bhyatta	khai
Owl	lātā chara लाटा चरा		lumbra
Own (adj.)	aphnu अफनु	mino	rose
Owner	dhani धनी		ploba
PACK (cards)	tās तास		
to	thankiaunu थनक्याउनु		
Packet	puntro पुन्तरो		
Pad, a	gaddā गद्दा		
Page	patrā पत्रा		
Pail (wooden)	theko ठेको		
Pain	dukh दुख		
Paint, to	rangāunu रंगाउनु		
Pair	jorā जोड़ा		
Palace	rājmahal राजमहल		
Palm (tree)	tār ko rukh ताड को रुख		
(hand)	hathkelo हथकेलो	hutpiak	yopla
Pane	aenā ऐना		
Panther	chituwā चितुवा		cheto
Paper	kāgaj कगज		
Parade	kawāj कवाज		
Paralysis	bān बान		
Pardon	māph माफ		

ENGLISH	KHAS	MAGAR	GURUNG
Parents	āmābābu आमाबाबु		
Parrot	shugā शुगा		
Part	bhāg भाग		
Particular	khās खास		
Partner	sangi संगी	lapha	āgu
Partridge	titrā तितरा	chāmre	tendre
Party	tolī टोली		
Pass, to (away)	bitnu, marnu बितनु मरनु	shi	shiy
(time)	kātnu काटनु	chi	to
(outstrip)	uchhinu उछिनु		
(by)	bāto jānu बाटो जानु		
, a (permit)	purza पुर्जा		
(mountain)	ghānti घांटी		
Past	biteko बितेको		
Paste	lei लेइ		
Pasture	kharka खरक		
Patch, to	tālnu टालनु		
Path	gorento or chor bāto गोरेंटो या चोर बाटो	dahar ; gorento lām	gorento kyya
Pathan	wākhlyā वाखल्या		
Patience	dhiraj धिरज		
Patwari	mukhiā मुखिया		
Pause, to	parkhanu परखनु	rung	pre
Paw	panjā पन्जा	hut	uri
Pay, to	tirnu तिरनु		
(noun)	talab, tanakā तलव, तनखा		
Pea	kerāu केराउ		
Peace	sunsān, sukh सुनसान, सुख mel मेल larāi na bhaya ko belā लड़ाई न भाको बेला		
Peach	āru आरू	gurli	kolo
Peacock	majur मजूर		
Peak	tipri टीपड़ो		
Pear	nāspāti नासपाती		

ENGLISH	KHAS	MAGAR	GURUNG
Pearl	moti मोती		
Peg	kīla कीला		
Pen	kalam कलम		
Pencil	pinsil पिनसिल		
Penknife	chakku चक्कू		
People	mānchheharu मानछेहरू		
Pepper	golmirich गोलमिरीच		
,, red	khursānī खुरसानी		
Per cent	sekarā pachhī सेकड़ा पछी		
Perhaps	sāhit, kunnī सायत, कुन्नी		
Personality	mohani मोहनी		
Perspiration	pasīnā पसीना	namchus	cheba
Persuade, to	phakāunu फकाउनु	hum	wha
Petal	phul ko pat फूल को पात		
Petition	binti बिन्ती		
Phlegm, nasal	sigān सीगान	nā	nā
Physical drill	akhārā अखाड़ा		
Pick, to	tipnu टिपनु	dhum	tu
, a	gainti गेंती		
Picture	taswir तसवीर		
Piebald	chhirbiryā छिरविरया		
Pierce, to	chhernu छेरनु	khoak	to
Pig (tame)	sungar सूंगर	wāk	tili
(wild)	banel बनेल		to
Pigeon (tame)	parewā परेवा		
(wild)	malewa मलेवा		
(,, big)	bajewa बजेवा		
(green)	halisa हलेसा		kuga
Pillar	khambā खम्बा		
Pillow	sirān सिरान		kreku
Pimple			
(big) (boil)	khatirā खटीरा	ma	po
(small)	phokā, bibrā फोका बिबरा		
	dandiphur डन्डी फौर		
(black)	kothī कोठी		
Pinch	chimātanu चिमाटनु	chimtili	

ENGLISH	KHAS	MAGAR	GURUNG
Pincers (crab)	sanāsu सुनासु		
Pine, a	sallā ko rukh सल्ला को रुख		
Pineapple	kāble kuthan काब्ले कुथन		
Pine martin	molsāpri मोलसाप्री		
Pipe	nalā, nalī नला, नली,		
(musical)	morali मोरली		
Pit	khālto खालटो		
Pitcher	gharā, ghailā घड़ा, घैला	kunra	kunra
Pity	chhimā, dayā छीमा, दया		
Place, a	thāun ठांऊ		klo
(good cool)	shital शीतल		
(bad hot)	aul औल		
, to	rākhnu राखनु	dā	the
Plague	putke rog पुठ के रोग		
Plains, the	des ; mādesh देस, मादेश		
Plan	yukti युक्ति		
Plane, to	tāchhnu ताछ्नु	jiak	chā
Plank	phalek फल्याक		
Plant	biruwā बिरुवा		
, to	ropnu, gārnu रोपनु, गाड़नु	chāg	ri
Play, to	khelnu खेलनु	ges	klo
Pleasant	ramāilo रमाइलो		
Please, to	ramāunu रमाउनु	marang	sain
Pleased	ramāyo रमायो	marānga	saiñ tai
Pleasure	ānand, bhog आनन्द, भोग		
Plot	yukti युक्ति		
Plough, a	halo हलो	har	
, to	halobāunu हलोबाउनु	sil	
	jotnu जोतनु		
Pluck, to	tipnu टिपनु	dhum	to
Pluck (noun)	dhiraj धिरज		
Plum	ālubokhrā आलुबोखरा		
Pocket	khalti खलती		
Pod	bālā बाला		
Poison	bikh बिष		nari
Poisonous	bisālu बिषालु		

English	Khas	Magar	Gurung
Poke, to	chhāmchhum, g. छामछुम ग		
Pole	danda डंडा		
,, (for carrying tigers, etc.)	nol नोल		
Polite	sushīl सूशील		
Pomegranate	dārim दाड़िम		
Pond	pokharī पोखरी		
Pony	tato टटो		
Pool	rah रह्		
Poor	kangāli कंगाली nirdhani निर्धनी		
Porcupine	dumsi दुमसी		tosi
Possible	hosakne हो सकने		
Post (mail)	dāk डाक		
,, (stick)	shito शितो		
,, (be posted	theknu ठेकनू		
Pot (earth)	hānri हांडी		pu
,, (brass and spout)	garuwā गड़ुवा		
Potato	ālu आलु		
Pour, to	jhārnu झाड़नु		
Power	bal बल		
Powerful	balio बलिवो		
Powder	dhulo धुलो		
Precipice	bhir भीर		pro
Pregnant	bhāri jyan भारी ज्यान gărbh गर्भ	tuk bumli	pho noimo
Present, a	dān दान		
(adj.)	hāzir हाजिर		
Press, to			
(down)	khāndnu खांदनु		
(print)	chhāpnu छापनु		ple
(squeeze)	ninchornu निचोड़नु		chura
(in crowd)	ghachcha dinu घच्चा दिनु dus antiāunu अत्याउनु	antidi	kaya anti

English	Khas	Magar	Gurung
Pretend, to	nuin g. न्यूंग ग bahānā g. वहाना ग		
Pretty	rāmro रामरो	sieche	chhiaba
Prey	airi अइरी		po
Price	dām दाम		se
Prick, to	ghochnu घोचनु	khowāk	malo
Pride	mijāt मिजात		
Prince	rajkumār राजकुमार rāja ko chhoro राजा को छोरो	raje mija	murai cha
Princess	rājkumāri राजकुमारी		murai chami
Print, to	chhāpnu छापनु		ple
Private	gupt गुप्त		
Procession	melā मेला		
Profession	beopār ब्योपार		
Profit	naphā नफा		
Promise, to	bāchā garnu बाचा गरनु		
Proof	pramān प्रमाण		
Protect (keep unharmed)	jogāunu जोगाउनु		
Proud	ghamandī घमन्डी		
Provision	sāmal सामल		
Pull, to	tānnuताननु	tāndi	
down, to	bhatkāunu भतकाउनु	bhāta	
Pulse	nāri नाड़ी		cha
Pumpkin	lauki लौकी		
Punishment	dand, sazā दंड, सजा		
Pure	sudo, nirmal सुदो, निरमलु		
Purge, to	jhāra phirnu ; झाड़ फिरनु hognu होगनु	penka	kli to
,, , a	julap जुलाप		
Purple	baijni बैजनी		
Purpose [1]	mansa मन्सा		

[1] "He did it on purpose"—"U le jane bhujera gario."

English	Khas	Magar	Gurung
Pursue, to	pachhi pachhi jānu पछी २ जानु	nuning	lilililiya
Push, to	ghachyā dinu घच्चा दिनु	dus	kay
Put, to	rākhnu राखनु	dā	the
, on	lagāunu लगाउनु	bil	ke
, out	mārnu मारनु	sāt	sai
QUAIL, A	bater बटेर		
Quarrel, a	jhagrā झगड़ा		
Queen	rāni रानी		
Queer	anautho अनौटो		
Quench, to	bujhānu बुझानु	sāt	sai
Question	sawāl सवाल		
Quick	chānri, chhito चांड़ै छिटो		
Quill	pwānkh प्वांख	mikar	peh
Quiver	dhongro ढोंग्रो		
Quoit	chakkar चक्कर		
RACE	bāzi बाजी		
Rafter	karang करङ्ग		
Rag	jhumro, luttā झुमरो, लट्टा		
Ragged (in rags)	thāngne थांगने		
Railway-line	rail ko lig रेल को लिग		
Rain, to	barsanu बरसनु		na yu
Rains, the	barkhā बर्षा		
Rainbow	indreni इन्द्रयानी		
Raise, to	uthāunu उठाउनु	sotāk	re
Ram, to	pitnu पिठनु	dātup	do
, a	bokya, sānde बोक्या, सांडे		
Ramrod	gaj गज		
Rank	darjā दर्जा		
Raspberry	aisālu ऐसालु	digāse	pala
Rat	musā मुसा	biu	namu
Rate	bhau भाव		
Ration	rasad रसद		
Raw	kācho काचो	mībil	siu
Read	parnu पड़नु	parish	khe, pardi

ENGLISH	KHAS	MAGAR	GURUNG
Ready	tayār तयार		
Real	khās खास		
Reap, to	kātnu काटनु	chi	to
Rebuke, to	dhamkānu धमकानु		
	hakānu हकानु		
Receive, to	pāunu पाउनु	din	yo
Recognise	chinnu चिननु		
Recruit	rangrut रंगरुट		
Recruiting	galla गल्ला		
Red	rāto रातो	geche	wālkia
Reflection	chhāyā छाया		
Refuse, the	kasingar कसींगर		
Regularly	barābar बराबर		
Reign, to	rāj garnu राज गरनु		
Relief	badalī बदली		
Religion	dharm धरम		
Remain	rahnu रहनु	mu, rung	ti
	parkhanu परखनु		
Remainder	ubryāko उबरयाको		gne
Remember	samjhanu समभनु		
Remind	samjhāunu समभाउनु		lo
Remove	lejāunu लेजाउनु	āl, sārdi	boya
	sārnu सारनु		
Rent	bhārā, kirāya भाड़ा, किराया		
Repair	sudhārnu सुधारनु		
Repent	pachhtāunu पछतानु		
Reproof	dhamki धमकी		
Request	bintī बिन्ती		
Resolve	thaharānu ठहरानु		
	āntnu ग्रांटनु		
Respectable	sajjan सज्जन		
	mānwālo मानवालो		
Responsible	jimāwāri जिमावारी		
, to be	utara dinu उतरादिनु		
Rest, to (*t*).	bisāunu बिसाउनु		
Result	phal फल		

ENGLISH	KHAS	MAGAR	GURUNG
Return (go)	pharkera janu फरकेरजानु		
(come)	pharki ānu फरकी आनु	leisma ra	
Revenge	paltō पलटो		
Rhinoceros	gainra गैंड़ा		shon
Rhodedendron	guruwans गुरूवांस		pora
Rib	kokha, karang कोखा, करङग		
Rice (cooked)	bhāt भात	chho	koin
(raw)	chāwal चावल	chhuru	si
(parched)	chiurā चिऊड़ा		
(growing)	dhān धान	chhosān	malāh
Rich	dhani धनी		
Riches	dhan धन		mui
Riddle	ahān अहान		
Ridge (hill)	dānrā डांड़ा		
Right			
(not left)	dāhinā दाहीना	dorche	kelo
(not wrong)	thik ठीक		
Ring, to	bajaunu बजाउनु	gn	rā
(finger)	aunti, mundra अउन्टी, मुंद्रा		chia
Nose and ear rings see under nose and ear.			
Ripe	pākyāko पाक्याको	mina	mīh
Ripen	paknu, phulnu पाकनु, फुलनु	wāt	sār
Rise, to	uthnu उठनु	so	re
River	gangā गंगा		
Road	bāto बाटो	lām	kyya
Roast, to	sekāunu सेकाउनु	āre	rô
	polnu पोलनु	jo	kro
Rob	chornu, lutnu चोरनु लुटनु	kus	yo
Robber	dāku डाकू		
Robber, a	chor चोर		
Rock, a	thulo dhunga ठुलो ढुंगा	karāncho lung	tebe yuma
Rod	tāngā, tangālo तांगा, तंगालो		
Roll, to	bernu, lapetnu बेड़नु, लपेटनु		
down, to	paltāunu पलटाउनु		
(as tea) to	mānrnu माड़नु	arju	ne

English	Khas	Magar	Gurung
Roof	chhānā छाना		
Room	kothā कोठा		
Root	jarā, जरा, mūla मुला		
up, to	ukhelnu उखेलनु	hot	siu
Rope	jiuri, dori जीउरी, डोरी, sutari सुतरी		cho
(porter's)	nāmlo नामलो	biri	topi
Rose, a	gulāb गुलाब		
Rot, to	kuhunu कुहुनु	gel	kraiya
Rough	khasro खसरो		
Round	ghero, gol घेरो, गोल bātulo बाटूलो		
Rouse, to	uthāunu उठाउनु	sotāk	re
Row, a	halla, hāhu हल्ला, हाहु		
Royal	rājāko राजाको		
Rub, to	michnu, malnu मिचनु मलनु	mol	ni
Rubbish	kasīngar कसींगर		
Rude	anghar अनघड़		
Rug	kāmlo, pānkhi कामलो, पांखी rāri राड़ी		
Ruin	nās नास	dasha	
Rule	ain ऐन		
, to	rāj garnu राज गरनू		
Rum	rakshi रकशी		
Run, to	dugurnu दुगुडनु	kher	bhagdi
Rupee [1]	kampanī कमपनी		muhi
Rust	khai खई		
SACK	thailo थैली	shana	nedo
Sacred	pabītra पवीत्र		
Sacrifice, to	chadhānu चढानू		
, a	balīdān बलीदान		
Sadness	udās उदास	birāha	birās
Saddle	zīn जीन		
Sake of	lāgi लागी		

[1] See footnote 1, p. 47.

ENGLISH	KHAS	MAGAR	GURUNG
Salt (noun)	nun नून	chhāh	chăza
(adj.)	nunīlo नूनीलो		
Salute, to	dhok g. ढोक गः	jor	phiyo
Sambhar	jaṛyāh जाड़्या		
Sand	bāluwa बालुवा		
Satisfied, to be	santusht सन्तुष्ट		
Satisfy, to (with food, etc.)	aghāunu अघाउनु	rās	mūr
Saucepan	tāuli ताऊली		
Saturday	shanicharbār शनीचरबार		
Saturn	shani शनी		
Savage	ghāmar घामड़		
	jangalī जंगली		
, a	banmānchha बनमान्छ		
Save (t)	bachāunu बजाउनु	jiwāk	
	rachhya garnu रक्षा गरनु		
(i)	bachnu बचनु	ji	so
Saw	āri, karāti आरी, करांती		
Say	bhannu भननु	di	bi
Scabbard	khol, dāb खाल, दाब		
Scale (of fish)	katla कतला		
Scar	tātā, dām टाटा, डाम		tāti
Scare, to	darāunu डराउनु	biri	gni
Scatter (t)	phijāunu फिजाउनु		
(i)	phijnu फिजनु		
Scissors	kainchi कैंचि		
Scent (good)	bāsin बसिन	nāma	thāh
(bad)	ganda गन्द		
Schoolmaster	guru गुरु		
Scoff	thatta garnu ठट्टा गरनु		
Scorn, to	ghin garnu घिन गरनु	jhir	
Scorpion	bichchhi बिच्छी		
Scotch	ghāgre घागेर		
Scrape, to	khurkaunu खुरकाउनु		
,, off, to (as in planing)	tāchhnu ताछ्नु		chai

ENGLISH	KHAS	MAGAR	GURUNG
Scratch, to	kaneāunu कन्याउनु	uk	ri
Scratched, to be	chithranu चीथरनु		
Scream, to	chịchiāunu चिच्याउनु	chiāk	
Screen, a	chhirki छिड़की		
Screw	pech पेच		
,, -driver	pechkas पेचकस		
Scurf	chāyā चाया		
Scythe	ānsi आंसी		
Sea	samundar समुन्द्र		
Seaweed	simāli सिमाली		
Seal	chhāp छाप		
Seasoned	chhipiāko छिपियाको	rāngche	
Seat	pirkā पीड़का		
Secret (adj.)	gupta गुप्त		
Secretly	luki lukera लुकी लुकेर	archim	loloi
See	dekhnu, hernu देखनु, हेरनु	dāng	nio, mär
Seed	biu बिउ	choiyo	plu
,, (tea)	gerā गेरा		
Seedling	biruwā बिरुवा		
Seek	khojnu खोजनु		
Seize	samātnu समातनु	jīm	kā
Seldom	kaile kaile mātri कैले २ मात्री		
Sell	biknu बिकनु	ārl	chu
Send	pathaunu पठाउनु	birin	bini
,, for	jhikāunu झिकाउनु	donāk	twi
Sentry	paharā पहरा		
,, box	gumti गुमटी		
Separate, to	chhutāunu छुटाउनु	dās	wāti
(adj.)	alag अलग		
September [1]	asoj असोज		
Servant	bāndā बांदा		
Sew	siunu सिउनु	rup	tu
Shade	chhāhāri छाहारी		

[1] See footnote 5, p. 33.

ENGLISH	KHAS	MAGAR	GURUNG
Shadow	chhāyā छाया		
Shake	halāunu हलाउनु	whek	lā
Shallow	shīm, janghāri शीम, जंघारी		
Shame	lāj लाज	kāra	pi
Shape	rup, dhāl रुप, ढाल		
Share	ansa, bhāg अंस, भाग		
Sharp (blade)	lagne, dhārīlo लागने, धारीलो		
(point)	tikho तिखो	gīmche	miu
Sharpen, to	dhār lagāunu धारलगाउनु udhārnu उधारनु	dhār ledik	dhār ledi
Sharpening stone	sili सिली		
Shave, to (hair)	chhurā le phālnu छुरा ले फालनु		
,, off (wood, etc.)	tāchhnu ताछ्नु		chai
Sheath	dāb दाब		
Shed	katerā कटेरा		
Sheep	bherā भेड़ा		kui
Sheet	chedar चेदर		
Shelf	khopā खोपा		
Shell (egg)	khapati खपटी		
(gun)	golā गोला		
Shelter	ār आड़		
Shepherd	gothālā गोठाला		prônchẽ mhi
Shield	dhāl ढाल		
Shin	nalihār नलीहाड़		
Shirt	bhoto, kurtha भोटो, कुर्था		
Shiver	kāmnu कामनु	hoi	tāra
Shoe	jutā जुता		
Shoot, to	goli le hirkānu गोली ले हिरकानु banduk charkāunu बन्दूक छरकाउनु	banduk phorek	
Shop	dukan दूकान		
Shore	pākhā, kinārā पाखा, किनारा		choko

ENGLISH	KHAS	MAGAR	GURUNG
Short	hocho होचो	tumche garche (of men)	maba
Shot	chharā छरा		
Shoulder	kum कुम		paido (lamjung) kānda (kaski)
Show, to	dekhāunu देखानु	tanāk	ūn
, a	barāti, ramītā बराती रमीता		
Shower	jhari झड़ि		
Shrine	thān थान		
Shrink	sāngrīnu सांगरीनु khumchīnu खूमचीनू		
Shut	thunnu थुननु	tu	thundi
Sick	birāmī बिरामी madhuro मधुरो	chāh	nāba
(to vomit)	wāknu; wāk wāk garnu, chādnu वाकनु; वाक २ गरनु चादनु	ok	rui
Sickle	ānsi आंसी		
Sickly			
(human)	rogi रोगी		
(plants)	sikro सिकरो		chāngra
Side (hill)	chheo छेव		
(ribs)	kākhi, kokhā काखी, कोखा,		
Sieve	chālno चालनो		
Sift	chālnu चालनु		
Sight (gun)	makkhi मक्खि		
(of eye)	nazar नजर		
Sign	chino चिनो		
Signal	sān सान		
Signature (to make)	sahi (lagāunu) सही (लगाउनु)		
Silence	sunsān सुनसान		
Silent (man)	gamīlo गमीलो		
Silk	resham रेशम		
Silver	chāndi चांदी		

ENGLISH	KHAS	MAGAR	GURUNG
Sin	pāp पाप		
Since	bāta बाट	ing	
Sinew	nasā नसा		
Sing, to	gānu गानु	ling	kwī prī
Singe	aile aile polnu अेले २ पोलनु		
Single	yota योटा	kāt	ghri
(bachelor)	kanne कनने		
Sink, to	dubnu डुबनु	thah	plai
Sister [1]	didi baini दिदि, बैनी		ani ; gnichu
Sit	basnu बसनु	mu	ti
Size	dal डाल		
Skill	sip सीप		
Skillful	sipālu सीपालु		
Skin	chhālā छाला		tīpi
Sky	akās, sarga अकास, सर्ग		mu
Slack	dhilo ढिलो		
Slate	jhīngitī झींगिटो		
Slave	kamārā कमारा		wāza
	bāndā बांदा		
Sleep, to	sutnu सुतनु	mis	ro
(noun)	nīnd नींद	mi	naru
Sleeve	bāulā बाउला		
Slip, to	larknu लरकनु	armet	plī
	chiphlinu चिफलिनु		
Slippery	chiphlo चिफलो	armetche	ple
Slow	dhilo, susto ढिलो, सुस्तो		
Slug	chiphlo kirā चिफलो किड़ा		kabo
Small	siāno स्यानो	garche (of men)	
		marche (always chion was)	
		tunche (became)	
Small-pox	biphar बिफर		
Smear, to	lipnu लिपनु	lāk	siala

[1] See footnote 2, pp. 35-36.

ENGLISH	KHAS	MAGAR	GURUNG
Smell, to	sungnu सूंगनु	ārmush	thahna
, a (bad)	ganda गन्द	māsieche nāma	achhiaba thāh
(good)	bāsin बासिन	jāpche nāma	chhiaba thah
Smoke	dhuwān धुवां		mikhu
Smooth	chillo चिल्लो		
Snail	chiphlo kīrā चिफलो कीड़ा		kabo
Snake	lāmkīrā, nāg लामकीड़ा, नाग	bul	pokri
(large).	ajīngar अजीङ्गर		
Snare, a	pānso पांसो		gno
Snatch away	khosnu खोसनु	shiad	piy
Sneak, a	khel halne खेल हालने	khel zātni	khel choni
Sneer	hishknu हिशकनु nāk nichornu नाक निचोड़नू		
Sneeze	chim garnu चिम गरनु		
Sniff	sungnu सुंगनु	ārmush	thahna
Snipe	chāha चाहा		
Snore	ghurnu घुरनु	ghurish	ghuridi
Snow	hiun हिऊं		
,, range	himāl हिमाल		
Soap	sāban साबन		
Sod	chhapri छपड़ी		
Soft	kāunlo काउलो		
Solder (to)	rāng (le jornu रांग ले जोड़नु		
Soldier	tilingā तिलङ्गा		
Sole (foot)	paitla पैतला		
Some	koi कोई	sui	kawe
Sometimes	kaile kaile कैले २	sien sien	khayan khayan
Somewhere	kahīn कहीं	kulak	kana
Son[1]	chhoro छोरी	mija	cha
Son-in-law	jawāin जवाई		

[1] See footnote 2 pp. 35-36.

ENGLISH	KHAS	MAGAR	GURUNG
Song [1]	gīd गीद	ling	kwī
Sore, a	ghāu घाव		
Sort	kisam किसम		
Soul	prān प्राए		
Sound, to	bajāunu बजाउनु		rā
, a	sabd सब्द		
(good)	nirogi, niko निरोगी, निको		
	tagro तगड़ो		
Sour	amilo अमिलो	bir	kiu
South	dakhan दखन		
Sow, a	sugarni सुगरनी		tili
to	biu chharnu बिउ छड़नु		
Spade	belcha बेलचा		
Spades	hukm हुक्म		
Spare, to	bachāunu बचाउनु		
(adj.)	phāltu फालतु		
Spark	olenī ओलेनी		
Sparrow	bhangera भंगेरा		kolme
Speak	bhannu भनन्	chiāk, de	bi
Spear	bhālā भाला		
Spectacles	chasmā चसमा		
Spend	māsnu मासनु		
Spice	masālā मसाला		
Spider	mākurā माकुड़ा	gharuwa	timru
Spill	pokhnu पोखनु	yat	niy
Spin, to	bhurung ghumāunu भुरुङ्ग घुमाउनु		
(thread)	bunnu बुननु	jāh	ro
	kātnu कातनु (cut=काटनु)	yet	rānt
Spinning machine	katuwā कतुवा		
Spine	darānlu दड़ान्लु		krezā
Spirit	sāns, prān सांस, प्राए		

[1] For the various songs see Songs (Part IV). To sing a song is Git jbiguu (M. Ling do. G. kwi pri). The tune is bhākha. The first line is Phet. The second line Tuppa.

English	Khas	Magar	Gurung
Spit	thuknu थुकनु	thuk	thuya
Spleen	phio फ्यो		
Splinter	tukro टूकड़ो		
Split, to	chirnu, phātnu चिरनु, फाटनु	che	plew
Spoke, a	pakheto पखेटो		
Spoil, to	bigārnu बिगाड़नु	bigardi	noā
	biraunu बिराउनु		
Spoon	dāru डाड़		
,, (bhat-mixing)	paneu पनेउ		
Spotted	chhiribiryā छिरबिरया		
Sprain, to	markanu मरकनु		kriya
Spread, to	phailānu फैलानु		pionya
Spring, to	uphrinu उफरीनु	phorju	uphridi
	phāl kātnu फाल काटनु	phal ka	phal ne
, a (water)	panero पनेरो	digātu	kāndu
(metal)	kamāni कमानी		
(season)	basant बसन्त		
Sprinkle (i)	burburinu बुरबुरीनु		
(t)	burburyānu बुरबुरयानु		
Sprout, a	tusā टुसा		
Square	chār patti चारपट्टी		
Squeak	chichiāunu चीच्याउनु	chiāk	
Squeeze	nichāunu निचाउनु		
	chepnu चेपनु		chiora
	antiāunu अंचाउनु		
Squint	serho सेड़ो		
Squirrel	lokhroke लोखोके		
Stab	ghochnu घोचनु		mlo
	chhuri dāsnu छुरी दासनु		
Stage (resting place at night)	bās बास		
Stagger	lotde lotde jānu लोटदै .२ जानू		
Stain, a	dāg दाग		
Stairs	sirhī lisno सीड़ी, लिसनो		
(stone)	bharyāng भऱ्याङ्ग		

English	Khas	Magar	Gurung
Stale	bāsi बासी		
Stalk, a	dānth डांट		
Stall, a	katerā कटेरा		
Stammer	bhagbhage garnu भगभगे गरनु		
Stamp, to	khutta mārnu खुट्टा मारनु		
Stand, to	ubhīnu उभीनु	torosh le	raï
	thāro hunnu ठाड़ो हुननु		
	arinu अड़िनु	tong	aridi
Star	tārā तारा	tuga	sāra
Statue	murtī मुरती		
Start, to			
(jump)	jhasaknu झसकनु		
(begin)	lāgnu, thālnu लागनु, थालनु		
Stay, to	rahnu रहनु	mu	ti
Steal, to	chornu चोरनु	kus	yo
Steam	bhāp भाप		
Steel	ispāt इस्पात		
Steep	bhirālo भिरालो		pro
Step, to	teknu टेकनु	tekdi	meya
Stick, to (in	alhhanu अलझनु	hārk	kawa
door)	atkanu अतकनु		
(adhere q.v.)	tāsnu, lāgnu टासनु, लागनु		
Stick, a	lauro, chhari लौरो छड़ी	dānga	pare
Sticks, small	choila चोइला		
Stiff	sāro सारो		
Still (adj.)	sunsān सुनसान		
(adv.)	aile, āji ऐले, आजी	chaha	tokan
Sting, to	toknu टोकनु	jik	chiya
Stingy	sum सूम		
Stomach	bhuri, pet भुंड़ि, पेट	tuk	po
Stone	dhungā ढुंगा	lung	yuma
Stool	morhā मोड़ा		
Stoop, to	niurnu न्यूड़नु	gum	kwāta
Stooping	ghopto घोपटो		kwā
Stop (t)	chheknu छेकनु	chekdi,	chekdi
	thāmnu थामनु	tun	

ENGLISH	KHAS	MAGAR	GURUNG
Stop (i) (remain)	parkhnu, rahnu परखनु, रहनु	rung, mu	ti
(i) (halt)	ubhīnu, arinu उभीनु, अड़ीनु		
Storey	talā तला		
,, top	ānti आंठी		
Storm	āndhi bhaunri आधि भौंरी		
Story	sawāi, katha सवाई कथा		
Straight [1]	sojho, surīlo सोझो, सुरीलो sarāsā सरासा		
Stranger	pardeshi परदेशी birāno mānchha बिरानो मांछ		
Strap	phitā फिता		
Straw	parāl पराल		
Strawberry	bhuinkāphal भूईंकाभल		
Stream	kholsi खोलसी		
Strength	bal बल		
Stretch (t)	pasārnu पंसार्नु	shiālik	sion
(legs)	tankāunu तनकाउनु		
(i)	tanknu तनकनु		
Strike, to	hirkānu हिरकानु	dathup	liya
(clock)	bajnu बजनु	gna	gniya
String	dhāgo धागो	sutta	ru
Strip, to	nikhārnu निखारनु		
(clothes)	kārnu काढनु	don	pli
Striped	dharkyā धरक्या		
Stroke, to	musārnu मुसारनु		
Strong	balio बलियो		pom
Struggle	larnu लड़नु	pun	niya
Stumble	thes lāgnu ठेस लागनु		tura
Stupid	ghāmar घामड़		
Subject, a	duniyā दुनिया		
Success	phalīt फलित		
Such	jasto जस्तो		

[1] Surilo is of trees, usually a tall, straight tree without branches near the bottom. A straight man is Sudho manchha. " Walk straight "—" Sojho hin." " Go straight there "—" Wahan sarasa jau."

English	Khas	Magar	Gurung
Suck, to	chusnu चुसनू	chup	chusti
Suck in, to	tutnu टुटनु		tutdi
Suddenly	ekāsi एकासी		
Sufficient	muktā मुकता		
Sugar	chini चीनी		
Sugarcane	unkhu ऊंखू	khum	ukhu
Sulphur	gandhak गन्धक		
Summer	ghāmko din घमको दिन		
Summit	tipri तीपरी		
Sun	ghām, surj घाम, सूर्ज	ṅamkhāṇ	ṭaï
Sunday	aitwār एतवार		
Sunrise	surj uday सुरज उदय	namkhān keoche	ṭai kai
Sunset	,, ast सुरज अस्त	namkhāṇ kima	tai buriye
Support, to (take care of)	samālnu समालनु		
(keep)	pālnu पालनु	kok`	wai
Support, a	teko टेको		
Surface (wall)	gāro गरो		
Surprised, to be	chhakha mannu छकमाननु		chak pardi
Surround, to	ghernu घेरनु		
Survive	jiunde rahnu ज्यूदै रहनु		
Suspicion	shankā शंका		
Swagger, to	shekhi g. शेखी ग		
Swallow, to	nilnu निलनु	nel	kloi
, a	gaunteli गौंतेली (bird)		chimli
Swarm, a	bagāl बगाल		
Swear (oath)	kiriya khānu किरियाखानु		
	gāli dinu गाली दिनु	dhi	
Sweat	pasīnā पसीना	namchas	chheba
Sweep, to	barhārnu बढारनु	sit	pheo
up, to	sohrnu सोहरनू		
Sweet (adj.)	mitho, gulio मिठो, गुलियो	jāpche, ji	li
(noun)	mīthāi मीठाई		
Swell	sunīnu सुनीनू	sok	roi

ENGLISH	KHAS	MAGAR	GURUNG
Swim, to	pāurnu पौरनु	pourish	pourti
Swing, to	jhulnu झूलनू		
Swoo ı	murchha मुर्छा		
Sword	tarwar तरवार		
Syphilis	bhiringi भिरिङ्ग		
TABLE	mez मेज		
Tahr [1]	jhāral झारल		
Tail	puchhār पुछार	meme	me
(coins)	chhāp छाप		
(turban)	phurkā फुर्का		
Take (catch)	linu, samātnu लीनु, समातनु	la, jim	ki, ka
(away)	lejānu, sarnu लेजानु, सरनु	al, sardi	bhoya
(off)	jhignu, karnu झिगनु, करनु	do	toī
(in)	dāntnu डांटनु	dantdi	lu
(out)	nikālnu निकालनु	chuk	twi
	jhignu झिगनु	do	toi
Tale	sawai, kathā सवाई, कथा		
Talk (noun)	kurā कुरा		ta
Tame	pāliako पालयाको	koka	
Tape	phitā फिता		
Tar	koltār कोलतार		
Target	tārā, chānd तारा, चांद		
Taste, to	chākhnu चाखनु	miang	miyo
Tavern	bhatti भट्ठी		
Tax	rakam, sermā रकम, सेरमा		
Tea	chāh चाह		
Teach, to	sikāunu सिकाउनु	pahāk	lo
Teacher	guru गुरु		
Teak	tunī टुनी		
Tear, to	phātnu फाटनु	chiāk	to
, a	ānsu आंसु	mikdi	mikli
Teat	kachono, thun कचोनो, थुन		gnie
Tehsil	addā अड्डा		
Temple (head)	kapāl कपाल	tālu	gnô

[1] A serow is called Tahr in Nepal.

English	Khas	Magar	Gurung
Tender	kāunlo काउंलो		
Tent	chholdāri छोलदारी		
,, peg	mekh, kilo मेख, कीलो		
,, pole	dandā डंडा		
Territory	khuwā खुवा		
Testicle	gullā गुल्ला	gere	kulphu
Than	bhandā भन्दा	denang	
Thank, to	gun mānnu गुनमाननु		
That	tio त्यो	hossa	cha
Thatch	khar खर		ki
Thaw, to	galnu गलनू		
Then	tab तब		
There	uthā उथा	holak	keyai
Thick	moto, bāklo मोटो, बाकलो khasro खसरो	desu	choima
Thief	chor चोर	khus	yoro mhi
Thigh	sānpro सांपडो	gaha	pa
Thigh-bone	pāsolā पासोला		
Thin	dublo, masīno दुबलो, मसीनो	rutma	chey
Thing	thok थोक		
Think	bichār garnu, sochnu बिचार गरनु सोचनु		
Thirsty	tirka lagio तिरखा लागयो di	sona	ku pi
This	yo यो	issa	chu
Thorn	kānrā काणा	ju	pojo
Thread	dhāgo धागो	sutta	ru
Thread (on wrist at Rikhi tarpan)	rākhi राखी		
Threat, a	dhamki धमकी		
Threaten	dhamkānu धमकानु	nār	
Throat	ghānti घान्टी	dunga	mlongo
Throne	gaddi गद्दी		
Throttle	achetnu अचेटनु sāns thunnu सांस, थुननू	dunga ik	mlongo niy
Throughout	bhari भरी		

English	Khas	Magar	Gurung
Throw	phālnu फालनु	loh	bheo
Thumb	buro aunto बुड़ो अंटी		
Thunder	garja गरज		
Thursday	bipaibār बिपेबार		
Tibet	bhot भोट		
Tick (dog)	kirnā किरना		
Tidy	thikthāk ठिकठाक		
Tie, to	kasnu कसनु	ïk	kasdi
Tiffin	arni अरनी		proke
Tiger [1]	dharāg, sher ढेड़ग, शेर bāgh बाघ		
Tight	sānguro सांगुड़ो		
Tighten	kasnu कसनु	ik	kasdi
Tile	jhingiti झींगिटी		
Till	samma सम्म jab samma जब सम्म		
Time [2]	belā बेला		
Tip	tuppo टुप्पो	midum	
Tiptoe	panjā tekerā पनजा टेकेर		
Tire, to [3]	thāknu थाकनु, galnu गलनु	mung	nār
To-day [2]	āj आज	chining	tinya
Toes	paitalo पैतलो	hil	pale ri
Toe-nail	khuttāko nang खुट्टाको नङग	hil-o-ārgin	pale yosi
Together	sangai सङ्गै	khatta	ni
Token	chinno चिन्नो		
Tomato	rāmbherā रामभेड़ा		
To-morrow [2]	bholi भोली	pihin	pana ; naon
Tongue	jibro जिबड़ो	millit, let	le
Tool	hāthiār हाथयार		
Tooth	dānt दांत		sa
Top	tippo, tuppo टिप्पो, टुप्पो thāplo थापलो		

[1] These three words are in order of size.

[2] See footnote 2, p. 31.

[3] Galnu (lit., to melt) is more of the arms and muscles.

English	Khas	Magar	Gurung
Torch	rāṅkho रांखो	ajar	metho
Torrent	ganga ko bel गंगाको बेल		
Tortoise	kachhuwā कछुवा		
Touch, to	chhunu, chhāmnu छुनू, छामनु	su	
Towards	tīra तीर	lak	te
Tower	burj बुर्ज		
Trace, track [1]	paielo, goho पाइलो गोहो patā पता		
Trade	beopār ब्योपार		
Trample	kuchnu कुचनु	puchhi	ple
Transparent	sangulo संगूलो		
Trap	pāso (or dharāp) पासो (धराप)		
,, , big	khor खोर		
Travel, to	dulnu दुलनु	dulish	
Treachery	kapat कपट		
Tread on	kulchi dinu कुलची दिनु	kulchi yā	ku khi pi
(grain)	mārnu माडनु	ājum	ne
Treasure	dhan, khajana धन, खजाना		
Treasury	dhansar धनसर		
Tree [2]	rukh, bot रुख बोट		shidu
Tremble, to	kāmnu कामनु	hoi	tāra
Trigger	librī लिब्री		
Trip, to (i)	thes khānu ठस खानु		
Triple	tehāro तेहरो		
Tripod (cooking)	odhān ओधान	āram	chombo
Trial	nisāph निसाफ ajmāis अजमाइस		
Trick, to	chhalanu, thagnu छलनु ठगनू		

[1] Goho is the beaten path an animal makes for itself when going through the jungle. Paielo is more footprint, etc.

[2] Trunk and bottom of tree is phed. Top is tippu. Leaf is Pat (M. and G. La). Branch is hanga. Trunk when cut is mura. Surillo rukh is a tall straight one with no branches near bottom. Sukhio rukh, a withered one.

Fruit trees are called by their fruits, *e.g.* Pangra ko rukh, a chestnut tree

ENGLISH	KHAS	MAGAR	GURUNG
Trouble	bethā, dukh बेथा दुख		
Trousers (drawers)	suruwāl सुरूवाल		
Trowel	khurpi खुरपी		
True	sāncho सांचो		
Trumpet	karnāl, bogate करनाल बोगते turi, narsinga तूरी, नरसींगा		
Trust, to	bishwās, patyaro garnu बिश्वास, पत्यारो गरनु		
Trunk (box)	sanduk, madhus संदूक मधुस		
(elephant)	sund सूंड़		
(tree)	phed, dhar फेद, धड़	miatum	
,, (cut)	mura मुरा		
Try, to			
(attempt)	mihnat g., मिहनत ग		
(test)	jānchnu जांचनू		
Tube	nali नली		
Tuesday	mangalbār मङ्गलबार		
Tune	rāg, bhākha राग, भाषा		
Turban	phitā फिता		
Turf	chapri चपड़ी		
Turmeric	besār बेसार		
Turn (t)	ghumāunu घुमाउनु	chharāk	
(i)	pharknu फरकनु	leis	tā
(noun)	bāri, pālo बारी, पालो		
Turns, by	pālo pālo पालो २		
Turtle	kachhuwa कछुवा		
Twins	jaunlia जौंलया		
Twinkle	chamkānu चमकानु		
(as window)	talkanu तलकानु		
Twist	bātnu बाटनु	ājek	kri
UNADORNED	bucho, rīto बुचो, रीतो		
Unawares	bethāh बेथाह najāndai नजानदै		
Udder	thun थुन		

ENGLISH	KHAS	MAGAR	GURUNG
Umbrella	chhātā छाता		
,, (grass)	shiāgu शिश्रागु		
Unclean	phohri फोहरी		
Uncle [1]	māmā मामा	kuba	
Under	talo तल	māklak	kuro
Understand	bujhnu बुझ्नु	wār	ko
Undo	jhingnu झिग्नु	don	twī
	phukāunu फुकाउनु	phorsak	pla
Unemployed (not enlisted)	dhākre ढाकरे		
Unfortunate	abhāgi अभागी		
Ungrateful	nirguni निरगुनी		
Uniform	urdi उर्दी		
Unite	sang jornu सङ्ग जोड़नु		
Unjust	anyai अन्याई		
	adharmi अधर्मी		
Unload	bhāri orālnu भारी ओरालनु		ti jārdi
Unripe	kācho काचो	mibil	siu
Untie	phuskāunu फुसकाउनु	phorsāk	pla
	phukālnu फुकालनु	,,	,,
Unwilling	aman, birāzi अमन, बिराजी		
Up	māthi, unbho माथी, उंभो	denām	kwaye
Uphill	ukālo उकालो		
Upper	māthilo माथीलो		takway
Uproot, to	ukhelnu उखेलनु	hur	suya
Upside-down	ulto-sulto उलटो सुलटो		
Upset			
(precipice)	khasāunu खसाउनु	jalāk	
(ground)	lotāunu लोटाउनु	korāk	pliya
Upwards	māthi tīra माथितीर	denam	kwaye
Urine	mut मुत	rosh	ku
Useful	kāmko कामको		
Useless	raddi रद्दी		
Uselessly	suddhai सुदधै		chelyan

[1] See footnote 2, pp. 35-36.

ENGLISH	KHAS	MAGAR	GURUNG
VACCINATE	khopāunu खोपाउनु	khopdi	khopdi
Vaccination	bhed भेद		
Vain (adj.)[1]	britta, suddhai वृथा सुदधै		
Valley	gairo, gaira गैड़ो गैरा		
Value	dām दाम		se
Vampire	pichās पिचास		
Vane (mekometer)	patri पत्री		
Vegetable	sāg, tarkāri साग,तरकारी gān		
Veil	mujātro मुजात्रो	lurupu	karamu
Vein	nasā नसा		
Velvet	makhmal मखमल		
Vengeance	badalā, sānto बदला, सांठो		
Venus	shukr शुक्र		
Very	dhere धेरै तैं		ley
Vessel (food)	bhānrā भाड़ा		
Vest [2]	bhoto भोटो		
Vice	pāp पाप		
Village	gāun गाऊं	lānga	nāsa
Vine	angur ko laharā अंगुर को लहरा		
Violet	baijnī बैजनी		
Virgin	kanya keti कन्या केटी	ārnām	rīme, čhami
Virtue	pune पुन्य		
Visit, to	darsan mā jānu दरसन मा जानु		
, a	bhet भेट		
Voice	sor, sabd सोर, सब्द		toyi
Vomit	chhādnu, wāk wāk garnu, ok wāknu छादनु, वाक वाक गरनु वाकनु		ri
Vow	kiriya किरिया		
Vulture	gidha गिद्ध		kure

1 "He tried in vain"—"U le alpatri gario (suddhai gario)." "They went in vain (to no purpose)"—"Uniharu suddhai goyo."

2 See footnote 1, p. 46.

ENGLISH	KHAS	MAGAR	GURUNG
WADE	tarnu तरनु	tarish	tardi
Wag, to	halānu हलानु	whek	lā
,, a	jhilkiyā झिलक्या		
Wages	jāgir, talab जागिर, तलब		
Waist	kamar कमर		
Waist-coat	āskat आसकट		
	bhoto भोटो		
Wait	parkhnu परखनु	rung	ti
Wake (t)	jagāunu जगाउनु	sotāk.	re
(i)	jāgnu जागनु	so	,,
Walk	dulnu डुलनु	dulish	
Walking-stick	lauro लौरो	dānga	pare
Wall	parkhāl परखाल		
	dewāl देवाल		
(inner)	gāro, bhitta गारो, भीत्ता		
Walnut	okhar ओखड़		
Wander, to	abāto lagnu अबाटो लगनु		
Want (verb)	māngnu मांगनु	gnīm –	rī
	khojnu खोजनु	pā	mai
Warm	mantāto, tāto मनतातो,तातो	kān	
Warn	chetāunu चताउनु		
Warp	tānā ताना		
Wart	musā मुसा	jish	chepora
Wash			
(clothes)	dhunu धुनु	hur	kru
(self)	nohānu नोहानु	resh	,,
(dishes)	pakhālnu पखालनु	hur	,,
Wash away	bagāunu वगाउनु	bagdis	bagdi
Wasp	bārulā बारुला	wāma	
Watch, to	chewā basnu चेवा बसनु	gnos	
	dhuknu ढुकनु		loy
Water	pāni, jel पानी, जेल	di	kiu
,, wheel	ghata घाट		
Wax	lei, mum लेई मूम		
Waterfall	chhāra छारा		
Weak	nirbalio निरबलयो		

ENGLISH	KHAS	MAGAR	GURUNG
Wear	lāunu लाउनु		
(clothes)	lagāunu.. लगाउनु	bil	khe
away (t)	khiyāunu खियाउनु		
(i)	khiunu खिउनु		
Web	mākurā jāli मानुराजाली	gharuwa jāl	timru jāl
Wednesday	budhbār बुधबार		
Weed	jhār झाड़		gno
(water)	simāli सिमाली		
Weep	runu रुनु	rāp	kro
Week	sātā, haftā साता, हफ़्ता		
Weigh, to	jokhnu जोखनु	jāp	kwe
Weighing-machine	kāntā, tulo कांटा, तुलो	pāra	pāra
Weight	bhār भार		
Well (noun)	kuwā, inār कुवा, इनार		
(good)	rāmro रामरो	sieche	chiab
(fit)	niko निको		
(adv.)	jāti जाती		
West	pachchim पश्चिम		
Wet	chilo, rujhiyo चिलो, रुझियो	chhima	
, to get	rujhnu रुझनु	chhim	pai
What ?	kya ? क्या ?	hi ?	to ?
Wheat	gahun गहुं		
Wheel	paiyā पैया		
When ?	kaile ? कैले ?	sien ?	khayan ?
When	jab जब		
Whence ?	kahān bāta ? कहां बाट ?	kulaki ?	kanabiti ?
Where ?	kahān ? कहां ?	kulak ?	kana ?
Where	jahān जहां ?		
Whither ?	kathā कथा ?	kulak ?	kana ?
Whiskers	khātā खाता		
Whistle, a	suskeri सुसकेरी		kupī
(noise)	shusilo शुसिलो		,,
White	seto सेतो	bochu	tarkya
Who ?	ko ? को ?	su ? kos ?	kāb ?

ENGLISH	KHAS	MAGAR	GURUNG
Whore	pātar, besyā पातर, ब्रेशिया		
Why ?	kina ? किन ?	hiki ?	tole ?
Wick (of lamp)	dār (batti ko) दार (बत्ती को)		
Wide	gajīlo गजीलो		
Widow	rānri रांड़ी		
Widower	rānro रांड़ो		
Wife	swāshnī श्वाशनी	māja	marī
Wife's house	mait मैत		
Wild	jangali, ban ko जंगली, बनको		
Wild boar	banel बनेल	wāk	tili
Wild dog	boānsi बोआंसी		piongo (Lamjung)
Will	ichchhā इच्छा		
Win	jitnu जितनु	jitdi	toy
Wind, the	batās बतास	namshu	namru
, to	ghumāunu घुमाउनु	chharāk	
(a turban)	guthnu गुथनु	chiäk	ti
Window	jhyāl झयाल		
Winnow	phatkanu फटकनू		hupdi
Winter	jāru ko din जारु को दिन		
Wipe	pochhnu, gasnu पोछनू, गसनू	sit	phiyo
Wisdom	buddhi बुद्धि		
With	sita, sang सित, संग	kata	pare
Withdraw	sarkanu सर्कनु		
Wither (i)	wailinu वैलिनु		
(t)	wailyānu वैल्यानु		
Withered	sukyāko सूक्याको	chokake	sôi
Within	bhitra भित्र		nâr
Without	bhaira भायर		
,, (not with)	binā बिना		
Witness	sākshi साकशी		
Woman[1]	swāshni श्वाशनी āimai आईमाई stri स्त्रि	māja	marī, rīme

[1] Swashni literally means wife; aimai, woman as opposed to man.

ENGLISH	KHAS	MAGAR	GURUNG
Wood (forest)	ban बन		
,, (substance)	dauro, kāth दौरो काठ	sing	si
Wool	un ऊन		
Work	kāj, kām काज, काम	zātke	ke
Working-party	khetara haru खेतरा हरु	hiami bharmi	moromhi
World	dunyā, jahān दुनया, जहान		
Worldly	sansāri ससारी		
Worn out (of people)	thötro थोतरो		
Worship	pujā पुजा		
Worthy	jogya जोग्य		
Wound	ghāu घाउ		
Wounded	ghaile घैले		
Wrap, to	lapetnu लपेटनु		
Wring, to			
(clothes)	nichornu निचोरनु	chupki	chiora
(hands)	halāunu हलाउनु	whek	lā
Wrist	nāri नाड़ी		
Write	likhnu लिखनू	rik	prī
Wrong (n.)	gaḷti गलटी		
YARD			
(measure)	gaj गज		
,, (court)	āgan आगन		
Yawn, to	hāi garnu हाई गरनू	hai rā	kā
Year [1]	sāl, san, baras साल, सन, बरस		
Yellow	pahilo पहिलो	orcho	urkya
Yesterday[1]	hiju हिजु	tisini	tela
Young	tanderi तन्देरी	renja	phrensi
Younger	kānchho कान्छो		āchiu
Youth (abs.)	joban, bhāis जोबान, भाइस		
(con.)	thitā ठिटा	renja	phrensi
	tanderi तन्देरी		
	taruna तरुना		
ZEALOUS	man paryā ko मन परयाको		

[1] See footnote 2, p. 31.

(b) KHASKURA-ENGLISH VOCABULARY

Note.—There are several words in this Vocabulary not shown in Chapter II(*a*), owing to their incapabilities of an easy English translation (*e.g.* Jhamta, Rodi).

The length of the vowel in the Roman word can be seen from the Hindi spelling.

Abato lagnu (v.) अबाटो लागनु	To stray from the road : to wander.
Abela (n.) अबेला	(Lit.) not in time ; lateness ; delay.
Abhagi अभागी	Not lucky ; unlucky.
Achchar (n.) अच्चर	Letter of the Alphabet.
Achetnu (v.) अचेटनु	To strangle, to choke.
Adha आधा	Half.
Adda (n.) अड्डा	A district, corresponding to an Indian tehsil.
Adhi bhaunri (n.) आधि भौंरी	A storm ; a tempest.
Adha bains आधा बाइसं	Manhood.
Aduwa (n.) अदुवा	Ginger.
Agan (n.) आगन	A yard (back-yard).
Agena (n.) अगेना	An oven.
Aghari अघाड़ी	(1) In front (adv.). (2) In front of (Genitive) (Prep.).
Aghaunu (v.) अघाउनु	To satisfy.
Aghillo (adj.) अघिल्लो	Foremost.
Aghinai (adv.) अघिनै	Before, previously.
Aghun (adj.) आघुं	Usually written fully—Aghun sal, next year. Aghun by itself, though is also used for next year.
Aglo (n.) आगलो	Bolt of a door ; wooden bolt.
Ago (n.) आगो	Fire.
Agulto (n.) आगुलटो	A fire-brand.
Aguni (adj.) अगुनी	Without thanks ; thankless ; ungrateful
Aguwa अगुवा	Guide, a
Agyan (n.) आज्ञा	An order, command.

Ahan (n.) अहान	A riddle.
Aher (n.) अहेर	Shikar, hunting.
Aile (adv.) अैले	Now ; immediately. "*Aile* thik bhayana"—"It isn't right yet" or "It's not quite right." "*Aile aile* kasnu"—"Tighten it just a little bit more." "Aile chhan"—"Still some more."
Ai mai (n.) आइ माई	Woman.
Ain (n.) अैन	An order ; a rule. "Rule No. 7"—"*Ain* sat."
Ainthaya bhangro अैथया भांग्रो	Nepalese material for clothes.
Airi (n.) अइरी	Prey. "M. *airi* khelnu goyo"—"I went shooting."
Aisalu (n.) ऐसालु	A raspberry.
Aitwar (n.) अैतवार	Sunday.
Aj (n.) आज	To-day. Ajbholi—nowadays.
Ajhai (adv.) अझै	Still ; yet. "Ajhai chhan"—"There are still some." "Ajhai thik bhayana"—"It isn't right yet."
Ajingar (n.) अजीङगर	A large snake ; a dragon.
Akas (n.) अकास	The sky.
Akhara (n.) आखाड़ा	Physical drill ; gymnastics.
Akhiri आखिरी	Last. "Sab—bhanda akhiri"—"Last of all." Sometimes used loosely instead of abela.
Akarnu (v.) अकड़नु	To become cramped.
Alag अलग	Separate.
Alainchi (n.) अलाइची	Cardamon.
Alchhi (adj.) अलछि	Lazy.
Alikati (adv.) अलीकती	A little. Alikheri, for a little while.
Aljhanu (v.) अलझनु	To stick in ; to become stuck in. (In the sense of to stick in one's throat, to stick in the doorway). See also Atkanu.
Alko (adj.) अलको	Tall, high. "Timi kati alko chhau ?"—"How tall are you ?"

Alai ; Alo (adj.) आलै: आलो	Fresh ; freshly-picked.
Altu-phaltu (adj.) आलतु-फालतु	Strange ; from outside. "Altu-phaltu manchha"—"A stranger."
Alunu अलुनु	Saltless.
Alu (n.) आलु	A potato.
Am (n.) आम	Mango. Also called anp.
Ama (n.) आमा	Mother.
Amaldar अमलदार	Naick.
Aman (adj.) अमान	Unwilling ; (lit.) against the mind or will.
Amel (ad.) अमेल	Odd, queer, strange.
Amilo अमिलो	Sour.
Amkhori (n.) अमखोरी	A plate.
Anand (n.) आनन्द	Joy.
Anari (n.) अनाड़ी	A fool.
Anchal (n.) आंचल	A knot. Anchal gantho, the marriage knot or tie.
Andaz (n.) अन्दाज	Guess. Andaz garnu, to guess. "Andaz le," "At a guess."
Andhyaro (n.) अंधयारो	Darkness.
Andra (n.) आन्द्रा	The entrails of an animal.
Ang (n.) आङ्ग	The whole body.
Angal halnu (v.) अङ्गल हालनु	To embrace ; to put one's arm round someone's neck.
Angeti (n.) अगेंटी	A chimney.
Angkusia (n.) अङ्गकुस्या	A hook.
Angur (n.) अंगूर	A grape. Angur ko lahara (or rukh), a vine.
Anguthi (n.) अंगुठि	A ring.
Anhwar (n.) अनव्हार	The face.
Anikal (n.) अनीकाल	A famine.
Ankha (n.) आंखा	The eye.
Ankhi-bhaun (n.) आखी भाऊं	The eye-brow.
Anlo (n.) अंलो	Finger, Buro, jetho or kalmi or chor, mainlo, sainlo, kanchho are thumb, fore, middle, fourth and little.

Anp (n.) आंप	A mango.
Ansa (n.) अंस	A share.
Ansar अन्सार	A guess.
Ansar le अन्सार ले	In accordance with ; according to.
Ansi (n.) आंसी	A scythe.
Ansu (n.) आंसु	A tear.
Anta (n.) अन्त	The end, finish.
Anti आंटी	Top storey.
Anthiaunu (v.) आंथ्यउनु	To squeeze.
Antilo आंटिलो	Daring.
Anyadesh (adj.) अन्यदेश	Belonging to another country ; foreign.
Apastma अपस्तमा	Among themselves.
Aphim (n.) अफीम	Opium.
Aphnu (pro.) अफनो	Own.
Aputa (adj.) अपुत	Childless.
Ar (n.) आड़	Shelter, cover.
Arhanu (v.) अढानु	To order, command.
Ahri (n.) आड़ी	Water-clock. A copper vessel called Ghari is placed in the Arhi (water vessel), and the time it takes to fill through a hole in its base, sink and strike a metal plate called Ghanta, is one Nepalese hour (Ghari).
Ari (n.) आरी	A saw.
Ariash lagaunu (v.) आड्यास लगाउनु	To lean against.
Aringal (n.) अरीगल	An ordinary hornet.
Arinu (v.) अड़िनु	To stop, halt, remain standing.
Arko (pro.) आरको	Other ; another.
Arni (n.) अरनी	Midday meal ; tiffin.
Artha (n.) अर्थ	Meaning (of a sentence or speech.)
Arthi (n.) अर्थी	Lesson.
Aru (conj.) अरू	And; more. "2 aru lau"—"Bring 2 more.
Aru (n.) आरू	A peach.
Asajilo (adj.) असजिलो	Difficult.
Asla असला	A fish.

Atkanu (v.) अटकनु — To stick in, be stuck in; same as Aljhanu.
Asar (n.) असाड़ — The month 15th June to 15th July.
Asik आसिक — Blessings (from a Superior).
Asina (n.) असीना — Hail.
Askot (n.) आसकोट — A waistcoat.
Asnan (n.) अस्नान — Bathing.
Asoj (n.) असोज — The month 15th September to 15th October.
Asra (n.) आसरा — Hope.
Asti (n.) अस्ती — Day before yesterday; also loosely for some days ago.
Asti (adj.) आस्ति — Slowly; gently.
Ataunu अताउनु — Fit, fit in.
Atinu (v.) आतीनु — To get nervous.
Aturi आतुरी — Lack of time, want of time.
Aukhadi (n.) — Medicine.
Aul (adj.) औल — Hot; this refers to climates. "Jacobabad aul thaun chha"—"Jacobabad is a hot place" meaning a bad, hot climate.
Aune (adj.) आउने — Future. "Aune haphta"—"next week."
Aya baba आया बाबा — Exclamation on a sudden pain.
Avir अबीर — Red water thrown in the Holi festival.
Ave अवे — Exclamation of regret or distress.
Ayo अयो — Exclamation. This is really the Past Part. of Anu to come. As an exclamation it comes to mean "Look out"; also often used when surprised by a sudden pain, *e.g.* when pinched.
Babaho ! बाबाहो — Exclamation of dread, and also to indicate surprise. Occasionally abbreviated to babe !
Babu (n.) बाबु — Father.
Bacha (n.) बाचा — A promise.
Bachaunu (v. tr.) बचाउनु — To save; to rescue; to protect or give shelter to.

Bachha (n.) बाछा	A non-ploughing bullock.
Bachhiu (n.) बछ्यू	A large hornet ; black body and yellow head.
Bachnu (v. inter.) बचनु	To be saved ; to escape (a disaster). Also used in the sense of "to be left over, to remain." "Yo kinera, kati rupeya bachio ?"—"After buying that, how many rupees were left over ?"
Badal (n.) बादल	A cloud.
Badala (n.) बदला	Change, exchange, relief. "Tis ko badala ma"—"In exchange for that." In connection with sentries. "Timro badala ayo"—"Your relief has come." Occasionally used for revenge. "Tis ko badala ma"—"In revenge for that."
Badam (n.) बदाम	An almond.
Bag (n.) बाग	A garden.
Bagal (n.) बगाल	A flock ; a herd. Hence loosely used referring to a crowd of men.
Bagaunu (v. tr.) बगाउनु	To carry away (by a river), lit. "To be 'flowed.'" "Ganga ma" lotera, pani le uslai bagayo"—"He fell down in the river and was carried away by the water."
Bagh (n.) बाघ	A tiger. This is used for a small tiger. *Darak* is the largest size. *Sher* is also larger than Bagh.
Bagulla (n.) बगुला	A heron.
Bagnu (v.) बगनु	To flow.
Bahanu (v.) बहनु	To flow.
Bahāna (n.) बहाना	Excuse.
Bahar (n.) बहड़	A young of cattle ; a calf.
Bahiro (adj.) बहीरो	Deaf.
Bahunne (n.) बाहुन्ने	A dwarf ; (lit.) a 52-inch man (Urdu word).

Baida (n.) बैद	A doctor or wise man.
Baijni (adj.) बैजनी	Purple.
Bain (adj.) बाञा	Left ; this is the Urdu word, the Khaskura being *Debro*, q.v.
Baini (n.) बैनीं	A younger sister.
Bairi (n.) बैरी	An enemy.
Baisakh (n.) बैसाख	The month 15th April to 15th May.
Baj (n.) or Baz बाज	A hawk.
Băjai (n.) बजेइ	Grandmother.
Bajaunu (v. tr.) बजाउनु	To sound or play a musical instrument.
Baje (n.) बजे	Time. "What is the time ?"—"Kati baje chha."
Bajewa (n.) बजेवा	A large wild pigeon.
Bājia (n.) बाज्या	A grandfather.
Bajnu (inter.) बजनु	Tc sound, strike (of a clock) "Ghanta bajio"—"The gong struck." "Kati bajio"—"What has struck ?" hence "What is the time ?'
Bajralep बजरलेप	Mortar.
Bajr बज्र	Thunder bolt, lightning.
Baklo (adj.) बाकलो	Thick. This word is chiefly used in reference to a thick mist or cloud, also a dense jungle ; not so much in the sense of *fat*.
Bakra (n.) Bakri (n.) बाकरा बाकरी	This is the general term for goat, male and female. For the distinctive terms see English-Gurkhali, note 2, p. 61.
Bal (n.) बल	Force, strength.
Bal (n.) बाल	The Urdu word for hair, often used.
Bala (n.) बाला	A bracelet.
Bala बाला	Pod (seed pod of plant).
Balakha (n.) बालख	A small child.
Baleni (n.) बलेनी	The eaves of a house.
Bali (n.) बाली	Harvest.

Balio (adj.) बलियो — Strong, powerful, firm. "Man balio rakh"—"Keep your mind strong: keep up your spirits."

Balla (adv.) बल्ल — At last.

Balmichai (n.) बलमिचाई — Compulsion.

Balnu (v.) बाल्नु — (intr.) to burn. "Ago balina"—"The fire didn't burn."
(tr.) to kindle. "Ago lai balnu"—"Light the fire."

Baluwa (n.) बालुवा — Sand.

Balwa (n.) बलवा — Mutiny, disturbance, tumult, insurrection (Urdu word).

Bam (n.) बाम — An eel. Rajbam is a large eel; chuchu bam a pointed one. Eels are considered good eating.

Bamgola (n.) बमगोला — A bomb.

Ban (n.) बन — Jungle, forest, wood.

Ban बान — Paralysis.

Banar (n.) बानर — A monkey.

Ban ko (adj.) बन को — (Formed from Ban). Of the jungle hence wild, savage.

Banmanchha (n.) बनमान्छा — A wild man; hence applied to a very ignorant man, as in English one says "So and so is a perfect savage."

Bancharo (n.) बनचरो — An axe.

Banda (n.) बांदा — A servant. This is not the same as a slave (Kumara). A Banda agrees to serve for a certain time for a certain sum of money, after which time he is free. A Kumara however belongs to a slave caste and is always a slave. He gets no pay except his board and lodging.

Bandhnu (v. tr.) बांधनु — To bind, tie, fasten.

Banduk (n.) बन्दूक — A gun. Banduk le hannu (hirkanu) is to shoot.

Banel (n.) बनेल	A wild pig.
Bangaro (n.) बांगरो	The jaw.
Bango (adj.) बांगो	Not straight, crooked.
Bani (n.) बानी	Habit. "Rakshi khana bani pario"—"He has got into the habit of drinking rum."
Banji (adj.) बांजी	Barren, without issue.
Banki (adj.) बांकी	Remaining. "Kati banki rahio"—"How many were left over?"
Bans (n.) बांस	Bamboo.
Banse (n.) बांसे	A Nepalese wooden hookah.
Bansuli बांसुली	Fife, picolo.
Bar (n.) बार	Day of the week. "Aja kia bar ho?" "What is the day to-day? Occasionally loosely used for date.
Bar (n.) बांड़	A hedge or boundary round a field, etc.
Barati (n.) बराती	A saw.
Bardan (n.) बरदान	A gift.
Barhaunu (v. tr.) बढ़ाउनु	To increase. "Tisko talab barhaunu parchha"—"His pay must be increased."
Barhnu (v. intr.) बढ़नु	To grow, to increase.
Bari (n.) बाड़ी	A garden, compound or place surrounded by a Bar (q.v.)
Bari (n.) बारी	Time, turn. "Tero bari ayo"—"Your turn has come."
Barkha (n.) बर्षा	The rains.
Barsnu (v.) बरसनु	To rain; not very often used.
Barula (n.) बारुला	A wasp.
Baruki बारूकी	A hiccough.
Basant (n.) बसंन्त	The season of Spring.
Basant Panchmi (n.) बसन्त पंचमी	The birth of Spring; a festival held at the commencement of Spring.
Basi (adj.) बासी	Stale, musty.
Basin (n.) बसिन	An odour, smell; this is chiefly applicable to a nice smell, a bad one being Gandha.

Basnu (v.) बसुन — To sit ; occasionally to abide. " M yota din Batoli ma basio "—" I stayed in Batoli for one day." It is also sometimes used for to stop (intr.) " Pani basio "—" The rain has stopped."

Bat (n.) बात — Talk, speech. Bat katnu, to contradict, cross-examine. Bat marnu, to talk.

Bata (prep.) बाट — From. " M Kathmandu bata gayo "— " I went from Kathmandu." " Yo tamasha kasko tira bata chha ? "— " (lit.) From whose direction is this show ? " hence " Who is giving this show ? "

Batas (n.) बतास — The wind.

Bataunu (v.) बटाउनु — To show : to winnow.

Batekri (n.) बतेकरी — A large female goat.

Bater (n.) बटेर — A quail.

Batha (adj.) बाठा — Wise. " Man bhanda challa batha "— " The chicken is wiser than the hen."

Bathan (n). बथान — A flock, herd.

Batnu (v.) बाटनु — To twist.

Bato (n.) बाटो — A road, highway. Chorbato or Gorento bato, a footpath or byway. Mul bato, a main road. "M bato birsio"— " I have forgotten the road," hence " I have lost my way."

Batuko (n.) बटुको — A cup.

Batulnu (v.) बटुलनु — To gather, collect together.

Baula (n.) बाउला — A sleeve of a coat.

Baunsa बौंसा — A wild dog.

Bawona (n.) बवोना — An oar.

Beglai (adj.) बेगलै — Different.

Beijati (adj.) बेइजती — Of no respect ; not to be respected; bad.

Bejor बेजोर — Odd-numbered (1, 3, 5, 7, etc.).

Bela (n.) बेला — Time ; " Tisto bela ma, na hansnu "— "At such a time, don't laugh." " Aile bela bhayana "—" It isn't the time yet."

Bela (n.) बेला — A cup.

Belcha (n.) बेलचा — A spade.

Beluka (n.) बेलुका — Evening.

Benr (n.) बेंड़ — A handle.

Beohara (n.) बयाहारा — Circumstance.

Beopar (n.) बयोपारा — Trade, profession.

Bernu (v.) बेड़नु — To roll.

Beru (n.) बेड़ु — A fig.

Besar (n.) बेसार — Huldi.

Besgari (adv.) बेसगरी — Utmost. "Besgari dugar "—" Run as hard as you can." "Timi rakshi ramro manchhau ? Besgari ! "—" Do you like rum ? Rather.

Besya (n.) बेसिया — A prostitute, whore.

Betha (n.) बेथा — Trouble, distress.

Bethaha (adv.) बेथाहा — Unawares.

Bhadu (n.) भदू — Millet.

Bhag (n.) भाग — Fate, luck.

Bhag (n.) भाग — Part.

Bhagat (n.) भगत — A devotee ; a man who spurns wordly things.

Bhagbhagi (n.) भगभगी — A stammerer.

Bhagaura (n.) भगौड़ा — A deserter, a runner-away.

Bhagiman (adj.) भाग्यमान — Lucky.

Bhagnu (v.) भागनु — To run away ; to escape.

Bhai (n.) भाई — Younger brother. Friendly term used to anyone.

Bhaini भाइनी — Younger sister.

Bhainsi (n.) भैंसी — A buffalo.

Bhaira (adv.) भायरा — Outside, without.

Bhais भाइस — Youth ; youthful health.

Bhakari भकारी — A large basket for keeping grain.

Bhakha (n.) भाषा — The tune of a song.

Bhakunda (n.) भकुन्डा — Hockey as played in Nepal.

Bhala (n.) भाला — A spear.

Bhalu (n.) भालु — A bear.
Bhalya (n.) भाल्या — A cock-bird ; a domestic cock.
Bhanda भन्दा — Than ; "Rupsing is better than Narbir" —" Rupsing Narbir bhanda ramro chha."
Bhaṇe (conj.) भने — If. Bhane dekhin also used. " M wahan gayana bhane, u marne thio "— " If I hadn't gone there, he would have died."
Bhanich (n.) भानोज — Son-in-law's son.
Bhanjyang (n.) भनज्यांग — A defile ; a narrow valley between two hills. There are several places of this name with different epithets in Nepaul.
Bhangera भगेरा — A sparrow.
Bhanra (n.) भांड़ा — Cooking-pots.
Bhanseghar (n.) भानसेवर — A cook-house.
Bhanse (n.) भानसे — A cook.
Bhannu (v.) भनन् — To say, tell, speak. The 1st person present often used at the end of a sentence for emphasis :—"Sara paltan bigardinchhas, Bhanchhu ! "—" You spoil the whole regiment, I tell you ! " The past participle is used largely where seemingly unnecessary :—M bholi janchhu bhanera bhanio ule "— " He said he was going to-morrow." " Report sick ! " would be—"M bimar chhu bhanera, report gar ! "
Bhanti (n.) भांती — Bellows (Sanscrit word).
Bhap भाप — Steam.
Bhapsila भापसीला — Hyaena.
Bhar भार — Indebtedness.
Bharai (n.) भरै — Evening. Baraisanjh also used.
Bhari (n.) भारी — A load, burden.
Bhari (prep.) भरी — Throughout the whole. " Din bhari"— " All day long."

Bharia (n.) भरिया	A man who carries loa.'s; a cooly, porter.
Bhariako (adj.) भऱ्याको	Full.
Bharkar (adv.) भरकर	Just now. "U bharkar ayo"—"He has just this minute come."
Bharm (n.) भर्म	Suspicion.
Bharnu (v.) भरनु	To fill.
Bharyang (n.) भरयांग	Stone stairs or steps.
Bhat (n.) भात	Boiled rice.
Bhatija (n.) भतीजा	Brother's son; nephew. Bhatiji, Brother's daughter, niece.
Bhatkanu (v. intr.) भतकनु	To collapse (of a wall, etc.)
Bhatkaunu (v.t.) भतकाउनु	To knock down. (a wall, etc.)
Bhatti (n.) भट्टी	An inn, tavern.
Bhaunra (n.) भौंरा	A bumble-bee.
Bhau (n.) भाव	Rate. Chawal ko bhau kati chha yahan?"—"What is the rate for rice here?"
Bhauju (n.) भाउजु	Elder brother's wife. E bhauju ho! Common method of calling to women!
Bhauno chhutna (v.) भाउनो छुटनु	To get giddy, faint.
Bhayo भयो	Past participle of Hunnu, to be. Used to denote "Finished" at the end of a work. Also as equivalent to Urdu word "bas"—"enough."
Bhed (n.) भेद	Vaccination, etc.
Bheli (n.) भेली	Gur sugar in a round lump (Urdu word).
Bhera, bheri (n.) भेड़ा भेड़ी	A sheep, male and female. Also for wild sheep.
Bhet (n.) भेट	A visit, meeting.
Bhetnu (v). भेटनु	To meet, visit.
Bhikhari (n.) भिखारी	A beggar.
Bhignu (v.) भीगनु	To get wet.
Bhinno bhinno भिन्नो भिन्नो	Different.

Bhir (n.) भीर — A very steep bit of hill ; a precipice.
Bhiralo भिरालो — Steep, precipitous.
Bhiringi (n.) भिरिङ्गि — Syphilis.
Bhittra (adv.) भित्र — Inside, within.
Bhog (n.) भोग — Pleasure, joy.
Bhognu (v.) भोगनु — To have pleasure.
Bholi (adv.) भोली — To-morrow.
Bhorto (n.) भोर्टो — Nepalese vest.
Bhot (n.) भोट — Tibet.
Bhubro (n.) भुबरो — Embers (of a fire.)
Bhuin (n.) भुईं — Ground, floor.
Bhuintala भुईंतल — Bottom storey, ground-floor.
Bhuin-chalo (n.) भुईं चालो — Earthquake.
Bhuin kaphal भुइँ काफल — Strawberry.
Bhukh (n.) भुख — Hunger. "Bhukh lagnu"—"To be hungry."
Bhul (n.) भूल — Piece of forgetfulness ; mistake.
Bhuknu (v.) भुकनु — To bark (as a dog.)
Bhunri (n.) भुंड़ि — Abdomen, stomach.
Bhuso (n.) भुसो — Chaff.
Bhyana (adj.) भ्यानै — Early (in the sense of early in the morning). Also used loosely for morning.
Bhyaunu (v.) भयाउनु — To finish.
Biah (n.) ब्याह — Marriage.
Biaguta (n.) ब्यागुता — A frog.
Biaz (n.) ब्याज — Interest (on money).
Bibro (n.) बिबरो — A small pimple.
Bichar (n.) बिचार — Thought. "Bichar Garnu"—"To think."
Bichchhi (n.) बिच्छि — A scorpion.
Bichhaunu बिछाउनु — To make one's bed.
Bida बिदा — Farewell, good-bye. "Ab bida bida hola"—"Now there will be good-bye."
Bigarnu (n.) बिगाड़नु — To spoil.
Bijli (n.) बिजली — Electricity, lightning.
Bikh (n.) बिष — Poison.

Biknu (v.) बिकनु — To sell.
Bilap (n.) बिलाप — Lamentation.
Bimra बिमरा — A pimple.
Bina (prep.) बिना — Without, not with. "U bina kukri ayo" —"He came without a kukri." But "He left without eating" would be "U na khayera gayo" (*lit.* he went not having eaten).
Bina (n.) बिना — The musk pod of a musk deer; musk.
Bina (n.) बिना — Elder sister's husband. A term of friendliness from a woman to a man. "E bina"—"O cousin."
Binti (n.) बिन्ती — Representation, request. "M binti garnu ayo"—"I have come to make a request."
Bipebar (n.) बिपेबार — Thursday.
Biphar बिफर — Small-pox.
Bir (adj.) बीर — Brave.
Biralu (n.) बिरालु — A cat.
Birami (adj.) बिरामी — Ill, sick.
Birano बिरानो — Stranger, unknown person.
Biraun (n.) बिराऊं — Error, mistake.
Biraunu (v.) बिराउनु — To make a mistake.
Biri (n.) बिरी — Black paintlike stuff put on teeth. It is supposed to show up the white, and also to keep the teeth strong.
Birko (n.) बिरको — Cork (of a bottle).
Birsnu (v.) बिरसनु — To forget. "M bato birsio"—"I forgot the road, I lost my way."
Biruwa (n.) बिरूवा — A small plant of any sort
Bisalnu (v.) बिसालनु — To take a rest; to rest.
Bishalu (adj.) बिषालु — Poisonous.
Bistar (adv.) बिस्तार — Gently.
Bitaidinu बिताईदिनु — To spend time.
Bitike (adv.) बितिकै — At that very time; at the same time.
Bito (n.) बिटो — Load of grass.
Bitta (n.) बित्ता — The span of hand.

Bitnu (v.) बितनु	To die.
Biu (n.) बिउ	Seed.
Bodho (adj.) बोढो	Blunt (of a knife).
Boknu (v.) बोकनु	To carry.
Bokra (n.) बोकरा	The bark of a tree.
Bokshi (n.) बोकशी	A witch. "Tio bokus-ma bokshi rechha"—"That box is haunted."
Bokya (n.) बोक्या	A ram.
Bolo (n.) बोलो	A beam (of wood).
Boso (n.) बोसो	Fat.
Bot (n.) बोट	A word sometimes used for a tree.
Bohari (n.) बोहारी	A daughter-in-law.
Buchka (n.) बुचका	Stubble.
Bucho (adj.) बुचो	Without ornaments, unadorned, plain.
Buddhi (n.) बुद्धि	Wisdom.
Buddhbar (n.) बुद्धवार	Wednesday.
Bujhaunu (v.) बुझाउनु	(1) To extinguish, put out (a fire). (2) To explain, make understand.
Bujhnu (v.) बुझनु	To understand.
Bulaki (n.) बुलाकी	The nose-ring on the piece of skin between the nostrils.
Bulbuli (n.) बुलबुली	A method of cropping the hair ("knuttish.")
Bunnu (v.) बुननु	To spin; to spin wool.
Burburya (adj.) बुरबुरया	Sprinkled, loose (of earth).
Burnu (v.) बुड़नु	To enter water, sink.
Buro (adj.) बुड़ो	Old, aged.
Buro Anlo (n.) बुड़ो अंलो	Thumb; big toe.
Burya (n.) बुड़िया	An old woman.
Chabaunu (v.) चबाउनु	To chew
Chabi (n.) चाबी	A key.
Chain चैं	An emphatic exclamation. "Ko chain ho?"—"Which is it *exactly?*"
Chadar (n.) चादर	A sheet. Also called chedar
Chah (n.) चाह	Tea.
Chahla चहला	Water-logged.

Chainu (v.) चाहिनु	To be necessary. " Is lài garnu chainchha "—" This must be done." " Koi aru manchhe chainchhàn ? "—" Are any more men required ? "
Chait (n.) चैत	The month 15th March to 15th April.
Chak (n.) चाक	The " seat " of a person, buttocks.
Chakhnu (v.) चाखनु	To taste.
Chaklo (adj.) चाकलो	Broad, thick, dense.
Chaku (n.) चाकु	A penknife (Urdu word).
Chal (n.) चाल	(1) Behaviour. " Tisko chal kasto chha ? "—" How does he behave ? " Chal Chalan frequently used. (2) Feeling. " Bhuinchalo ko chal payis ki payenas ? "—" Did you feel the earthquake or not ? "
Chalan (n.) चलन	Behaviour. See Chal.
Challa (n.) चल्ला	A small chicken.
Chalno (n.) चालनी	A sieve.
Chalnu (v.) चालनु	To sift.
Chamera (n.) चमेड़ा	A bat (bird).
Chamkanu (v.) चमकनु	To be startled.
Chanakho (adj.) चनाखो	Smart, clever, alert, brisk.
Chand (n.) चांद	Target (Urdu word).
Chandi (n.) चांदी	Silver.
Chankya (n.) चंखिया	Clever.
Chanri (adv.) चांड़ै	Quickly, swiftly ; also used for early " Timi chanri ayau "—" You came quickly or early."
Char (num.) चार	Four ; the word for tea is Chah.
Charaunu (v.) चराउनु	To graze, to pasture.
Charbar (n.) चाड़बाड़ा	A festival.
Charkhaunu (v.) चरखाउनु	To fire.
Charkha (n.) चर्खा	A spinning wheel.
Charko (adj.) चरको	Aloud. " Aile charko bhan "—" Talk a little louder."

Charnu (v.) चढ़नु	To climb, ascend; to mount a horse or carriage. "Ghora mathi charera"—"On horseback."
Chara (n.) चरा	A bird.
Charo (n.) चारो	Bait, for fishing.
Charkinu (v.) चरकिनु	To crack (of a wall, etc.).
Charpatti (adv.) चारपट्टी	All four quarters.
Chartira (adv.) चारतीर	All four directions. "Chartira pani thio"—"There was water all around."
Chasma (n.) चसमा	Spectacles, glasses.
Chatnu (v.) चाटनु	To lick with the tongue.
Chaubandi (n.) चौबन्दी	Nepalese dress (as Jhampanis wear).
Chauro (adj.) चौड़ो	Broad (Urdu word).
Chawal (n.) चावल	Rice (uncooked).
Chaya चाया	Scurf.
Cheli (n.) चेली	A girl.
Chepnu (v.) चेपनु	To press.
Chepto (adj.) चेपटो	Flat.
Cherana (n.) चेरना	A girl.
Chetaunu (v.) चेताउनु	To warn.
Chewa (n.) चेवा	A hiding place, ambush.
Chhadnu (v.) छादनु	To be sick, to vomit, to eject.
Chhahari (n.) छाहारी	Shade; shadow.
Chhala (n.) छाला	Skin, leather, hide.
Chhalinu (v.) छलिनु	Deceive.
Chhamnu (v.) छामनु	To touch, feel.
Chhana (n.) छाना	Ceiling, roof.
Chhango (n.) छांगो	A torrent, rapids.
Chhantnu (v.) छांटनु	To select, choose.
Chhap (n.) छाप	(1) Print. (2) The tail of coins. (3) A seal.
Chhaphăni top छफनी तोप	A large cannon of 6 maunds powder.
Chhapnu (v.) छापनु	To press, to print.
Chhapri (n.) छपरी	A sod of turf.
Chhara (n.) छारा	A waterfall, cascade.
Chhara (n.) छरा	Shot.
Chharnu (v.) छड़नु	To sow.

Chhata (n.) छाता	An umbrella.
Chhati (n.) छाती	The chest.
Chhatkya (adv.) छटक्या	Diagonally, at an angle.
Chhaya (n.) छाया	Shadow, shade.
Chhegnu (v.) छेंगनु	To stop, prevent.
Chhenr (n.) छेंड़	A hole.
Chheo (n.) छेव	The side (of a place), the edge, bank.
Chheparo (n.) छेपाड़ो	A lizard.
Chherauti (n.) छेरौटी	Diarrhœa.
Chhima (n.) छिमा	Mercy.
Chhimal छिमाल	Grass on a tree.
Chhimeki (n.) छिमेकी	A neighbour, acquaintance.
Chhin (n.) छिन	A moment. "Ek chhin"—"Half a mo."
Chhina (n.) छीना	A chisel.
Chhipia ko (adj.) छिपियाको	Wrinkled.
Chhiribirya (adj.) छिरबिऱ्या	Piebald, spotted.
Chhirki (n.) छिड़की	The chik (on a door).
Chhirnu (v.) छिरनु	To pierce, bore, go through; also to split (wood).
Chhito (adv.) छिटो	Quickly, swiftly.
Chholdari (n.) छोलदारी	A tent.
Chhopnu (v.) छोपनु	To cover; to catch.
Chhornu (v.) छोड़नु	To loose, loosen, let go, forsake. "Na chhor" "Don't let go," *i.e.* "Hold tight."
Chhor: chhori (n.) छोरो छोरी	Son, daughter. Also for stepson, step-daughter.
Chhunu (v.) छुनु	To touch.
Chhura (n.) छुरा	A razor.
Chhuskya (n.) छुस्क्या	A backbiter, sneak.
Chhutaunu (v. tr.) छुटाउनु	To dismiss, divorce.
Chhutnu (v. intr.) छुटनु	To leave, forsake
Chhutti (n.) छुट्टि	Holiday, leave.
Chichiaunu (v.) चीच्याउनु	To scream.
Chihan (n.) चिहान	A cemetery, burial-ground.
Chil (n.) चील	A kite (bird).
Chilaunu (v.) चिलाउनु	To itch.

Chilaunu (n.) चिलाउनु	A tree that grows in Nepal.
Chilm (n.) चीलम	The upper part of a hookah.
Chimalnu (v.) चिमलनु	To close the eyes. Also chim garnu used.
Chinkh garnu (v.) चिखं गरनु	To sneeze.
Chimatnu (v.) चिमाटनु	To pinch, nip.
Chimchim (n.) चिमचिम	A wink. "U le mlai chimchim gario"—"He winked at me."
Chin (n.) चीन	China.
Chinajana (n.) चीनाजान	Acquaintance.
Chinnu (v.) चिननु	To recognize.
Chino (n.) चिनो	A sign, signal.
Chiphlinu (v.) चिफलनु	To slip. This and the next two words can be written with p instead of ph :—चिफलो
Chiphlo (adj.) चिफलो	Slippery, slimy.
Chiphlo kira (n.) चिफलो	A slug or snail (lit. a slimy insect.)
Chirko (adj.) चिरको	Senseless.
Chiso (adj.) चिसो	Cold (to the touch). "Pani chiso chha" —"The water is cold." But "It is cold to-day" would be "Aja jaru bhayo."
Chitharnu (v.) चीथरनु	To get scratched.
Chitti (n.) चिट्ठी	A letter.
Chituwa (n.) चितुना	A leopard, panther.
Chiunro (n.) च्यूंडो	The chin.
Chiura (n.) चिऊड़ा	Rice (parched).
Chobaunu (v.) चोबाउनु	To dip (tr.)
Chobnu (v.) चोबनु	To dip (intr.).
Choila (n.) चोइला	Small sticks.
Chokho (adj.) चोखो	Clean.
Cholo (n.) चोलो	A bodice.
Chor (n.) चोर	A thief.
Chor ankha (n.) चोर श्रांखा	Thief eye. "Chor ankha le hirnu"—"To give a sidelong look" or "to steal a glance."
Chor anlo (n.) चोर श्रंलो	The fore-finger.

Chor bato (n.) चोर बाटो — A byway, foot-path.
Chornu (v.) चोरनु — To steal, thieve.
Chuchubam (n.) चुचुबाम — A pointed eel.
Chula (n.) चुला — A cooking-place.
Chuli (n.) चुली — A cliff.
Chuna (n.) चुना — Lime.
Chunrnu (v.) चुड़नु — To nip off
Chunu (v.) चुनु — To leak
Chura (n.) चुरा — Bracelet.
Chusnu (v.) चुसनु — To suck.
Chyau (n.) च्याऊ — A mushroom.
Dabaunu (v.) दबाउनु — To hide, hide away.
Dab (n.) दाब — A sheath, scabbard.
Dabilo (n.) दाबीलो — A disc.
Dada (n.) दादा — An old servant.
Dag (n.) दाग — A stain.
Dagi (n.) दागी — Punishment.
Daha (n.) डाह — Envy, hate.
Dahi (n.) दही — A kind of sour milk curd.
Dai दाई — Elder brother.
Daijo (n.) दाइजो — A dowry.
Dailo (n.) दैलो — A door, gate.
Dainya (adj.) दाइन्या — Right (not left).
Daju (n.) दाजु — An elder brother, also pronounced dazu and dai.
Dak (n.) डाक — The postal service ; a system of couriers.
Dakhan (n.) दखन — The south.
Dakkar दक्कार — A belch. "Dakkar ayo"—"a belch came."
Daknu (n.) डाकनु — To call "Tis lai daknu" —"Call him"
Daku (n.) डाकू — A robber, highwayman.
Dalchini (n.) दालचीनी — Cinnamon.
Dalin (n.) दलीन — A beam (wood).
Dalo (n.) डालो — A basket.
Dallo (n.) डल्लो — A round lump of anything ; a berry.
Dam (n.) दाम — Price, value.
Dam (n) डाम — A scar.

Damru डमबरू	Hourglass-shaped drum.
Dan (n.) दान	A gift ; charity.
Dana (n.) दाना	Grain.
Dand (n.) डंड	A fine.
Danda (n.) डन्डा	An axle.
Dandá (n.) डन्डा	A pole.
Dandiphor डन्डीफोर	A pimple.
Dangra डाङगरा	A shiver.
Dangre डाङगरे	A mina bird.
Danra (n.) डाड़ां	A ridge, spur of a hill, a razorback hill ; a hill.
Dans (n.) डांस	A horse-fly.
Dant (n.) दांत	A tooth.
Danth (n.) डांठ	A stalk (of a plant).
Daphe (n.) डाफे	A minal.
Dar (n.) डर	Fear ; danger.
Daraunu (v.) डराउनु	To frighten.
Darnu (v.) डरनु	To fear.
Dari (n.) दाड़ी	A beard.
Darim (n.) दाड़िम	A pomegranate.
Darkanu (v.) दरकनु	To split or be scarred (of hillside).
Dărsăn दरसन	Visit to superior.
Daru (n.) डाड़ु	A spoon.
Daru (n.) डारू	A sort of rum made in the Terai.
Das (num.) दस	Ten.
Dasein (n.) दसाईं	The festival of the Dasehra, held at the end of September or in October. Consists of dancing, singing, etc. On the first day sacred rice is sown. On the seventh day the sacred flowers are brought, and on the ninth, goats and buffaloes are sacrificed. The tenth day, (Tika) caste marks are placed on the forehead (of rice) ; a good deal is also drunk that day. The rice has a permanent guard over it. The

Malshiri and Ramayan books are read and sung during this festival.

Dasnu (v.) डसनु — To enter into, pierce.
Data (n.) दाता — A philanthropist ; a spendthrift.
Dauro (n.) दौरो — Wood (the substance) ; fire-wood.
Dazu (n.) दाजु — An elder brother.
Debro (adj.) देबरो — Left.
Dekhnu (v.) देखनु — To see, look.
Des (n.) देस — Country. Any ades or pardes is foreign country. Des is also used for the Plains of India in comparison with the hills. Also written desh.
Desan (adj.) देसान — Infectious.
Desi (adj.) देसी — Indian ; belonging to the Plains.
Dewal (n.) देवाल — A wall.
Dhago (n.) धागो — Thread.
Dhaja (n.) धजा — A small flag over a temple.
Dhakar (n.) धाकर — A basket for grain.
Dhaknu (v.) ढाकनु — To cover, close.
Dhakre (n.) ढाकरे — One without a permanent profession.
Dhalkanu (v.) ढलकनु — To lean over.
Dhălnu (v.i.) ढलनु — To topple over.
Dhālnu (v.tr.) ढालनु — To knock over.
Dhamkanu (v.) धमकानु — To threaten.
Dhamki (n.) धमकी — A threat.
Dhan (n.) धान — Growing rice.
Dhan (n.) धन — Riches.
Dhankhani (n.) धनखनी — A woman who is a spendthrift.
Dhantnu (v.) ढांटनु — To deceive, take in " Dhantia ko kura " —" A lie."
Dhanu (n.) धनु — An arrow.
Dhapaunu (v.) धपाउनु — To drive away.
Dhar (n.) धाड़ — The stem, bottom of anything.
Dhar (n.) धार — The blade of a knife.
Dharag (n.) डराग — A large tiger.
Dharilo (adj.) धरिलो — Sharp. Edge-ways.
Dharknu (v.) धरकनु — To throb (of heart).

Dharkya (adj.) धरक्या	Striped.
Dhawa (n.) धावा	An attack. "Dhawa paret"—"An out parade."
Dhere (adj.) धेरै	Many. Too much. "Timi le dhere diyo"—"You gave too much."
Dheruwa (n.) धेड्वा	A langoor monkey.
Dhilo (adj.) ढिलो	The opposite to Chanri. Slow, late.
Dhiraj (n.) धिरज	Courage.
Dhito (adj.) ढीटो	Obstinate. Stubborn.
Dhobi (n.) धोबी	A washerman.
Dhobini (n.) धोबिनी	(1) A washerwoman. (2) A bird.
Dhok (n.) ढोक	Worship. "Dhok garnu"—"To worship, to bow down to (in form of salutation)."
Dhoka (n.) ढोका	A door.
Dhoknu (v.) ढोकनु	To worship, bow.
Dhoti (n.) धोती	Loin-cloth.
Dhuiro धुइरो	A crowd.
Dhuknu (v.) ढुकनु	To watch, lie in wait for.
Dhukur (n.) ढुकुर	A dove.
Dhukuti (n.) धुकुटी	Treasure chest, treasury.
Dhulo (n.) धुलो	Dust.
Dhumilo (adj.) धुमिलो	Not clear, hazy, dirty (of water).
Dhumiro (n.) धुमीरो	A white ant.
Dhumsi (n.) धुमसी	Mildew.
Dhunga (n.) ढुंगा	A stone, rock.
Dhungra (adj.) ढुंगरा	Hollow.
Dhungro (n.) ढुंगरो	A megaphone.
Dhunu (v.) धुनु	To wash (of clothes, mouth and hands etc., not to have a wash).
Dhuwan (n.) धुवां	Smoke.
Dhyan (n.) ध्यान	Notice, attention. "Us lai dhyan dinu chainchha"—"Attention must be paid to that."
Didi (n.) दिदि	Elder sister.
Dikhanu (v.) दिखानु	To show.
Din (n.) दिन	Day.

Dinu (v.) दिनु — To give ; allow. "Tis lai jane na dinu" —"Don't let him go."

Diuso (n.) दिऊसो — Daytime.

Diwali (n.) दिवाली — A festival, often called Tiwar ; the feast of lamps in honour of the goddess Bhawani at the new moon of the month of Kathik, October or November.

Diyo (n.) दियो — A small lamp made of earthenware.

Divasilai (n.) दियासलाई — A match.

Do bhashe दो भाशे — One who does things from both sides ; an interpreter.

Dobriaunu (v.) दोबऱ्याउनु — To fold.

Doharo (adj.) दोहरो — Double.

Doko (n.) डोको — A basket.

Donra (n.) डोंड़ा — The gutter in a roof.

Dopahar (n.) दोपहर — Midday (the middle of the watches).

Dori (n.) डोरी — A rope.

Dornu (v.) दोरनु — To know how to.

Doryaunu (v.) डोऱ्याउनु — To lead by the hand or on a string, etc.

Dosh (n.) दोष — Blame, suspicion.

Dosan (n.) दोसान — The frontier, border of a country.

Dotho डोठो — Bucket

Dubaunu (v. tr.) डुबाउनु — To drown, make sink.

Dublo (adj.) दुबलो — Thin, lean.

Dubnu (v.) दुबनु — To drown, sink.

Dubo (n.) दुबो — Turf.

Dudh (n.) दुध — Milk ; the female breasts ; udder.

Dugarnu (v.) दुगड़नु — To run.

Duita (num.) दुइटा — Two, both.

Dukha (n.) दुख — Trouble.

Dukhnu (v.) दुखनु — To ache, pain, trouble.

Dulha (n.) दुलहा — Bridegroom.

Dulhani (n.) दुलहानी — Bride.

Dulnu (v.) डुलनु — To wander, walk, travel.

Dulo (n.) दुलो — A hole.

Dumsi (n.) दुमसी — A porcupine.

Dunga (n.) डुङ्गा	A boat (small).
Dunro (adj.) डुड़ो	Lame.
Dunya (n.) दुनिया	The world.
Ekka (n.) एक्का	The ace in cards.
Ekkasi (adv.) एक्कासी	Suddenly.
Eknasai (adv.) एकनासै	Alike.
Gadah (n.) गदाह	A donkey ; also a term of abuse as in English.
Gadda (n.) गद्दा	A mattress.
Gagri (n.) गागरी	Copper jar.
Gagro गागरो	Earthenware jar.
Gahana (n.) गहना	An ornament.
Gahun (n.) गहूं	Wheat.
Gai (n.) गाई	A Cow.
Gail (adj.) गैल	Absent, missing.
Gainra (n.) गैंड़ा	A rhinoceros.
Gainti (n.) गैंती	A pickaxe.
Gairo (adj.) गैरो	Deep.
Gairo (n.) गैरो	Nullah, small valley.
Gaj (n.) गज्	A yard (3 feet).
Gajilo (adj.) गजीलो	Broad.
Gajul (n.) गाजुल	The black stuff put round the eyes.
Gajur (n.) गजुर	A dome, minaret.
Gala (n.) गाला	A necklace.
Gali (n.) गाली	Abuse, swearing, bad language.
Galich (n.) गालीच	Braces.
Galla (n.) गल्ला	Recruiting.
Galnu (v.) गलनु	To melt, dissolve ; hence to tire (often of the arms).
Galti (n.) गलती	Fault, mistake.
Gambhir (adj.) गम्भीर	Polite.
Gamilo गमीलो	Silent.
Gabana (n.) गबन	An oar.
Ganaunu (v.) गनाउनु	To smell, stink (usually of a bad smell) " Kia ganayo ? "—" What is smelling ? "
Gandha (n.) गन्ध	Smell, scent (usually bad). " Us ko

gandha pario "—" It smelt." " Us ko gandha payo "—" Got its scent."

Gandhak (n.) गन्धक — Sulphur.

Ganga (n.) गंगा — A river.

Ganganānu (v.) गनगनानु — To murmur. Gangani, a murmurer.

Gangata (n.) गंगटा — A crab.

Gannu (v.) गन्नु — To count.

Ganra (n.) गांडा — Goitre. " Kana des ma ganra tanderi " —" In a blind country a goitre looks nice."

Gantho (n.) गांठो — (1) A knot. (2) A knuckle.

Ganu (v.) गानु — To sing.

Ganwari (adj.) गंवारी — Foolish.

Gara गड़ा — A terraced field

Gari (n.) गाड़ी — A carriage.

Gari (n.) गड़ी — A fortress, tower.

Garja (n.) गरज — Thunder.

Garnu (v.) गरनु — To do. This is used with many nouns to form a verb : " Katam garnu,"— " To finish, etc." Also for frequentative verbs : " Bokdai garnu,"—" To be in the habit of carrying."

Garnu (v.) गाड़नु — To bury. Purnu is more polite. To penetrate.

Garo (n.) गारो — A wall, partition.

Garo (adj.) गारो — Severe, irksome. " M paret khelnu la garo manchhu "—" I think that it is rather hard to go on parade."

Garul गरुल — Eagle.

Garungo (adj.) गरुंगो — Heavy.

Garuwa (n.) गड़ुवा — Brass pot with spout.

Gaun (v.) गाऊं — A village.

Gaura गौडा — Shelter, redoubt.

Ghachya (n.) घच्या — A push.

Ghado घादो — Nepalese garment knotted in front of chest.

Ghaile (adj.) घैलें — Wounded.

Ghainta घैन्टा	Earthenware pot ; gharra.
Ghalek (n.) घलेक	A cloth worn over the shoulder.
Gham (n.) घाम	Sunshine ; heat of the sun ; also loosely as sun.
Ghamandi (adj.) घमन्डी	Proud.
Ghamar (adj.) घामड़	Ignorant, foolish, stupid.
Ghamora (n.) घमोड़ा	Heat rash.
Ghan (n.) घन	A large hammer.
Ghanta (n.) घन्टा	Gong, bell, clock.
Ghanti (n.) घांटी	A mountain-pass. The throat.
Ghar (n.) घर	A house, home.
Ghari (n.) घड़ी	A watch. Ghari ghari (adv.), frequently.
Ghas (n.) घास	Grass.
Ghasnu (v.) घसनु	To anoint, pour on.
Ghat (n.) घाट	Landing place, ferry.
Ghataunu (v. tr.) घटाउनु	To decrease.
Ghati (n.) घटी	Want, lack.
Ghatnu (v. intr.) घटनु	To decrease.
Ghau (n.) घाव	A wound.
Ghera (n. & adj.) घे ा	A circle ; round.
Ghernu (v.) घेरनु	To surround.
Ghichra (n.) घिचरा	The nape of the neck.
Ghinn (n.) घिन्न	Contempt, disgust.
Ghisarnu (v.) घीसाड़नु	To drag along the ground.
Ghochnu (v.) घोचनु	To pierce, prick.
Ghoptaunu (v. tr.) घोपटाउनु	To upset, capsize.
Ghoptnu (v. intr.) घोपटनु	To upset, capsize.
Ghopto (adj.) घोपटो	Bent, stooping.
Ghora (n.) घोड़ा	A horse.
Ghotnu (v.) घोटनु	To rub.
Ghui (n.) घ्यूं	Ghee ; clarified butter.
Ghuchuk (n.) घुचुक	Back of the neck.
Ghumaunu (v. tr.) घुमाउनु	To turn round. "Mero tauko ghumayo"—"I am giddy" (Urdu phrase, Khaskura being ringaunu, q.v.).
Ghumnu (v. intr.) घुमनु	To turn round (Urdu word).

Ghunra (n.) घुंड़ा	The knee.
Ghurinu (v.) घुरीनु	To snore.
Ghus घुस	A bribe.
Gid (n.) गीद	A song.
Gidda (n.) गिद्द	A vulture.
Gidi (n.) गिदि	The brain.
Gijaunu (n.) गिजाउनु	To laugh at, jest at, cheek.
Gin (n.) गीन	A ball.
Gita (n.) गीटा	A species of creeper.
Gobar (n.) गोबर	Fresh cow-dung.
Gobara (n.) गोबारा	(1) A beetle. (2) Balloon.
Gobi (n.) गोबी	A cabbage.
Gogan (n.) गोगन	A vessel made of grass.
Gohar (n.) गोहार	Help.
Gohara (n) गोहड़ा	A biscobra ; large lizard.
Goho (n.) गोहो	A pathway made by animals in jungle
Gola (n.) गोला	A shell (gun).
Goli (n.) गोली	Urdu word for ball ; bullet.
Goli ganta (n.) गोली गांठा	The ankle.
Golmirich (n.) गोलमरीच	Black pepper.
Gora (adj.) गोरा	Fair complexioned : also (n.) for a British soldier.
Gorentho bato(n.)गोरठो बाटो	A pathway ; byway.
Gorsh गोरश	Milk (curd).
Goru (n.) गोरु	A bull.
Goth (n.) गोठ	A cowshed.
Gothala (n.) गोठाला	A cowheard.
Goti (n.) गोटी	A piece in a game like chess, draughts, etc.
Gu (n.) गू	An animal's droppings.
Gudi (n.) गुदी	Kernel (of a nut).
Guhi (n.) गुहि	A crocodile.
Gulam (n.) गुलाम	Knave in cards. (Urdu).
Gulamchor गुलाम चोर	A card game like "Old Maid." (Urdu)
Gulap (n.) गुलाब	Rose (flower).
Guleli (n.) गुलेली	A small bow which shoots mud pellets.
Gulio (adj.) गलियो	Sweet.
Gulla (n.) गुल्ला	Testicle.

Gumti (n.) गुमटी	The butts on the range ; a sentry box.
Gun (n.) गुन	Thanks.
Guna garnu (v.) गुना गरनु	To multiply. Also duiguna is two times etc. (Multiplication).
Gunda (adj.) गुन्दा	Clever.
Gunga (adj.) गुंगा	Dumb.
Gunr. (n.) गूंड़	A bird's nest.
Gupt (adj.) गुप्त	Secret, private.
Guru (n.) गुरु	A teacher, learned man.
Guruwas (n.) गुरुवास	Rhodedendron.
Guthnu (n.) गुथनु	To wind round (a turban).
Gyan (n.) ग्यान	Knowledge, wisdom.
Hagnu (v.) हगनु	To purge.
Hai (n.) हाई	A yawn. " Hai garnu "—" To yawn."
Haiza (n.) हैजा	Cholera.
Hakanu हकानु	To drive away.
Halo (n.) हलो	A plough.
Halungo (adj.) हलुंगो	Light (not heavy).
Halanu (v. intr.) हलनु	To move.
Halaunu (v. tr.) हलाउनु	To move.
Halisa (n.) हलीसा	A green pigeon.
Halnu (v.) हलेसा	To put. " Tis lai utha hal "—" Put this there." Also in the Completive verbs as an alternative to Saknu : " Maile uslai gari halio "—" I finished doing that."
Hami (pro.) हमी	We ; also honorific for I.
Hamro (pro.) हमरो	Our ; also honorific for my.
Hango (n.) हांगो	The branch of a tree.
Hani (n.) हानी	Destruction, damage.
Hannu (v.) हाननु	To hit, strike. " Khutta le hannu "—" To kick " (of humans). For an animal " to kick " is " lat le hannu.'
Hanri (n.) हांड़ी	A pot.
Hâns (n.) हांस	A duck. " Thulo hans "—" A goose."
Hansnu (v.) हंसनु	To laugh.
Har (n.) हाड़	A bone.

Harami (n.) हरामी — A term of abuse.
Haraunu (v.) हराउनु — To lose a thing. "Maile mero chaku harayo"—"I lost my penknife."
Harbar (n.) हड़बड़ — Confusion.
Hari (n.) हरी — God.
Harikangal (adj.) हरी कंगाल — Destitute.
Harikatha (n.) हरीकथा — A sermon; (lit.) A God lesson.
Haryo (adj.) हरियो — Green.
Harsha (n.) हर्ष — Pleasure.
Harmani हारमानी — Astonished.
Harmoni (n.) हारमोनी — A sort of guitar.
Harnu (v. intr.) हारनु — To lose. "Bazi ko katam bhayo; hami haryaun"—"The match is over; we lost."
Haskanu (v.) हस्कनु — To become pleased.
Hath (n.) हाथ — The hand; the fore-arm. Also as a measure, the span of the hand.
Hathbhari (adj.) हाथभरी — Handful.
Hathi (n.) हाथी — An elephant.
Hathkari (n.) हाथकड़ी — Handcuff.
Hathkelo हाथकेंलो — Palm of the hand.
Hathyar (n.) हाथयार — A tool.
Hatoro (n.) हतोडो — A hammer.
Hawas (adv.) (imp.) हवस — (1) The polite form of the auxiliary imperative. "Basnu hawas"—"Please sit down." (2) An exclamation in answer to a request, etc. "Mero luga liau"—"Bring my clothes"; "Hawas"—"All right."
Hela (n.) हेला — Disgrace.
Hernu (v.) हेंरनु — To look.
Hiju (n.) हिजु — Yesterday.
Hijuasti (adv.) हिजुअस्ती — Some days ago. "Hijuasti hamile testo garinaun"—"We have not been doing so these latter days."
Hilo (n.) हिलो — Mud.
Himal (n.) हिमाल — A snow-peak.

Hinamina (adv.) हिनामिना — Scattered about.
Hira (n.) हिरा — A diamond.
Hirkaunu (v.) हरकाउनु — To hit, strike. "Maile banduk le hirkayan"—"I shot (it.)."
Hishknu (v.) हिसकनु — To be startled, frightened.
Hit (n.) हित — Kindness; friendship.
Hitnu (v.) हिटनु — To move, to start on a walk, etc.
Hiun (n.) हिऊं — Snow.
Ho हो — 3rd person sing. Present indicative of Hunnu, to be; used as "yes": "Tero naun Ranbir ho?"—"Is your name Ranbir?" "Ho"—"Yes."
Hocho (adj.) होचो — Short, low.
Hoina होइन — The negative of Ho above and used in the same way. It is more emphatic than the ordinary "ne," "no."
Hosakne (adj.) होसकने — Possible.
Hori होरी — The Holi festival.
Hukm (n.) हुक्म — (1) Command, order, decree, authority. (2) The spade suit in cards.
Hunnu (v.) हुनु — To be; become; auxiliary verb, see Grammar.
Hurri (n.) हुर्री — A storm, tempest.
Ichchha (n.) इच्छा — Wish, desire, "Maile aphnu ichcha le garyan"—"I did it of my own accord."
Inar (n.) इनार — A well.
Indreni (n.) इन्द्रयानी — Rainbow.
Int (n.) ईंट — A brick.
Inta (n.) ईंटा — The diamond suit in cards.
Isalu (n.) ऐसालु — Raspberry (really Aisalu, q.v.)
Ispat (n.) इस्पात — Steel.
Isto (adv.) Issari एस्तो — Thus (really esto q.v.)
Itha (adv.) एथा — Hither (really yetha q.v.)
Ityadi इत्यादि — Et cetera.
Jab (adv.) जब — When.
Jaephul (n.) जाईफुल — Nutmeg.

Jagaunu (v.) जगाउनु	To arouse, wake up (tr.)
Jagir (n.) जागिर	Pay ; land given on account of service. " Jagir khanu "—" To get pay."
Jagnu (v. intr.) जगनु	To awake.
Jahan (adv.) जहां	Where ; wherever.
Jahan (n.) जाहान	Person in one's home.
Jairya (n.) जैन्या	A fool, idiot.
Jal (n.) जाल	Net, cobweb.
Jalthal जलथल	Flood.
Jalnu (v. intr.) जलनु	To burn, be kindled.
Jamani जमानी	An answerer back.
Jamnu (v.) जमनु	To freeze.
Jan (n.) जान	Life.
Jana (n.) जना	Man, person.
Janchnu (v.) जांचनु	To examine, prove.
Janeu (n.) जनेउ	The Hindu thread.
Jangal (n.) जंगल	Jungle.
Jangali (adj.) जंगली	Wild, savage.
Janghar (n.) जंघार	A ford, crossing place.
Janghari (adj.) जंघारी	Shallow.
Janibujhera (adj.) जानीबु झेर	Knowingly ; wittingly, on purpose.
Janmasthami जन्मास्टमी	Birthday of Shri Krishna.
Jannu (v.) जाननु	To know a thing.
Janr (n.) जांड़	An intoxicating drink made out of rice, rather like beer.
Jantu (n.) जन्तु	An animal, creature.
Janu (v.) जानु	To go. Past tense " gayan etc. ' Used as in Urdu to form the Passive Voice.
Janwar (n.) जनवार	An animal.
Jara (adv.) जरा	A little. Pronounced zara. " Jara debro tira sar "—" Move a little to your left."
Jarayo (n.) जड़ायो	A sambhar.
Jaro (n.) जरो	Fever.
Jaro (adj.) जाड़ो	Cold (of climate, etc.). " Aja jaro bhayo "—" It is cold to-day." " The

	water is cold" would be "Pani chiso chha."
Jasilo (adj.) जसीलो	Famous.
Jasari जसरी Jasto जस्तो	These two adverbs both mean "as."
Jat (n.) जात	Caste.
Jatan (adj.) जतन	Careful, care.
Jati (adj.) जाती	Lit: "casty," so "good," "excellent."
Jati (adv.) जती	As many as.
Jau (n.) जौ	Oats, barley.
Jaunlia (n.) जौंल्या	Twins.
Jawai (n.) जवाइ	Son-in-law.
Jela जेला	Tax, labour.
Jeth (n.) जेठ	The month 15th May to 15th June.
Jethan (n.) जेठान	Wife's elder brother. Jethani = his wife.
Jetho (adi.) जेठो	The eldest of a family; elder. Jethi ama = elder maternal aunt. Jetha ba = elder paternal uncle.
Jhagra (n.) झगड़ा	A quarrel, dispute.
Jhain (adv.) झैं	As.
Jhalla (adj.) झल्ला	Mad.
Jhamre झामरे	Any quick song.
Jhamta (n.) झामटा	A place where sticks remain after the large parts of a felled tree are removed.
Jhan (adv.) झन	All the more. "Jhan sikaunchhu, jhan jandenas"—"The more I teach you, the less you know."
Jhandi (n.) झन्डी	A flag.
Jhanto (n.) झांटो	A water-mill.
Jhank (adj.) झांक	Male (or all wild animals, except birds).
Jhar, Jhari (n.) झाड़, झाड़ी	A small bush; tuft, etc.
Jhara (n.) झाड़ा	A stool, purge.
Jhari (n.) झाड़ि	A shower of rain.
Jharnu (v.) झड़नु	To come down, descent. "U rukh bata

jhario "—" He came down from the tree."

Jhasang झसंग — Jhasanghunu, to be afraid.
Jhatt (adv.) झट्ट — Instantly.
Jhelkhana (n.) झेलखाना — Prison
Jhignu (v.) झिगनु — To take out. "Ule chaku khalti bata jhigyo "—" He took a knife out of his pocket." Also "Git jhignu "—" To sing a song.
Jhikaunu (v.) झिकाउनु — To call, summon.
Jhilkia (n.) झिलक्या — A wag, funny man.
Jhinga (n.) झिङ्गा — A small fly, such as a sandfly.
Jhingiti (n.) झींगिटी — A tile, slate on roof.
Jhitimiti (n.) झिटीमिटी — Belongings, one's things.
Jholi (n.) झोली — A haversack.
Jhuknu झुकनु — To bow down, bend forward.
Jhukira (adv.) झुकीर — By accident.
Jhulnu (v.) झुलनु — To nod.
Jhumro (n.) झुमरो — A rag
Jhundaunu (tr.) झुंडाउनु — To hang.
Jhundnu (v. tr.) झुन्डनु — To hang, be hanging.
Jhuppa (n.) झुप्पा — A bunch.
Jhuro (adj.) झुरो — Brittle.
Jhus (n.) झूस — Hair (as on a woolly-bear caterpillar).
Jhutha (adj.) झुठा — False, untrue.
Jhyal (n.) झ्याल — A window.
Jhyang (n.) झयांग — Small scrub, bushes.
Jhyau (n.) झ्याऊ — Moss.
Jibro (n.) जिबड़ो — The tongue. " Jibro pharkanu —" To have the correct pronunciation.
Jiju जीजृ — Great-grandfather.
Jijubaje (n.) जिजुबाज्ये — Ancestors.
Jimi (n.) जिमी — Ground.
Jimwal जिमवाल — Headman but below a Mukhia, chief.
Jiring jiring जिरिङ्ग २ — Trembling at beginning of fever or cold.
Jitnu (v.) जितनु — To win, conquer.
Jiundai (adj.) जिउंदै — Alive.

Jiunu (v.) जिउनु	To live, be alive.
Joban (n.) जोबन	Puberty, youth.
Jogaunu (v.) जोगाउनु •	To protect, save from damage (as a box keeps its contents).
Jokhnu (v.) जोखनु	To weigh.
Jogi (n.) जोगी	A religious mendicant.
Jor (n. & adj.) जोड़	A pair ; even ; even (of numbers). A join.
Jori (n.) जोड़ी	A friend, chum.
Jornu (v.) जोड़नु	To add, join.
Jotnu जोतनु	To plough.
Jotishi (n.) जोतिशी	Astronomer.
Juko (n.) जुको	A leech ; worm.
Julap (n.) जुलाप	A purge.
Jumra (n.) जुमड़ा	A louse. White louse that infests the body.
Jun (n.) जुन	The moon.
Juneli (adj.) जुनेली	Moonlit ; also for noun moonlight.
Junga (n.) जुंगा	The moustache.
Junkiri (n.) जुनकिड़ी	A firefly, glow-worm.
Jureli जुरेली	A nightingale.
Juta (n.) जुता	A shoe.
Juwa (n.) जुवा	A gamble, betting. "Juwa khelnu"—"To gamble."
Jyan (n.) ज्यान	Life.
Jyu (n.) ज्यू	Body.
Kabja (n.) कबजा	A hinge.
Kachhar (n.) कछार	Foot of a hill.
Kachhuwa (n.) कछुवा	Tortoise, turtle.
Kachkachia (n.) कचकचा	A chatterer.
Kacho (adj.) काचो	Unripe.
Kachona (n.) कचोना	A teat.
Kadhai (n.) कढ़ाइ	Cauldron.
Kag (n.) काग	(1) Cork. (2) A crow.
Kagaj (n.) कागज	Paper.
Kahan (adv.) कहां	Where ?
Kahin (adv.) कहीं	Anywhere.

Kaile (adv.) कैले	When ?
Kaile kaile (adv.) कैले २	Sometimes.
Kaj (n.) काज	Work, business.
Kakh (n.) काख	Lap.
Kakhara (n.) कखरा	The Alphabet.
Kakhi (n.) काँची	Armpit.
Kakrinu ककरीनु	To be huddled up.
Kakryo ककरीयो	Huddled up.
Kal (n.) काल	Death ; the figure of death. "Tero kal ayo"—"Your end has come."
Kalam (n.) कलम	Pen.
Kalejo (n.) कलेजो	The liver.
Kalij (n.) कालीज	The Pheasant of that name.
Kalo (adj.) कालो	Black.
Kalilo (adj.) कलीलो	Young and supple.
Kălmi ko aunlo (n.) कलमी को आउंलो	The fore-finger.
Kam (n.) काम	Work, business.
Kamal ko phul (n.) कमल को फुल	A lily.
Kamani (n.) कमानी	A spring (metal).
Kamara (n.) कमारा	A slave, who belongs to the slave caste. They are bought and sold and always belong to the slave caste. They get no pay but board and lodging. A kamari who has a child by her master may demand to be freed, but the child is a kamara.
Kamaunu (v.) कमाउनु	To cultivate.
Kamero (n.) कमेरो	Lime.
Kamilo (n.) कमिलो	Ant.
Kamlo (n.) कामलो	A blanket.
Kamalo (adj.) कमलो	Soft.
Kamar (n.) कमर	The waist.
Kamnu (v.) कामनु	To tremble, quake, shiver.
Kampani (n.) कम्पनी	Nepalese word for Indian rupee.
Kan (n.) कान	The ear.

Kana (adj.) काना	One-eyed; blind.
Kancaunu (v.) कन्याउनु	To scratch.
Kanchho (n. & adj.) कान्छो	The youngest of a family; younger. "E Kanchha!"—"O! Littl' one." Kanchhi ama=younger paternal aunt. Kanchhaba—younger paternal uncle.
Kandi (n.) कन्डी	Box, made of wickerwork.
Kando (n.) कन्डो	Back.
Kangali (adj.) कंगाली	Poor, destitute.
Kangiyo (n.) कांगियो	Comb.
Kankro (n.) कांकडो	(1) Cucumber. (2) Chicken-pox (also written 'kankara').
Kanra (n.) काएा	A thorn. "Kanre tar"—"Barbed wire."
Kansutlo (n.) कनसुतलो	An earwig.
Kapal (n.) कपाल	The forehead, skull.
Kapas (n.) कपास	Cotton plant, cotton.
Kapasi (adj.) कपासी	Immoral.
Kapat (n.) कपट	Deceit, treachery.
Kaphal (n.) काफल	A tree, with fruit like a strawberry (which is called bhuin kāphal).
Kaphar (n.) काफर	A coward.
Kapti (adj.) कपटी	Double-faced, deceitful.
Kapur (n.) कपूर	Camphor.
Kar (n.) कर	Obligation.
Kar (n.) काड	An arrow.
Karati (n.) कराती	A saw.
Karan (n.) कारए	Cause, reason.
Karang (n.) करङग	The ribs. Rafter in a house.
Karaunu (v.) कराउनु	To carry out: to call (of an animal or bird)
Karda (n.) कर्द	The small knife on a kukri
Kareli करेली	Bridle.
Karmi कर्मी	Carpenter.
Karnu (v.) करनु	To do. This is an alternative to Garnu, q.v.
Karnu (v.) काढनु	To take off.

Kartik (n.) कार्तिक	The month 15th October to 15th November.
Kasingar (n.) कसीगंर	Rubbish, dirt.
Kasnu (v.) कसनु	To tighten, tie.
Kasari : Kasto (adv.) कसरी कस्तो	How ? In what manner ?
Kastura (n.) कस्तूरा	The musk deer. Musk is 'kasturi.'
Kata (adv.) कटा	Whither.
Katera (n.) कटेरा	A shed, stall.
Kath (n.) काठ	Wood, timber.
Katha (n.) कथा	A story, tale.
Kathin (n.) कठिन	Difficulty.
Kati (adv.) कती	How many ? How much ?
Katnu (v.) काटनु	(1) To cut, reap. "Bat katnu"—"To interrupt, cross-examine."
कातनु	(2) To spin.
Katora कतोरा	A cup.
Katro (adv.) कतरो	How big ?
Katuwa (n.) कतुवा	An instrument on which wool, etc., is spun.
Kaunlo (adj.) काउंलो	Soft, meek.
Kawaj (n.) कवाज	Parade.
Kera (n.) केरा	A banana.
Kerau (n.) केराउ	A pea.
Kesara (n.) केसरा	The pig of an orange.
Keta (n.) केटा	A child, boy ; Keti, girl ; Keta keti, children.
Khachchar (n.) खच्चर	A mule.
Khachyang khachyang (adv.) खच्यांग खच्यांग	Limping, lame.
Khai (n.) खई	Rust, corrosion.
Khairo (adj.) खैरो	Brown.
Khajur (n.) खजुर	Palm-tree, also called Tar ko rukh.
Khajuro (n.) खजुरो	A centipede.
Khalati (n.) खलाती	Bellows.
Khalti (n.) खलती	A pocket.
Khalto (n.) खालटो	A pit, hole.

Khamba (n.) खम्बा	A pillar, pole.
Khancho (adj.) खांचो	Necessary.
Khandnu (v.) खांदनु	To press down.
Khani (n.) खानी	A mine.
Khannu (v.) खननु	To dig.
Khanu (v.) खानु	To eat, drink.
Khapaunu (v.) खपाउनु	To place carefully.
Khar (n.) खर	Thatch.
Kharah (n.) खराह्	A hare.
Kharani (n.) खरानी	Ashes.
Kharbhuja (n.) खरभुजा	A melon.
Khari (n.) खड़ी	Chalk.
Kharka (n.) खरक	Pasture.
Khas (adv.) खास	Really, certainly, for sure.
Khasnu (v.) खसनु	To fall (from a height): cf. Lotnu.
Khasro (adj.) खसरो	Thick.
Khassi (adj.) खस्सी	adj. Castrated. (n.) An eunuch ; castrated goat.
Khata (n.) खाता	Whiskers.
Khataunu (v.) खटाउनु	To appoint.
Khawl (n.) खावल	A loom.
Khatira (n.) खटीरा	A boil.
Khatrang khutrung (adv.) खतरांग खुतरुग	With a clatter. Not with one noise.
Khet (n.) खेत	A field. Kheti, cultivation. Kheti garnu, to cultivate.
Khetara (n.) खेतारा	A working party.
Khili (n.)खीली	A corn, callosity (on feet).
Khishaunu (v.) खिशाउनु	To scorn, laugh at, make ashamed.
Khiyaunu (v. tr.) खियाउनु	To wear away.
Khitkhiti (n.) खितखिती	Giggling.
Khiyinu (v. intr.) खिउनु	To be worn away.
Khojnu (n.) खोजनु	To search, look for; to want. "Yahan kya khojchhas"—"What are you looking for here ?" or "What do you want here ?"
Khoki (n.) खोकी	A cough.

Khokalo (adj.) खोकलो — Loose, not secure, not firm.
Khol (n.) खोल — Scabbard, sheath.
Kholsa (n.) खोलसा — A stream, smallish river. Kholsi also used.
Khopi (n.)खोपी — A drawer (furniture).
Khopaunu : khopnu (v.) खोपाउनु खोपनु — To vaccinate, inoculate, tattoo.
Khor (n.) खोड़ — A large trap.
Khosnu (v.) खोसनु — To take away, snatch away.
Khot (n.) खोट — Blemish, flaw.
Khuilo (adj.) खुइलो — Bald.
Khumáni (n.) खुमानी — An apricot.
Khumchaunu खुमचाउनु — To bend.
Khumchinu खुमचिनु — To be bent.
Khundo (adj.) खुन्दो — Blunt, without an edge.
Khurkaunu (v.) खुरकाउनु — To scrape.
Khurpi (n.) खुरपी — A trowel, weeding-knife.
Khursani (n.) खुरसानी — Chilli, red pepper.
Khurundo (adj.) खुरुन्डो — Lame, maimed.
Khutruka (adv.) खुतरुक — Huddled up.
Khutta (n.) खुट्टा — Leg, foot.
Khuwa (n.) खुवा — Territory.
Ki की — (1) Prep. fem. "of." (2) Conj. "that." "Ule bhanio ki—"—"He said that—." (3) "or" "Ye ramro ho ki naramro" —"Is this good or bad?" Also "Pani anchha ki ? "—" Is it going to rain or (not going to) ? "
Kil (n.) कील — A nail.
Kilo (n.) कीलो — Tent peg.
Kimu (n.) किमू — A mulberry. Kimu ko rukh, mulberry tree.
Kina (adv.) कीन — Why ? Also : " T sakchhas ? "—" Can you ? " " Kina na sakne "—" Of course I can " (lit. Why can't I ?).

Kinaki किनकी	Because.
Kinkitya (adj.) किनकिटया	Stingy, miserly.
Kinnu (v.) किनन्	To buy.
Kira (n.) किड़ा	Insect, worm, maggot.
Kiria (n.) किरिया	Oath.
Kirna (n.) किरना	A dog tick.
Kisani (n.) किसानी	A farmer, cultivator.
Kodali : kodalo (n.) कोदाली	A hoe. Kodali is bigger than Kodalo.
Kodo (n.) कोदो	A black coarse grain.
Koel (n.) कोयल	A bird.
Koi कोई	(1) Any, some. (2) Idiomatically for where? "Ranbir koi?"—"Where is Ranbir?" (3) Idiom for my turn now, *e.g.* If *A* is looking at something through field glasses and *B* wants to look, *B* might say "koi" meaning "give me the glasses" or "let me have a look now."
Koila (n.) कोइला	Coal.
Kokha (n.) कोखा	The ribs, side.
Kopila (n.) कोपीला	A bud.
Korara (n.) कोरड़ा	Whip, lash.
Kori (n.) कोड़ी	A leper. Kori khana, leper asylum.
Korka (n.) कोरका	A conical basket.
Kornu (v.) कोरन्	To scratch.
Kot (n.) कोत	Strong-room; bells of arms.
Kotarnu (v.) कोतरन्	To scratch.
Kotha (n.) कोटा	A room.
Kotryo (adj.) कोतरयो	Scratched.
Kothi (n.) कोठी	A black mole or spot on the skin.
Kowanri (n.) कवांरी	A kind of grass.
Kuwa (n.) कुवा	A well.
Kubro (adj.) कुबड़ो	Hunchbacked; deformed.
Kuchal (n.) कुचाल	Misconduct.
Kuchcho (n.) कुच्चो	A broom, brush.
Kuchnu (v.) कुचनु	To dent. Kuchia ko, dented.
Kuhiro (n.) कुहिरो	A fog, mist.

Kuhunu कुहुनु — To rot.
Kuina (n.) कुइना — Elbow.
Kukra (n.) कुकड़ा — A fowl, chicken.
Kukur (n.) कुकुर — A dog. Kukurni, a bitch.
Kulchi dinu (v.) कुलची दिनु — To tread on.
Kulkutumb (n.) कुलकुटम्ब — Family, relations.
Kulkuli कुलकुली — Tickling.
Kulo (n.) कुलो — A drain, channel, ditch.
Kumlo कुमलो — Load of grass.
Kunda (n.) कुन्दा — The butt of a rifle.
Kuna (n.) कुना — Corner, angle.
Kunni कुन्नी — An expression which might be translated by "perhaps" or "dunno," *e.g.* "Pani ala ki ?"—"Will it rain ?" "Kunni !"—"It may."
Kura (n.) कुरा — Talk, speech, language.
Kurani कुरानी — A sort of cream.
Kurkucha (n.) कुरकुचा — The heel.
Kuro (n.) कुरो — Spear-grass.
Kutnu (v.) कुटनु — To beat, pound.
Kuto (n.) कुटो — A small hoe.
Kya ? क्या — What ?
Lagaunu (v.) लगाउनु — To put ; to apply ; to put to work ; to wear ; put on.
Lagi (prep.) लागी — For the sake of. Mero lagi, for my sake, for me.
Lagne (adj.) लागने — Sharp of a knife.
Lagnu (v.) लागनु — To begin, see Initial verbs in Grammar. To hit : "Chand lai lagyo ki lagina?" —"Did it hit the target or not ?" To be applied. "Timilai laj lagchha ?"—"Are you shy ?"
Lagnu (v.) लगनु — To carry.
Lahara (n.) लहरा — A creeper.
Lasun (n.) लसुन — Garlic.
Lahure (n.) लाहुरे — Service in the army.

Lai लाई	Postposition the sign of the Dative and Accusative.
Laj (Laz) (n.) लाज	Shame, modesty.
Lakh (n.) लाख	A hundred thousand.
Lam (n.) लाम	The road to a war ; hence war itself.
Lamchhe (adj.) लामछे	Oval.
Lamchuchia (n.) लामचुच्या	A bird with a long beak.
Lamkhutya (n.) लामखुट्या	A mosquito.
Lamkira (n.) लामकीड़ा	A snake (lit. a long worm).
Lamo (adj.) लामो	Long.
Langothi (n.) लंगोठी	A loin-cloth, worn between the legs.
Lapetnu (v.) लपेटनु	To roll, fold, wrap up.
Larai (n.) लड़ाई	War, strife, fighting.
Larknu (v.) लरकनु	To slip.
Larnu (v.) लड़नु	To fight, struggle.
Lat (n.) लात	The sole of the foot. "Lat le hannu"—"To kick like an animal."
Lata (adj.) लाठा	Deaf and ḍumb ; dumb.
Lathepra (n.) लठेपरा	A fool, blockhead.
Latta (n.) लट्टा	A rag, cloth for cleaning rifles.
Lattha (n.) लट्ठा	A pillar ; boundary pillar on frontier.
Launu (v.) लाउनु	To wear.
Lauro (n.) लौरो	A walking stick.
Le ले	The postposition of the Agent case ; also instrumental. (2) "Take it." "Catch hold" (imperative of Linu).
Lei (n.) लेइ	Paste.
Lejanu (v.) लेजानु	To take away. Past tense, lagyan.
Lekh (n.) लेख	A mountain.
Liaunu (v.) ल्याउनु	To bring, fetch.
Lig (n.) लिग	A track, rail.
Likhnu (v.) लिखनु	To write.
Linu (n.) लिनु	To get, take.
Liphapha : Lipha (n.) लिफाफा लिफा	An envelope.
Lipnu (v.) लिपनु	To smear, plaster.
Lisnu (n.) लिसनु	A ladder.

Lobra (n.) लोबरा — Chips, bits of the bark of a tree, etc.
Logne (n.) लोगने — A husband, male human.
Lokharke (n.) लोखरके — A squirrel.
Loso (adj.) लोसो — Slack.
Lotaunu (v. tr.) लोटाउनु — To upset on the ground, knock down.
Lothro (adj.) लोथरो — Clumsy.
Lotnu (v. intr.) लोटनु — To fall, fall down (being on the ground the whole time).
Luga (n.) लुगा — Clothes, cloth.
Lukaunu (v. tr.) लुकाउनु — To hide, conceal.
Lukiluki (adv.) लुकी २ — Secretly.
Luknu (v. intr.) लुकनु — To hide.
Lukne thaun (n.) लुकने ठाऊं — Hiding place, ambush.
Lulo (adj.) ललो — Maimed, crippled.
Lutnu (v.) लुटनु — To plunder.
Luto (n.) लुतो — The itch.
Luwang (n.) लुवङग — A clove.
M (pro.) म — I.
Ma (prep.) मा — At, in, among, on top of (Locative sign).
Machha (n.) माछा — Fish.
Machungi (n.) माचुंगी — A jew's harp.
Madal (n.) मादल — A tomtom, used at dances, etc.
Madali (n.) मादली — The man who plays the tomtom.
Madhuro (adj.) मधुरो — Weak, dim (used as regards light).
Madesh मादेश — The plains compared to the hills.
Madhyan (n.) मध्यान — Midday.
Magh (n.) माघ — The month 15th January to 15th February.
Magro (adj.) मगरो — Cross, discontented; obstinate.
Mah (n.) मह — Honey.
Mahango (adj.) महंगो — Expensive.
Mahi (n.) मही — Butter-milk.
Mahina (n.) महिना — Month.
Maiju (n.) माइजु — Mother-in-law.
Mait (n.) माइट — Mother-in-law's house.
Majh (n.) माझ — Midst. middle. "Uniharu ka majh ma"—"In their midst."

Majur (n.) मजुर — A peacock.
Makai मकाई — Maize.
Makkhi (n.) मक्खि — The sight of a rifle.
Makha (n.) माखा — A fly, house-fly.
Makura (n.) माकुड़ा — A spider.
Mal (n.) मल — Dirt.
Mala (n.) माला — Necklace.
Malami मलामी — Funeral.
Malchara (n.) मालचड़ा — A large bird.
Malewa (n.) मलेवा — A wild pigeon.
Mallam (n.) मल्लम — Ointment.
Mallo (adv.) मल्लो — Above, upper.
Malmatta (n.) मालमत्ता — Belongings, property.
Malnu (v.) मलेनु — To rub.
Mama (n.) मामा — Maternal uncle.
Man (n.) मान — Honour, respect.
Man (n.) मन — Mind, heart, soul; eighty pounds weight.
Manchha (n.) मनछ — A man, person, human being.
Măndăl marnu मन्दल मारनु — To circle as a hawk.
Mandra moli (n.) मन्द्र मोली — Old name for the Mohr (8-anna piece).
Mandro (n.) मान्द्रो — A mat.
Mangal (n.) मङगल — Mars (the planet).
Mangalbar (n.) मङगलवार — Tuesday.
Mangni (n.) मांगनी — Proposal, asking in marriage.
Mangnu (v.) मांगनु — To ask for, demand.
Manis (n.) मानिस — Person, man, human being.
Manjhari (n.) मंझारी — The part of the floor just inside the door of a house.
Mannu (v.) माननु — To obey; respect; have as an opinion. "Uslai kasto manchhas?"—"How do you like him?"
Mansuba (n.) मनसुवा — Desire; scheme.
Mantato (adj.) मनतातो — Luke-warm. But "Man tato rakh"—"Keep alert" (lit. keep your mind hot).
Mantra (n.) मनत्र — Charm, spell, incantation.

Markanu (v.) मड़कनु	To sprain.
Marm (n.) मरम	Vital place.
Marnu (v. tr.) मारनु	Beat, strike, kill.
Marnu (v. intr.) मरनु	To die.
Maruni (n.) मरुनी	The female dancer in Dasehra dances.
Mas (n.) मास	A sort of black pulse. There is also Setomas (white), Ratomas (red).
Masala (n.) मसला	Spices.
Masi (n.) मासी	Excreta.
Masi (n.) मसी	Ink.
Masino (adj.) मसीनो	Thin. "Pani masino ayo"—"Gentle rain came."
Mangsir (n.) मङ्गसीर	The month 15th November to 15th December.
Maskaunu (n.) मसकाउनु	To tighten.
Masnu (v.) मासनु	To spend (money).
Mastira (adv.) मासतीर	Above, up. A contraction of Mathi tira.
Masu (n.) मासु	Flesh, meat.
Mata (n.) माता	A hermit.
Matengra (n.) मटेंग्रा	An arrow, dart.
Mathi (adv.) माथी	Above, up, upper, upon. "Mathi jau"—"Go above, go up." "Mej mathi chha"—"It is on the table." "Mathi tala"—"The top story" (here it is short for Mathilo). "Thulo chand ko mathi"—"At the large target."
Mathilo (adj.) माथीलो	Adjective from Mathi. Upper.
Mato (n.) मतो	Opinion.
Mato (n.) माटो	Earth.
Matrai (adv.) मात्रै	Only. "Dui matrai lejau"—"Only take away two."
Matwala (n.) मतवाला	Drunkard.
Matyako (adj.) मात्याको	Drunk.
Mauri (n.) मौरी	Bee.
Maya माया	Love.
Mekh (n.) मेख	A nail, peg, wedge.

Mero (pro.) मेरो	My.
Metnu (v.) मेटनु	To be effaced, wiped out, lost.
Michnu (v.) मिचनु	To rub.
Mirga (n.) मिर्ग	A deer.
Mishavnu मिशाउनु	To mix.
Mitho (adj.) मिठो	Sweet.
Mohali (n.) मोहली	A pipe (made of hookah bowl and two pipes).
Mohni (n.) मोहनी	Personality, fascination.
Mohr (n.) मोहर	A seal.
Moiai (n.) मोआइ	A kiss.
Molsapri (n.) मोलसाप्री	A pine martin.
Morha (n.) मोड़ा	Native stool of straw.
Moto (adj.) मोटो	Fat.
Mukh (n.) मुख	Mouth. "Mukh jornu"—"To answer back." "Mukh jorne"—"An answerer back.
Muktai (adj.) मुक्त	Plentiful.
Mukhya (n.) मुखिया	Chief, headman. Mukhyani, chieftess.
Mul (adj.) मूल	Main, chief. "Mul bato"—"Main road."
Mula (n.) मूला	A root, drug, radish.
Mundro (n.) मुंद्रो	An ear-ring.
Muni, Muntira (adv.) मुनी मुनतीर	Below, under, underneath, down.
Mungro (n.) मुंगरो	A mallet.
Munto (n.) मुन्टो	The head.
Murchha (n.) मुरछा	A faint, swoon.
Muro (n.) मुड़ो	Tree-trunk cut down.
Murda (n.) मुर्दा	A corpse.
Murkha (n.) मुर्ख	A fool, blockhead.
Muri hath (n.) मुड़ी हाथ	The length of forearm with fist clenched.
Murilo मुड़िलो	Hatless.
Murli (adj.) मुर्ली	Female of all animals except human, birds and domestic animals.

Murti (n.) मुर्ती	(1) Heads of coins. (2) An idol, statue, picture.
Musa (n.) मुसा	(1) A rat, mouse. (2) A wart.
Musarnu (v.) मुसारनु	To stroke.
Mutthi मुट्टी	The fist. "Mutthi parnu"—"To clench the fist."
Mutnu (v.) मुतनु	To micturate. Mut (मुत) urine.
Muto (n.) मुटो	The heart.
Nachnu (v.) नाचनु	To dance ; to hover (of birds).
Nag (n.) नाग	A snake, serpent.
Nagphini (n.) नागफिनी	A cactus (lit. flat snake).
Naito (n.) नाइटो	Navel.
Nak (n.) नाक	Nose.
Nakali (adj.) नकली	Nice.
Nali (n.) नाली or नली	Pipe, tube.
Nam (n.) नाम	Name.
Nalihar (n.) नलिहाड़	Shin, shinbone.
Namja : Namlo (n.) नामजा नामलो	A coolie's rope.
Nanauli (adj.) ननाउली	Obscene. Nanauli kura=improper talk
Nang (n.) नङग	A nail (toe or finger).
Nangnu (v.) नाङगनु	To jump over. "Ye le tio lai nangio"-"This exceeded this" (when comparing the size of two things.
Nango (adj.) नांगो	Naked.
Nani (n.) नानी	A baby, small child. "E nani!"—"O Sonny!"
Nantina (n.) नानतीना	Children.
Napha (n.) नफा	Profit, gain.
Naramro (adj.) नरामरो	Bad.
Nari (n.) नाड़ी	The wrist ; pulse.
Naruwal (n.) नरुवल	A cocoanut.
Nas (n.) मास	Damage, loss, destruction.
Nasa (n.) नसा	A vein, muscle.
Nasnu (v.) नासनु	To suffer damage, loss, destruction.
Naspati (n.) नासपाती	A pear.
Nati नाती	Grandson ; Natini, grand-daughter.

Naula (adj.) नौला	Different, new.
Naun (n.)नाऊं	Name.
Nauni (n.) नौनी	Butter.
Nel (n.) नेल	Fetter.
Neoli (n.) नेग्रोली	A black-coloured bird with distinctive cry.
Nepte (adj.) नेपटे	Obtuse-angled ; flat (nose).
Nibhanu (v.) निभानु	To blow out.
Nidhar निधार	Forehead.
Nigali (n.) निगाली	A sort of grass, like thin bamboo.
Nij निज	The same, the above mentioned, own. personal.
Nikalnu (v.) निकालनु	To take out.
Nikharnu (v.) निखारनु	To take away.
Niko (adj.) निको	Good, sound, healthy.
Nilnu (v.) निलनु	To swallow.
Nilo (adj.) निलो	Blue.
Nimaunu (v.) निमाउनु	To complete.
Nimtho (n.) निमठो	Brim.
Ninchanu (v.) निचनु	To squeeze, wring.
Nind (n.) नींद	Sleep.
Ninda garnu नीन्दा गरनु	To spread scandal.
Ningale (n.) निगाले	A small leopard.
Niphannu (v.) निफननु	To choose.
Nira (adv.) निर	Near, close.
Nirbalio (adj.) निरबलयो	Weak.
Nirdhani (adj.) निर्धनी	Poor.
Nirmal (adj.) निरमल	Pure.
Nirogi (adj.) निरोगी	Free from disease ; healthy.
Nithur (adj.) निथुर	Cruel.
Niu (n.) न्यू	Excuse, pretence.
Niuto dine (n.) निउतो दिने	Host.
Niuranu (v.) न्यूड़नु	To stoop.
Niuraunu (v.) न्यूड़ाउनु	To bend (tr.).
Nohanu (v.) नोहानु	To wash, bathe.
Nok (n.) नोक	End, point.
Nol (n.) नोल	A pole such as a tiger is carried on.

Nun (n.) नून	Salt.
Nunilo (adj.) नूनीलो	Salty.
Nyolo musa न्योलो मुसा	Mongoose.
Nyano (adj.) न्यानो	Hot (of climate, etc., as a rule).
Obano ओबानो	Drought, dryness.
Ochchhyan (n.) ओच्छ्यान	Bedding.
Odan (n.) ओदान	A tripod for putting a cooking pot on.
Oho ! ओहो	Alas ! Exclamation of sadness.
Okhar (n.) ओखड़	A walnut. " Okhar ko rukh "—" Walnut tree."
Oleni ओलेनी	A spark.
Onth (n.) ओंट	The lip.
Oralnu (v.) ओरालनु	To bring down.
Oralo (n. & adv.) ओरालो	Descent, downhill.
Orar (n.) ओरार	Cave.
Oraunu (v.) ओराउनु	To cover up.
Os (n.) ओस	Dew.
Pa प	This is untranslatable ; it gives a little more force to a sentence :—" Uniharu isto kina gardenan ? "—" Why don't they do thus ? " " Kya pa ho "—" (Why on earth don't they) I don't know."
Pachharnu पछाड़नु	To knock down.
Pachchhim (n.) पच्छिम	The West.
Pachhi (adv. & Prep.) पछी	Afterwards, late ; after, behind.
Pachhtaunu (v.) पछताउनु	Repent.
Pahara (n.) पहरा	A guard, sentry.
Pahilo (adj.) पहिलो	Yellow.
Pahuno पहुनो	A guest.
Pailo (n.) पाइलो	Track, foot-print.
Pairo (n.) पैरो	A landslip.
Paitla (n.) पैतला	The sole of the foot.
Paiyan (n.) पाईयां	A cherry. " Paiyan ko rukh "—"Cherry tree."
Pakaunu (n.) पकाउनु	To cook.

Pakha (n.) पाखा	The side, bank. " Goli pakha ma goyo" —" The bullet went to one side."
Pakhalnu (v.) पखाल्नु	To wash (plates, etc.)
Pakheta (n.) पखेटा	(1) A spoke. (2) A fin. There is also a fish called Pakheta because of its pronounced fins.
Pakhi (n.) पाखी	A blanket.
Pakhura (n.) पाखुड़ा	The upper arm.
Paknu (v.) पाक्नु	To be cooking, be cooked, ripen.
Pakya ko (adj.) पाक्याको	Cooked.
Paleti marera (adv.) पलेटी मारेर	Cross-legged.
Pallo (adv.) पल्लो	That side, the other side, across, the further (one).
Palnu (v.) पाल्नु	To keep, maintain, bring up, preserve ; to tame.
Palo पालो	Turn. " Palo palo "—" In turns."
Palta पल्ट	Time in sense of how many *times*, etc.
Paltaunu (v.) पलटाउनु	To upset.
Palya ko (adj.) पाल्याको	Tame.
Pan (n.) पान	The betel-nut leaf. (2) Heart suit in cards.
Panchhi (n.) पंछी	A bird.
Panero (n.) पनेरो	A spring (of water).
Pangra (n.) पांगरा	(1) The knee cap. (2) A wheel. (3) A chestnut. " Pangra ko rukh "— " A chestnut tree."
Pani (n.) पानी	Water.
Pani (adv.) पनी	Also.
Panio (n.) पनेव	A spoon.
Panja (n.) पनजा	The toes. " Panja ma tekera "—" On tip-toe."
Pansa (n.) पांसा	Dice.
Panso (n.) पासो	A trap.
Pap (n.) पाप	Sin, evil, wrong deed. " Papi "—" A sinner."
Paral (n.) पराल	A straw.

Paraunu (v.) पढ़ाउनु	To cause to read, to teach.
Parayko (adj.) परायाको	Strange, foreign.
Parbat (n.) परबत	A hill, mountain, hilly district. A district in Nepal.
Pardes (n.) परदेस	A foreign country ; distant land.
Pardeshi (adj.) परदेशी	Foreign.
Parela (n.) परेला	An eyelash.
Parewa (n.) परेवा	A tame pigeon.
Pargattai (adv.) परगट्टै	Publicly.
Pari (adv.) पारी	Across. "Ganga pari"—"Across the river." This is also a term for Nepal, when speaking in India, the actual word "Nepal" being reserved for the Valley of Nepal.
Pari (n.) परी	A fairy.
Parkar (n.) परकार	Manner, method, way.
Parkhal (n.) परखाल	A wall.
Parkhanu (v.) परखनु	To wait, remain.
Parnu (v.) पढ़नु	To read ; to learn.
Parnu (v.) पारनु	To clench.
Pasaunu (v.) पसाउनु	To reap.
Pashu (n.) पशू	An animal, creature.
Pasina (n.) पसीना	Sweat.
Pasnu (n.) पसनु	To enter, go in.
Pasola (n.) पासोला	The thigh bone.
Pat (n.) पात	A leaf.
Pata (n.) पत्ता	A clue, mark, address.
Patha (n.) पाठा	A young goat.
Pathaunu (v.) पठाउनु	To send.
Patar (n.) पातर	A whore, prostitute.
Patri (n.) पत्री	A narrow strip, the vein on a mekometer.
Patti (n.) पट्टी	(1) A puttee, bandage. (2) The direction :—pallo patti, the other side.
Pattyanu (v.) पत्याउनु	To believe, trust.
Patuka (n.) पतुका	A cloth worn round the thighs, something like a kilt.
Patuwa (n.) पटुवा	Hemp.

Paunu (v.) पाउनु	To get, receive. Also: "M bhannu payena"—"I didn't get an opportunity to speak."
Pech (n.) पेच.	A screw. Pechkas, screw-driver.
Pet (n.) पेट	The stomach; also for mind occasionally.
Petaro (n.) पेटारो	A round basket.
Peti (n.) पेटी	Waist-belt.
Phagun (n.) फागुन	The month 15th February to 15th March.
Phailanu (v.) फैलानु	To spread.
Phakaunu (v.) फकाउनु	To coax, persuade.
Phal (n.) फल	Fruit. Result. The blade of a knife.
Phalam (n.) फलाम	Iron.
Phalana (adj.) फलाना	Certain, some.
Phalphul (n.) फलफुल	Fruits.
Phalnu (v.) फालनु	To throw, throw away. "Chura le phalnu"—"To shave."
Phaltu (adj.) फालतु	Of no special class, odd.
Phalyak (n.) फल्याक	A plank.
Pharkaunu (v.) फर्काउनु	To cause to return or turn round.
Pharknu (v.) फर्कनु	To turn round, return.
Phatnu (v.) फाटनु	To tear, rend.
Phed (n.) फेद	The base, foot (of a tree).
Phijaunu (v.) फिजाउनु	To scatter (tr.).
Phijnu (v.) फिजनु	To be scattered (intr.).
Phiô फियो	Spleen.
Phirat (n.) फिरात	Complaint.
Pheri (adv.) फेरी	Again.
Phirnu (v.) फिरनु	To eject.
Phirpata (n.) फिरपाटा	The hip.
Phita (n.) फिता	Tape, turban.
Phohri (adj.) फोहरी	Dirty, obscene.
Phoke tara (n.) फोके तारा	A large star.
Phokso (n.) फोकसो	The lung.
Phukalnu (v.) फुकालनु	To untie, unravel.
Phukaunu (v.) फुकाउनु	To untie, unravel.
Phuknu (v.) फुकनु	To blow.

Phuko dhulo (n.) फुको धुलो — A powder.
Phul (n.) फुल — An egg; a flower.
Phulgopi (n.) फुलगोपी — A cauliflower.
Phuli (n.) फुली — (1) A funnel (for pouring liquids). (2) A nose-ring worn on the outside nostril.
Phulnu फुलनु — To ripen.
Phupu फुपु — Elder paternal aunt.
Phuskaunu (v.) फुसकाउनु — To become untied.
Phusro (adj.) फुसरो — Grey.
Phutkanu (v.) फुतकनु — To escape.
Phurka फुरका — Tail of turban.
Phutnu (v.) फुटनु — To burst.
Phyaunro (n.) फ्यांउंरो — A small type of fox.
Piaj (n.) पियाज — An onion.
Pichas (n.) पिचास — A ghost.
Pidi (n.) पीडि — A balcony.
Pilo (n.) पिलो — An abcess.
Pindo (n.) पिन्डो — A mound, lump.
Pinjaro (n.) पिंजरो — A cage.
Pinnu (v.) पिननु — To grind.
Pip (n.) पिप — Matter, pus.
Pipa (n.) पीपा — A cask, barrel; a kalasi.
Piraulo पिरौलो — Calf of leg. Also called tikhra (तिखरां).
Pirthibi पिरथीबी — The earth, world.
Pitnu पिटनु — To hit, pound.
Pitho (n.) पिटो — Flour.
Piut (n.) पिउट — Lance Naick.
Pochhnu (v.) पोछनु — To wipe.
Pokhari (n.) पोखरी — A lake, pool.
Pokhnu (v.) पोखनु — To spill, upset.
Polnu (v.) पोलनु — To burn.
Pornu (n.) पोरनु — To swim.
Postak (n.) पोस्तक — A book.
Pothi (n.) पोथि — A female bird, a hen.
Pothra पोथ्रा — Scrub, bushes, young tree.
Powa (n.) पोवा — An inn.

Prameshwar (n.) प्रमेश्वर — God.
Pran (n.) प्राण — Soul, spirit, life.
Prantu (conj.) प्रन्तु — If.
Preg (n.) प्रेग — Nail.
Prem (n.) प्रेम — Love.
Priti (n.) प्रीति — Love.
Puchhar (n.) पुछार — A tail.
Pugnu (v.) पुगनु — To arrive, approach.
Puja (n.) पुजा — Worship.
Pulik (n.) पुलिक — A red stone like a cherry, which when worn round the neck is said to stop nose-bleeding.
Puntro (n.) पुन्तरो — A packet, parcel, bundle.
Purano (adj.) पुरानो — Old, ancient.
Puraunu पुराउनु — To take anything to a place. "Tislai mero ghar ma pura"—"Take this to my house."
Purja (n.) पुर्जा — A slip of paper.
Purnu (v.) पुरनु — To bury.
Pursenge (n.) पुरसङ्गे — Male dancer in Dasehra dances.
Pus (n.) पूस — The month 15th December to 15th January.
Putali (n.) पुतली — A butterfly.
Putke rog (n.) पुठके रोग — The plague.
Pwankh (n.) पांख — A feather.
Pyaro (adj.) प्यारो — Beloved, dear.
Ra (conj.) र — And. "Ranbir and Jangbir"—"Ranbir ra Jangbir."
Rag (n.) राग — A tune.
Ragharnu (v.) रघड़नु — To pull along the ground. Also to work extra time.
Ragat (n.) रगत — Blood.
Ragat masi (n.) रगत मासी — Dysentery.
Rah (n.) रह — A pool.
Rahechha राईछ — From Rahnu. This is in very common use: "U pāni ma porne na janne rahe chha"—"He doesn't know how to

swim." The "rahechha" gives the sentence a more continuative meaning.

Rahnu (v.) रहनु — To remain, reside. This is the verb used for Continuative tenses:, see Grammar.

Raj (n.) रांज — Reign. "Raj garnu"—"To rule."
Raja (n.) राजा — A king.
Rajbam (n.) राजबाम — A large eel.
Raji (adj.) राजी — Satisfied, pleased, contented.
Rajkumar (n.) राजकुमार — A prince.
Rajmahal (n.) राजमहाल — A palace.
Rakkhya (n.) राकख्या — The amulet string tied round wrist in the Rikhi Tarpan.

Rakhnu (v.) राखनु — To place, put, keep, possess, preserve.
Rakshi (n.) रकशी — Rum.
Ramarumi (n.) रामारुमी — Dawn.
Ramailo (adj.) रमाइलो — Pleasant.
Ramaunu (v. tr.) रमाउनु — To please, amuse.
Rambans (n.) रामबांस — Aloe plant.
Ramita (n.) रमीता — Play; fun; jolly show.
Rambhera (n.) रामभेड़ा — Tomato.
Ramro (adj.) रामरो — Good, well.
Rando (n.) रांड़ो — A widower.
Răng (n.) रंग — Paint.
Rāng (n.) रांग — Solder.
Rangaunu (v.) रंगाउनु — To paint.
Rango (n.) रांगो — A male water buffalo.
Ranko (n.) रांको — A torch.
Rani (n.) रानी — A queen.
Ranri (n.) रांड़ी — A widow.
Rari (n.) राड़ी — A blanket.
Ras (n.) रस — Juice.
Rashes (n.) राशेस — A giant.
Rashik (n.) रसिक — Joy.
Rat (n.) रात — Night.
Rato (adj.) रातो — Red.
Ratti (n.) रत्ति — A weight equal to 8 barley corns.

Raun (n.) रौं	Hair.
Resham (n.) रेशम	Silk.
Rimejhime (adv.) रिमेझिमे	" Pani pario rimejhime "—" Slight rain fell " : this is only used in connection with rain.
Rin (n.) रिण	A debt.
Ringato (n.) रिङगाटो	Giddiness, dizziness.
Ringaunu (v.) रिङगाउनु	To get giddy, dizzy.
Ris (n.) रीस	Anger.
Risaunu (v.) रिसाउनु	To get angry.
Riti (n.) रीति	Custom, habit.
Rito (adj.) रितो	Bare, unadorned.
Rodi (n.) रोदी	The place where dancing, etc., goes on in a village.
Rog (n.) रोग	Sickness, disease.
Rogi (adj.) (n.) रोगी	Sick, ailing ; an invalid.
Ropnu (v.) रोपनु	To plant.
Roti (n.) रोठी	Bread, chipati.
Ruchaunu (v.) रूचाउनु	To please, delight.
Ruga (n.) रूगा	A cold, chill.
Rujhnu (v.) रूझनु	To get wet.
Rukh (n.) रूख	A tree.
Rukho (adj.) रूखो	Barren (ground).
Runu (v.) रूनु	To weep, cry.
Sabal (n.) साबल	A crow-bar. Also written सब्बल
Sabai (adj.) सबै	All, every.
Sabd (n.) सब्द	A noise, sound.
Sadhain (adv.) सधैं	Always.
Sag (n.) साग	Vegetables, greens.
Sagun (n.) सगुन	An omen.
Sahajan (adj.) साहाजन	Noble.
Sahango (adj.) सहंगो	Cheap.
Sahanu (v.) सहनु	To endure, to suffer.
Saharo (n.) सहारो	Bold.
Sahas (adj.) साहस	Support, assistance.
Sahi (n.) सही	Signature. " Sahi lagaunu "—" To sign."

Sainlo (adj.) सइंलो	The third in a family.
Saiyat (n.) सायत	Propitious time.
Sajaunu (v.) सजाउनु	To repair, mend.
Sajilo (adj.) सजीलो	Easy.
Sajun सजनु	A tree in Nepal.
Saknu (v.) सकनु	To be able; also as to finish in the Completive verbs, see Grammar.
Sakya (n.) साक्या	The Buddhist teaching.
Sal (n.) साल	A timber tree ; a year.
Sala (n.) साला	(1) Younger brother-in-law, (2) Cousin from maternal uncle. Sali is the feminine.
Salah (n.) सलाह	Advice.
Salau (n.) सलौ	A locust.
Salghari सलघारी	A pine forest.
Salkaunu (v.) सलकाउनु	To set fire to, to light.
Salla (n.) सल्ला	A pine. "Salla ko rukh"—"A fir tree, deodar."
Samalnu (v.) समालनु	To collect in one place, take care of.
Samatnu (v.) समातनु	To seize, catch hold.
Samaunu (v.) समाउनु	To seize, catch hold.
Samet (prep.) समेत	With, together with, including.
Samjhanu (v.) समझनु	To understand.
Samjhaunu (v.) समझाउनु	To make understand, to explain.
Samma सम्म	(1) Up to, as far as. (2) Level, flat.
Samundar (n.) समुद्र	The sea, ocean.
San (n.) सन	Year.
San (n.) सान	A sign, signal.
Sanasu (n.) सनासु	Pincers (as a crab).
Sancho (adj.) सांचो	True, real.
Sancho (n.) सांचो	A mould.
Sang (prep.) संग	With.
Sanghu (n.) सांघु	A bridge.
Sangi (n.) संगी	Friend, chum.
Sanglo (n.) सांगलो	A chain.
Sangrinu (v.) सांगरीनु	To shrink.
Sanguro (adj.) सांगुड़ो	Narrow, tight.

Sanjh (n.) सांझ	Evening.
Sanka (n.) संका	Doubt, suspicion.
Sanki सनकी	Bad tempered.
Sanpro (n.) सांपड़ी	The thigh.
Sansa संसा	Fit, well.
Sans (n.) सांस	Breath.
Sansari (adj.) संसारी	Worldly ; also married.
Sant (adj.) सान्त	Quiet.
Santnu (v.) सांठनु	To change, exchange.
Santusht (adj.) सन्तुष्ट	Satisfied.
Sapana (n.) सपना	A dream.
Săpha (adj.) सफा	Clean.
Sarasar (adv.) सरासर	Straightway ; without a pause.
Sarg (n.) सर्ग	The sky, heavens.
Sarangi (n.) सारंगी	Fiddle.
Sarkaunu (v.) सरकाउनु	To make withdraw, remove.
Sarkinu (v.) सरकिनु	To withdraw.
Sarir (n.) सरीर	Body, figure.
Sărnu (v.) सरनु	To move (intr.)
Sārnu (v.) सारनु	To make move, move (tr.), place.
Sarai (adv.) सारै	The whole, all.
Saro (adj.) सारो	Hard, not soft.
Saru chara (n.) सारू चरा	A mina (bird) ; also called Dangre. (दाङ्गरे).
Sasura ससुरा	Father-in-law.
Sashu साशु	Mother-in-law.
Sata (n.) साता	A week, a 7 days.
Satkanu (v.) सटकनु	To go away.
Sato सातो	Presence of mind.
Satur सतुर	Enemy.
Sawal (n.) सवाल	A question.
Sekara सेकड़ा	Per cent, %. "Sekara pachhi"—"Per cent."
Sekaunu (v.) सेकाउनु	To roast (tr.)
Seknu (v.) सकेनु	To get roasted, roast (intr.)
Selaunu (v.) सेलाउनु	To cool.
Serho (adj.) सेड़ो	Squinting.

Seto (adj.) सेतो	White.
Sewa (adj.) सेवा	Attendance on superior.
Shakshi (n.) शाक्षी	A witness.
Shakti (n.) शक्ति	Strength, ability.
Shani शनी	Saturn.
Shanicharbar (n.)शनीचरबार	Saturday.
Shekhi (n.) शेखी	Boastfulness ; insolence.
Sher (n.) शेर	A large tiger, but smaller than Dhara ; a lion.
Shiaku (n.) शिआकु	An umbrella made of large leaves.
Shieli (n.) शेथली	A whetstone. Also called Sili (सीली).
Shikka (n.) शिक्का	A Nepalese coin.
Shilapatthar (n.) शिला पत्थर	A sacred stone.
Shim (n.) शिम	A marsh ; also called Shim shar.
Shisa (n.) शिसा	Glass, bottle.
Shital (n.) शीतल	A good, cool climate.
Shito (n.) शितो	A post.
Shok (n.) शोक	Anxiety.
Shuga (n.) शुगा	A parrot.
Shukrbar (n.) शुक्रवार	Friday.
Shukr शुक्र	Venus.
Shusilo (n.) शुसिलो	The noise of a whistle, a whistle.
Shwang (n.) श्वांग	Acting, wittiness, mimicry. " Shwang garne manchha."—" A wag, actor."
Shwasni (n.) श्वासनी	Wife, woman.
Siano (adj.) स्यानो	Small. " Siani ama "—" Younger maternal aunt."
Siddhyo (adj.) सीदधीयो	Finished.
Sigan (n.) सीगान	Nasal phelgm, saliva.
Sikaunu (v.) सिकाउनु	To teach.
Siknu (v.) सिकनु	To learn.
Sikri (n.) सिकरी	A link in a chain.
Sikro (adj.) सिकरो	Sickly, poorly (of plants).
Sikuwa (n.) सिकुवा	A balcony.
Simali (n.) सिमाली	A waterweed.
Simi (n.) सिमी	A bean.
Sinduri rog (n.) सिन्दुरी रोग	Mildew.

Sinkaula (n.) सिनकौला — Cinnamon.
Sinko dhago (n.) सनको धागो — The ceremony for getting divorced, also called Sinko pangra.
Sino (n.) सीनो — An animal's carcase.
Siunri (n.) स्यूणी — Cactus.
Sip (n.) सीप — Cleverness, ability.
Sipalu (adj.) सीपालु — Clever, able, skilful.
Siran (n.) सिरान — A pillow.
Sisa (n.) सीसा — Lead.
Sisno (n.) सिसनो — Nettles.
Sit (n.) सीत — Dew.
Sita (prep.) सित — **With**, in company with.
Siunu (v.) सीउनु — To sew.
Siyal (n.) स्याल — A jackal.
Siyo (n.) सियो — A needle.
Sochnu (v.) सोचनु — To think.
Sodhnu (v.) सोधनु — To ask (a question).
Sohaunu (v.) सोहाउनु — To mean right (of a word). To fit, become (as a hat).
Soharnu (v.) सोहरनु — To sweep, clean.
Sojho (adj.) सोझो — Straight.
Solti (n.) सोलटी — Cousin from maternal uncle, marriageable.
Sombar(n.) सोम्बार — Monday.
Sonpi (n.) सोंपी — Care, charge.
Sor (n.) सोर — Voice, sound.
Stri (n.) स्त्री — A woman.
Subhan सुभः — May everything be pleasant! This is the usual ending to a letter.
Sudharnu (v.) सुधारनु — To repair, mend, adjust.
Sudi (adv.) सुदई — In vain, to no purpose.
Sudo (adj.) सुदो — Pure.
Sugghar (adj.) सुग्घर — Clean, neat.
Sukaunu (v.) सुकाउनु — To dry (tr.).
Suknu (v.) सुकनु — To get dry, to dry (intr.), to wither.
Sulto (adj.) सुल्टो — Aright, not upside down or wrong way round.

Sum (n.) सूम — A miser.
Sun (n.) सुन — Gold. The number "O."
Sunar (n.) सुनार — A goldsmith.
Sund (n.) सुंढ — The trunk of an elephant.
Sungar (n.) सुंगर — A tame pig.
Sungnu (v.) सुंगनु — To smell (tr.), to sniff.
Suninu (v.) सुनिनु — To swell.
Sunno (adj.) सुन्नो — Solitary, lonely (place).
Sunnu (v.) सुननु — To hear, listen.
Sunsan (n.) सुनसान — Quiet, peace.
Suntala (n.) सुनतला — An orange.
Surilo (adj.) सुरीलो — Straight, especially of a tall tree, with no branches low down.
Surta (n.) सुरता — Anxiety.
Surti (n.) सुर्ती — Tobacco for chewing.
Surung (n.) सुरुंग — A mine (explosive).
Suruwal (n.) सुरुवाल — Trousers, long drawers.
Suskeri (n.) सुसकेरी — A whistle.
Susti सुस्ती — Gently, softly.
Sutnu (v.) सुतनु — To sleep; lie down; also to go to sleep of limbs.
Sutari सुतरी — Rope.
Suto (n.) सुटो — Ginger.
Swatai (adv.) स्वाटै — All at once, the whole at once.
T त — Thou.
Tab (adv.) तब — Then; also used idiomatically and translatable by "There, I told you so" or "That's what I mean."
Tachhnu (v.) ताछनु — To scrape off, plane off.
Tachak basnu (v.) तचक बसनु — To squat on the ground, with seat on ground.
Tagaro (n.) तगारो — A bar, forming a gate such as are used in stalls.
Tagro (adj.) तगड़ो — Fit, healthy, strong.
Tahan (adv.) तहां — There (correlative).
Taknu (v.) ताकनु — To aim, aim at.

Taktakaunu (v.) टकठकाउनु — To shake.
Tal, talau (n.) ताल तलाउ — A lake.
Tala (adv.) (n.) तल — (Adv.) Down, below, under (similar meanings as prep.). (n.) A storey in a house.
Tala (n.). ताला — A lock.
Talnu (v.) टालनु — To patch.
Tama (n.) तामा — Copper.
Tambar (n.) तम्बर — A drum.
Tan (n.) तान — A warp.
Tana (n.) तना — A lace, bootlace.
Tandheri (n.) तन्धेरी — A youth, lad, boy.
Tanga, tangalo (n.) तांगा, तंगालो — A rod, fishing-rod.
Tank (n.) टांक — A button.
Tankaunu (v.) तनकाउनु — To stretch (tr.)
Tanki (n.) टांकी — A kind of grass.
Tanknu (v.) तनकनु — To stretch (inter.), grow long.
Tannu (v.) ताननु — To pull, drag. Tanatan, a tug of war.
Tapain (n.) तपाईं — Honorific, "your honour."
Tapasi (adj.) तपास्री — Moral.
Tapnu तापनु — To get warm.
Tara (n.) तारा — (1) A star. (2) A target.
Tara (adj.) टाड़ा — Far, distant.
Tăra (conj.) तर — But.
Tarkanu (v.) तड़कनु — To brush, brush off (dust, etc.).
Tarnu (v.) तरनु — To pass across, ford, wade across.
Tarsaunu (v.) तरसाउनु — To frighten, threaten.
Tarul तरुल — A sort of creeper.
Taruni तरुनी — A girl.
Tas (n.) तास — A card.
Tasnu (v.) टासनु — To adhere, stick to.
Taswir (n.) तसबीर — A picture.
Tata (n.) टाटा — A scar.
Tataunu (v.) तताउनु — To heat, make hot.

Tato (adj.) तातो — Hot (of water, etc.), "Man tato rakh" —"Keep alert." "Kan tato rakh" —Keep your ears open."

Tauli (n.) तौली — Saucepan.
Tauko (n.) टाउको — The head.
Tawa (n.) तावा — Flat dish for cooking chappatis on.
Tekan (n.) टेकन — A prop, support.

Teknu (v.) टेकनु — To step. "Panja ma teknu"—"To go on tiptoe."

Tel (n.) तेल — Oil.
Tero (pro.) तेरो — Thy.
Tero (adj.) टेड़ो — Not straight, crooked, bent.
Terso (adv.) तेरसो — Along the level. "Terso jau."— "Keep along the same level."

Testo (adv.) तेस्तो — So (correlative).
Tewa chara (n.) तेवा चड़ा — Jay.
Tewhar (n.) तेवहार — A ceremony.
Thagnu (v.) ठगनु — To cheat, deceive.
Thah (n.) थाह — Information, knowledge.
Thaharaunu (v.) ठहराउनु — To get informed.
Thailo (n.) थैलो — A sack, bag.
Thaknu (v.) थाकनु — To tire, get tired.
Thali (n.) थाली — A large flat brass dish.
Thalnu (v.) थालनु — To begin, commence.
Thamnu (v.) थामनु — To stop, cease.
Than (n.) थान — A temple.
Thangne (adj.) थांगने — Ragged, in rags.
Thankiaunu (v.) थनक्याउनु — To put in order.
Thaplo (n.) थापलो — Top (of anything).
Thapnu (v.) थापनु — To give to, hand to.
Thapri (n.) थपड़ी — A clap. "Thapri marnu"—"To clap"
Tharki (n.) थरकी — A game something like "Ludo."
Tharo (adj.) ठाड़ो — Upright, standing up.
Thatta (n.) ठट्ठा — A joke, jest, fun.
Thattaunu (v.) ठट्ठाउनु — To make fun at, take in.
Thaun (n.) ठाऊं — A place.

Theki (n.) ठेकी	Round wooden receptacle for holding ghee, etc.
Thes (n.) ठेस	A stumbling, trippling up. "Thes khanu."—"To stumble, trip up." "Thes lagaunu"—"To trip up, upset."
Thinkia (n.) ठिनक्या	A sudden occurrence like a match bursting into flame.
Thirnu (v.) थिरनु	To hover, settle.
Thita (n.) ठिठा	A youth, lad.
Thond (n.) ठोंड	A beak (of a bird).
Thok (n.) थोक	A thing.
Thokar (n.) ठोकर	A clash, blow, collision.
Thopo (n.) थोपो	A drop (of water, etc.).
Thotro (adj.) थोतरो	Old, worn out.
Thotya ठोत्या	A grass, with large leaves.
Thuknu (v.) थुकनु	To spit. A spit is a sign of contempt.
Thulo (adj.) ठुलो	Great, big, large.
Thun (n.) थुन	A teat, udder.
Thunnu (v.) थुननु	To shut, close.
Thunse (n.) थुंसे	A certain kind of grass.
Thuprinu (v.) थुपरिनु	To assemble, crowd.
Thupro (n.) थुपड़ो	A crowd.
Thutnu (v.) थुतनु	To suck in, draw through.
Tika (n.) तिका	Caste mark.
Tikho (adj.) तिखो	Pointed, sharp.
Tikhra (n.) तिखड़ा	The part of the leg behind the shin. The calf.
Tilinga (n.) तिलिंगा	A soldier.
Tili (n.) तिली	A small mole.
Tio (pro.) त्यो	That, the further ; he.
Tipnu (v.) टिपनु	To pick up.
Tipri (n.) टिपरी	Top, summit, peak.
Tira (prep.) तीर	Towards, in the direction of.
Tirkha (n.) तिरखा	Thirst. "Tirkha lagnu"—"To be thirsty."
Tirnu (v.) तिरनु	To pay back.

Tirza (n.) तिरजा — An allotment.

Tissi (adv.) टिस्सी — Aimlessly, without a purpose. "Timi kina isto garchhau ?"—"Why do you do thus ?" "Tissi" meaning O ! I just do it (without any particular reason).

Tith (n.) तिथ — Love.

Tithi (n.) तिथी — A date.

Tito (adj.) तितो — Bitter.

Titra (n.) तितरा — A partridge.

Tiun (n.) तीउन — Meat and vegetables, etc., accompanying a dish.

Toknu (v.) टोकनु — To bite.

Toli (n.) टोली — A batch, party.

Topi (n.) टोपी — A hat, cap.

Tornu (n.) टोड़नु — To break (tr.)

Tosak (n.) तोसक — A mattress.

Tostan (n.) तोस्तान — Accoutrements.

Tras (n.) त्रास — Fear.

Tachituchi ताची तुची — Shavings.

Tuhinu (v.) तुहिनु — To miscarry.

Tuhura (n.) टुहूरा — An orphan.

Tukruko basnu (v.) तुकरुक बसनु — To squat on the thighs.

Tulo (n.) तलो — A weighing machine.

Tuni (n.) टुनी — (1) A kind of grass. (2) Teak.

Tuyanlo (n.) तुयांलो — Heat haze.

Tupi (n.) टुपि — The Hindu pigtail.

Tupo (n.) टुपो — Top, summit.

Tuppa (n.) टुप्पा — The second line of a verse or song.

Tusa (n.) टुसा — A sprout.

Tusaro (n.) तुसारो — Frost.

Twak (n.) तवाक — A measure for rum (tot).

Twakai (adv.) टवाकै — Exactly.

U (pro.) उ — He ; that.

Ubhinu (v.) उभीनु — To stand, be standing.

Ubhrinu (v.) उभ्रिनु	To remain over. "Ubhrva ko" "The remnants."
Uchalnu (v.) उचालनु	To raise up.
Uchhinnu (v.) उछिननु	To overtake, to pass.
Uchita (adj.) उचित	Fair, just.
Udas (n.) उदास	Sadness.
Udasilo (adj.) उदासीलो	Dull, sad.
Udekh (n.) उदेख	Astonishment.
Udekh ko (adj.) उदेख को	Strange, wonderful.
Udhyaunu (v.) उध्याउनु	To grind ; sharpen on a stone.
Ugharnu (v.) उघाड़नु	To open, uncover.
Uile (adv.) उइले	Long time ago.
Uile Uile उइले उइले	Days ago, years ago.
Ujaryo (adj.) उजाड़यो	Ruined, desolate (house, etc.)
Ujyalo (adj.) उज्यालो	Light, bright.
Ukalo उकालो	Uphill, ascent.
Ukhelnu (v.) उखेलनु	To uproot.
Ulto (adv.) उलटो	Reversed, the wrong way. "Ulto-sulto"—"Upside-down."
Umalnu (v.) उमालनु	To boil (tr.)
Umar (n.) उमर	Age.
Umkanu (v.) उमकनु	To escape.
Umkaunu (v.) उमकाउनु	To let escape.
Umranu (v.) उमरनु	To grow.
Un (n.) ऊन	Wool.
Unbho (adv.) (prep.) ऊंभो	Above.
Undho (adv.) (prep.) ऊंधो	Below.
Unglnu (v.) उंगलनु	To boil (intr.), be boiling.
Uni (pro.) उनी	They.
Unkhu (n.) ऊंखु	Sugar-cane.
Unpiya (n.) ऊंपीया	A flea.
Unt (n.) ऊंट	A camel.
Upai (n.) उपाय	A plan, means.
Upas (n.) उपास	Fasting, a fast.
Upharnu (v.) उफाड़नु	To jerk, jerk up.
Uphrinu (v.) उफड़ीनु	To jump up, jump about, hop.
Urnu (v.) उड़नु	To fly (as a bird).

Urus (n.) उड़स	A bug, bed-bug.
Usinnu (v.) उसीनन्	To boil (intr.), not used of liquids.
Utar (n.) उत्तर	The North.
Utara (n.) उतरा	An answer.
Utha (adv.) उथा	Thither.
Uthaunu (v.) उठाउन्	To arouse, awake (tr.)
Uthnu (v.) उठन्	To rise, wake (intr.)
Utranu (v.) ऊतरन्	To descend out of.
Wak wak garnu (v.)	To vomit—waknu (वाकन्) also used.
Wakhlia (n.) वासल्या	A Pathan.
Wallo (adv.) वल्लो	On this side (opposite to pallo).
Yahan (adv.) यहां	Here.
Yo (pro.) यो	This.
Yota (adj.) योटा	One.
Yukti (n.) युक्ति	A plan, scheme.

CHAPTER III.

MISCELLANEOUS.

PROVERBS.

Note.—The literal translation is in brackets.

Aphi thangne ghora bata mangne
(He being in rags begs from horseback).

Agulto dekhi darayo ko kukur bijli dekhi tarsinchha
(The dog once frightened by a firebrand fears lightning).
Once bitten twice shy.

Arko ko shwashni ramro dekinchha
(Another's wife seems best).
Stolen fruits are sweetest.

Umkia ko machha thulo hunchha
(The escaped fish seems big).

Mau bhanda challa batho.
(The chicken is wiser than the hen).

Indra sanga barkha ko kura
[Talking of rain to Indra (the God of rain)].
Carrying coals to Newcastle.

Bhera bhera sang bakra bakra sang
(The sheep together, the goats together).
Birds of a feather flock together.

Ghanti dekhera har nilnu
(Look at the throat before swallowing the bone).
Look before you leap.

Jasto lai testai.
Tit for tat.

Jasto des testo ves
(As the country so the dress).
Do in Rome as the Romans do.

Na hunne mama bhanda kana mama niko
(A one-eyed uncle is better than none).
Half a pint is better than no beer.

Bichchhi ko mantra na jane sarpa ko dulo ma hath halne
(Not knowing how to charm a scorpion he puts his hand into a snake's hole).

Khane mukh lai junga le chhekdaina
(A moustache won't stop a hungry mouth eating).
Where there's a will there's a way.

Na dinne baraju budhbar parchha
(The father-in-law who doesn't want to give, says "come on Wednesday").
To-morrow never comes.

Jahan dherai biralu hunchhan, wahan musa mardainan
(Where there are many cats the mice don't die).
Too many cooks spoil the broth.

Lanka ma sun chha mero kan rito
(There is gold in Ceylon but my ears are unadorned).

Pet pasi khutta tanchha
(Having entered the stomach he stretches his legs),
i.e., having once got a hold on someone by kindness he puts the screw on.

Dullu ko ulu Dailekhi chor
(The owl comes from Dullu, the thief from Dailekh).

Kana des ma ganra tanderi
(In a blind country a goitre looks nice).

Kaphar hunne bhanda marnu ramro.
(It is better to die than to be a coward).

LETTER WRITING.

The following are the usual methods of starting and ending letters :—

BEGIN :—Swosti shri (sarba poma yoge ityadi sakal guna garisht
स्वोस्ती श्री (सर्ब पोमा योगे इत्यादी सकल गुण गरीस्ट
raj bhar samrath ita shri) 3 (*a*) age m (*b*) ko taraph
राज भार साम थ इत श्री) ३ आगे म को तरफ
bata bahut bahut karera (*c*) (*d*) sewa (*e*) chha ji aru
बाट बंहुत बहुत करेर सेवा छ जी अरु
bachi linu hola ji—(text of letter follows).
बाची लीनु हांला जी

ENDING :—Kalam ko bhul chuk maph garnu hola. Subham.
कलम को भुल चुक माफ गरनु होला सुभ्म.

ADDRESS ENVELOPE.—Yo chitti jaega——(*f*)

Paega——(*g*)

Bejha——(*h*)

Notes.—(*a*) Ordinarily 3, but 4 for enemy and 5 for teacher or special person.

(*b*) Writer's name or relationship to reader.

(*c*) Reader's name or relationship can be entered here (not necessary).

(*d*) Frills such as "hath jori" may be entered here.

(*e*) Here enter "dhok" if writing to superior or "ashik" if to inferior.

(*f*) Place. (*g*) Receiver's name. (*h*) Sender's name.

Swosti means, Peace to you. Shri means great. Sewa = superior. Dhok = worship.

Ashik means blessings for inferior. Subham means, May everything be pleasant.

The part in brackets may be omitted.

EXAMPLES OF SONGS.

These songs may be roughly divided into two classes—ordinary songs sung any time (called Jhamre), and those sung at festivals as the Dasehra. Jhamre songs differ according to their tunes not according to the words. Each tune however has its own chorus. The words of the verses of one jhamre song can be sung in any other song provided they are adapted to the tune. Thus in the following examples the verses given under the SAINLADAI song do not belong to that song only ; they are merely examples of suitable verses and could equally well be sung to the MASANI tune, having been adapted to suit that tune.

To sing is "ganu" or "git jhignu." The first line of the verse is called " phet " ; the second line, which usually contains the joke of the verse, is called "tuppa." The tune is called "bakha." " Siano sor le jhignu " is to sing in seconds as the women do. The tomtom is called " madal."

The Dasehra songs are more hymn-like and are chiefly extracts from books such as the Ramayan, Chalitra, etc. The male dancer is called "prosengi" or "pursengi" and the female dancer " maruni."

SAINLADAI (Third eldest brother).

Tune No. 13 (see Music at end.)

Each verse begins with " Sainladai " and ends with "Mayalo."

Dêdho rāmro khāna mitho hiun chelli ko pāni
Āja mêro kăpal dukhio rakshi khāna bāni.

Gêro sainlo, gêro mainlo mādal lūke gêro
Rakshi khāna bāni rahechha layo chhorun phêro.

Tul pă rio ko pukro mā nil pă rio ko pāni
Chelli sīta gide gānda rakshi khāna bāni.

Dailo muni titio pāpa gai le khaio khāla
Eki rāt ke pira ti le jahān gayo jāla.

Yota guru Dubtāna mā, yota guru Bhānko
Jāgira khāna jaun to chelli tirza launla gaun ko.

Rāto māto chiplo bāto gai ko khutta lărkio
Cherăna le gānda kheri măn to mero dărkio.

Tuchi tuchi guleli ta hāth mā layo dhănu
Gide gāna cherana lai maile kăti bhănu.

Hookah mêro nări wala chilam to Bengāli
Chelli sita gide gāna m jasto kăngāli.
Dhān ko bāla hărio to kodo bāla kungri
Āja dinu hānsi khêli bholi dekhi hongri.
Dhān ko bāla hărio to pāni pări pări
Timro jawān bithaidunla isse gări gări.
Tinko sāra Nepāl mā hāthi kina jhulio
Săbi săngi hānsi kheli m ta kina bhūlio.
Dhobi dhăra pănera dhobi luga dhunchha
Bhairo mănma hānsa khela bhīttra mănma runchha.
Batuki ko tāto dudha phūki phūki khaunla
Chelli sīta pirā tītha lūkilūki launla.
Ullăghar birālu le pallă ghara dhūkchha
Chelli ju ko tambācu le āja kăpal dukhchha.
Pālio ko bhālia pōthi bākum bākum bhănchha.
Chelli ju ko dekhda kheri dākum dākum lăgchha.
Ukāli ko chiso pāni gogăn bāta piunla
Chelli ju ko sir ko jobān mero hāthi liunla.
Poli khāna mītho hunne bākari ko pio
Āja rāt sapăna mā mêro kākhmā thyo.
Pokra ko sirāni mā pāni tāri khêta
Kāhan ko chelli kāhan ko m ta āja bhayo bhêta.
Hādi pāri unchi dhunga gori sukaio dhān
Hāti ko churi chinchin bāzi murkha na bujhe san.
Kācha pāta sura tita poli khāna bhaina
Jānchhu bhăni chelliju lai chhori jāne bhaina.

Chorus—Sainladāi kāhan goyo he hai pāni ghata Neole karāyo
Or, Sainladai pherī bheta hola ki yesai marunla ki mayālo.

JABRI.

(*a*) Pirāthi Launla yāri bāne ma resāmi māni.

Tune No. 1 (see Music at end).

This is the chorus.
Any ordinary verse can be adapted to this tune.

"Resami nānī" really precedes the rest of the chorus though when sung it appears to come at the end.

(b) JANDA JĀNDA LAHURYA NAUTUNWA MĀ BĀTO BIRĀYO.

Tune No. 2 (see Music at end).

This is the chorus.
Any ordinary verse can be adapted to this tune.
Nautunwa is a place on the road to Batoli.

(c) LALI MAYA.

Tune No. 7 (see Music at end).

Verses must be adapted to this tune.

(d) MARCHING SONG.

Tune No. 10 (see Music at end).

Chorus—Ho ki hoi*nā* ho kareli *mā* ho jhiama māyalo

This song is formed from any Sainladai verse (page 3) by correct emphasis where underlined, *e.g.*, Sainladai verse No. 1 would run :—

Dedho rām*ro* ho khāna mi*tho* ho, hiun chelli ko pāni
Aja me*ro* ho kapal dukhi*o* ho, rakshi khāna bāni.

Other verses similar.

Another chorus with slightly contracted tune as given in Music at end is "Ho ki hoina dī dai kareli ma jhiama māyālo."

(e) CHUTKE JABRI.

Tune No. 8 (see Music at end).

This song is also formed from any Sainladai verse, by making a pause (/) in the middle of each line and starting the second half with "E." The second half of the second line forms the chorus (underlined). *E.g.* Sainladai verse No. 2 would run :—

Gero sāinlo gero māinlo/E mādal luke gero.
Rakshi khāna bāni rahechha/E *lāyo chhorun phero.*

MISCELLANEOUS.

Chi jana tapain le maya pa mario ki ?

1. Pāni ra pario, rima ra jhima, ban bhāyo ha rio
   Khāna ra pinia, daulati thio, joi bina mario.

2. Āja maile ta, bhātera khāyo, kelara pāti mā
   Hitera nāni, gumnara jāu, juneli rāti mā.

3. Khola rawāri, khola rapāri, dhunga le hānna hān
   Yota lognia, diute shwāshni, langothi tānna tān.

This can be adapted to Tune No. 9.

Lalpati Jaunla. (Lalpata).

Chorus—Lālpāti jāunla bholi nāchunla.
Mās bāri māshiri totra kasāri shiaulo gisāri
Chulto batāre gonra pasāri puto techāri
Ho rāhi banai mā, jochha manai mā, bhanole.

MĀSĀNI.

Tune No. 3 (see Music at end).

These verses also adapt themselves to Sainladai and Jhamre (*b*). One Sainladai verse forms two Māsāni verses. The second line of each verse is the chorus for that verse.

E mitho surti pāyena, maile
E kācho pāta khāyena, Māsāni.
E Māsāni ko shwāshni chhena
E issa pāli liaunla, Māsāni.
E dulo khelne titari dīr
E mandal mārne bāza, Māsāni.
E charan sita gauna lāi
E kya ko thyo lāza, Māsāni.
E Nadi pāri bhainsi kinio
E sutari le tānna Māsāni.
E sutari le bhayena bhani
E piriti le tānna, Māsāni.

E bhalo mari bela lāyo
E umbho khole shiashia, Māsāni.

E Hazur bhayo raitani
E Hami para desi, Māsāni.

E Gide gaunda hazur sanga
E Pito na lāgi gayena, Māsāni.

The dance accompanying this song is danced mainly standing on the head, time being kept by waving the legs in the air.

SALIJU (Wife's younger sister).

Tune No. 5 (see Music at end.)

Pito lāgio māchungi mero (E Sāliju) bātera bajāunla
Māchungi mero (E Sāliju)
Gide gānde chelli ju lāi (E Sāliju) sāthera lejāunla.
Chelli ju lāi (E Sāliju) ,, ,,

Hānsera mukha jabāne gayo ( ) khabari paundena
Sāthi ko sangi bijuti gayo ( ) ramailo lagdena.

Din māthi dina bajeni bhāyo ( ) bātera bajāunla
Bela nā ruyio chelliju lāi ( ) sāthera lejāunla.

Bhyāna pokho jalaku ghāma ( ) dānra ko sirāna
Ekira chorun gidera gaido ( ) hoina birāna.

Sirapati kukri, Manipuri dāba ( ) dahini pati birunla
Māya ko chelli kahān pugio bhani ( ) rukha chari hirunla.

Batoli bāta Tiribini samma ( ) kampani chellauna
Chelli ju gharbāri rahechha ( ) dobai balauna.

Lekha bāta Tātopāni samma ( ) tije muni bakhara
Pachhi prānta kepāro ~unchha ( ) chhota māya na gara.

Nepale jānia Nepale dāje ( ) Nepalai kasto chha
Suna ra chāndi jhili ra mili ( ) taruni sasto chha.

Each of the lines of this song is sung twice as in example 1.

Between the brackets—( ) "E Sāliju" comes. Women join in the chorus singing a sort of second higher up.

RATOLI SONG.

Sung at a marriage festival by women only. No males allowed.

1. Wari baḷāyo baje, pāri balāvo baje, baje ko jhāta le biskun challāyo.
2. Khopi ta khopi kursān rākhne khopi, Ratoli hirna auna lai, phukāune ko topi (phokunda).

MAGARKURA SONG.

No special tune.

Siri ma siri mān ,mān ko biri lākhwa bunang bārale
Sadhain mā rāle ita mātri chanle gnā do yera mā rāle.

GURUNGKURA SONG.

No special tune.

Kanari yāmo kāmi dāi golari yāmo nāni jerdo sāi.

DASEHRA SONGS.

Maruni is female dancer; prosenge or pursenge, male dancer; madali, tomtomer.

MAGAR

Ramayan.

Tune No. 14 (see Music at end.)

Dasarāt rāja ko tinota rāni, kānchhi Kiake ko bārasti bhāyo
Rāmā Lachhmi bani bani bāsa likhio, bārasti chhatru, ko rajai.
Tumita ayela dewara gusain dāji lāi kahā chori ayaun
Ho: dāji ta gaye miraga pachhi hāmu āve ghat ko rakhwa le

Āshish.

(Giving blessings to the person who rewards the dancers).

Tune No. 12 (see Music at end.)

Ho Bakhatale siri rām Isswor le puryaon
Ho barhia ma barhio Dhanara darbe gai got ha barhio ho
(Repeat 1st line).

Chalitra.

Tune No. 6 (see Music at end).

Ho ! Dudhayo ko bālakha mero kauna le hari lagio
He ! Kita Hari lagio Langka pati raun le
Ye ho kita Hari lagio bāsu deo le
Jamāna ko nira tira Dhyāno gai chario
Kamu Dhyāno rupara gari ho baru hirna ayo
Homeri lila rui ma rui rati bhyayo.

GURUNG.

Surāti.

Tumu ta rāja chale la bidesa.
Yue jyān marunla.
Choriāna katiori.
Katiori na dāsi marunla.
Kamari birani kukri dāsi marunla.
Băru hirani jau.
Kāli ko tira Moti ko sira.
Surāti rāni ko ghar.

Hirana māmoi Surāti rāni ko ghar.

Bhujeli ko dabero jasto	As a large kukri's sheath
Surāti rāni ko chulāti.	So is Surati's hair.
Kera ko thaman jasto	As the banana plant is
Surāti rāni ko sarira.	So is Surati's body (figure).
Bārula ko kamar jasto	As the wasp's waist
Surāti rāni ko kamara.	So is Surati's.
Pipala ko pāta jasto	As the pipal tree's leaves
Surāti rāni ko onth,	So are Surati's lips.
Kankro ko bia jasto	As the cucumber's pips
Surāti rāni ko danita,	So are Surati's teeth.
Parewa ko ānkha jasto	As the pigeon's eyes
Surāti rāni ko ānkhi,	So are Surati's.
Sāru ko khutta jasto	As the mina bird's legs
Surāti rāni ko khuttao	So are Surati's.
Kukra ko phul jasto	As the fowl's eggs
Surāti rāni ko kurkucha,	So are Surati's heels.

Purānio jun jasto
  Surāti rāni ko lilāta,
Hiran māmio Surāti rāni ko
  lilāta.
Thore rupa dekhi dekhi
Mero man bhāigavo santokha.

As the full moon
So is Surati's forehead.
Behold O uncle Surati's fore-
  head.

Kiala.

(Sung by both Magars and Gurungs).

Tune No. 4 (see Music at end.)

Sāmjhi rahe maruni sāme mā, hoi {jaunla / rahunla} bhet.

Hā hā purube ko maruni pachhim ko mādale sāme mā hoi {jaunla / rahunla} bhet.

Jauna Bhana Je.

Tune No. 11 (see Music at end).

1. (*a*) Jāuna bhāna je, jāuna bhāna je, kamala ko phuli tipi liauna bhāna je
   (*b*) Jānna māma, jānna māma, pāyar mero dukhi ānchha, jānna māma.
2. (*a*) Jāuna bhāna je, jāuna bhāna je, pāvar lāune juta diunla, jāuna bhāna je
   (*b*) Jānna māma, jānna māma, sira mero dukhi ānchha, jānna māma.
3. (*a*) Jāuna bhāna je, jāuna bhāna je sira urne chhāta diunla, jāuna bhāna je
   (*b*) Jānna māma, jānna māma, ānkhi mero dukhi ānchha jānna māma.
4. (*a*) Jāuna bhāna je, jāuna bhāna je; ānkhi lāune chasma diunla, jāuna bhāna je.

Notes.—Bhāna je means bhānich.
For " kamala ko phuli lina " in line 1(*a*) the following can be substituted " bhāgini ko dudha lina."
" Laune " is contracted from " lagāune."

The following may be substituted at end :-

" Sămjhu bā le, samjhu bā le, āma ra bābu lai, samjhu bā le."

PHARSE KURA.

(1) Invert the syllables in a word :—

M bholi jānchhu

M libho chhujān.

(2) (Bipharse). Insert " bi " between each syllable :—

Timi bholi jānu parchha

Bitibimi bibhobili bijābinu biparbichha.

(3) (Chari). Insert " Chari " in place of " Bi " in (2).

(4) (Bhāi). Insert " Bhāi " before each word, and before the " Bhāi " repeat the word less the first consonant.

Notes.—" Chha " becomes " a."

If the word begins with a vowel it is usual to add " n " at the beginning.

E.g.—Timi kina āyau ?

Imi bhāi timi ina bhāi kina nāyau bhāi āyau ?

Daphtar mā kya kām chha ?

Aphtar mā bhāi daphtar mā e bhāi kya ām bhāi kām ā bhāi chha ?

CHARM (in Pharsekura).

Leju kum lerju rungsa nidai shibok lota pa sodar Suri hama ode ki chaba putam pu. Rasi khumra sira rumbhai nakha khumra nakar rumbhai khamu khumra timukh rumbhai hath khumra kakar rumbhai pau khumra dagun rumbhai Suri hama ode ki chaba putam pu. Leju kum lerju rundsa nidai shibok lotapa sumdar Suri hama ode ki chaba putam pu. Rugude ragude Mabrah Nuvish Risuhema nam gadir Vide apantut taun thumka tadun thumka, Suri hama ode ki chaba rugu nathokgor ki chaba putam pu.

Such a charm is supposed to frighten ghosts.

RIDDLES (Ahan).

Question.	*Answer.*
Hario chara ko dui pati puchhar ?	Duna.
Diuso sutchha rāti utchha ?	(*a*) Dāmlo. (*b*) Chamera.
Bina mukh ko petāro ?	Anda.
Gangani buriya ko thāplo māthi āgo ?	Chilum.
Kalo rah, sinko na sah ?	Ānkha.
Ghar tira āunda chilo, ban tira jāunda phusre ?	Ghara.
Bhairo khasro, bhitra masino ?	Kapās.
Āma bhanda chhori bokshi ?	Kursāni.
Siāno siāno rukh charne ko dukh ?	Sisno.
Ek rukh ko 12 hāngo, ek hāngo ko 30 pāt ?	Baras.
Yota buriya ko pet bhari hilo ?	Jānr.
Rāti hālchha, bhyāna nikālchha ?	Tāla.
Basda siāno hinda lāmo ?	Juko.
Lāmo lahari ko mitho phāl ?	Māchha.
Ek bhāi ko 2 bhāi ?	Mās.
,, ,, ,, 3 ,,	Odān.
,, ,, ,, 4 ,,	Thun.
Gangani buriya ko bhāt tyun mitho ?	Mauri.
Tāmi nal palāmi phal ?	Pāpa.
Yota doli mā sauota rāni ?	Tori.
Bhyāna uthera āmā le chhori lāi dhok garchha ?	Pāni sario ko

TWO GURKHALI STORIES.

Taken down verbatim from a Gurkha.

1. Yota shwāshni thyo, yota lognia thyo ; shwāshni le nātā khellaune thyo. To shwāshni le lognia lāi bhanio ban mā dauro jāndakheri tio mura lāi " dwāng " gari hāna, tab mero lognia ban mā gāyo bhani chāl paunla ; pheri āndakheri " dwāng " hāna tab mero lognia ban bāta āyo bhanunla ; titi bhanio ko thyo. Tab nāta lāi mitho mitho khulaune, burha lai kehi pani na dine.

Tab pandra mahina din mā tio burha lulo bhāyo khāna na pāyera ; to ek din māita jānchhu bhani bhanio ra gāyo. To usko sāla le bhanio " Bina, timi kina iti tutio ? Bimār bhāyo ki kina ho ? " bhandakeri " Ne, sāla, bimār bhāyo ko chhena ; dauro garne jānchhu timro didi le mura lāi dwāng gari hān bhanchha, tab hanera jānchhu ban ma, tab āndakheri pani hānera ānchhu " bhanera bhanio. " Bholi ta m pani jānchhu timi sita bina " bhanera. Arko din sāla ra bina ayo. To " daura garnu jau, bina " bhanera bhanio. Tab duita sāla bina gāyo ban mā. Tab ui mura lāi hānio bina le. Tab " timi dauro kātne jau, bina " bhanio " m ta ghari janchhu ; bimar hunchhu ki " bhanera. Tab ghar mā gāyo. Usko didi ko dusra lognia āyo ko rahechha ; kamal muni dhākio bhai āyo bhanera. Tab " didi, m lai jaru āyo " bhanio bhai le " tio kamal de, m urchhu." " Ne bhai kamal urne chhainna " bhanio " razai ur " bhanera, dina lagio. " Ne m ta kamal urchhu " thulo binti gario u le. Tab u le kāshi koshi gari gorash ko bhitra lukāidio dusra lognia lāi. Tab u pheri kamal urio " m ta niko bhayo, didi m gorash khānchhu " bhandakheri. " Hiju āsti tatāyera rākhia chha ye usindinchhu ra ye khālas " bhana lagio didi le. " Ne m ta chhutera khānchhu " bhanera bhanio bhai le yota thulo lati samātera. Ui gorash ko bhitra basālio ko thyo ; jahān u lukio ko thyo, u le hāna gāyo ; ui manchha lāi hānio pānch chha phera ; sārine dukhio bhāgio. Tab arko din bhāyo. To m didi ko bina ju ko sau barta lagaunchhu bhanera dhere pakāyo. Har ek manchha āla bhanera hukm sunaidio gaun ko kotwāl le ; to bhāt khāne ayo ; to tio manchha āyo ki āyena bhani talāsh gario-ayo ko thyo. Usi ko sāla pheri bhānse thyo, tab bāntna lāgio. Tab shikār bāntne gayo usko chheo pugio. Tab usi ko mukh mā hāth lāgio thyo. " Gorash ko bhitra mā chhuti māngne timi ho ki ? " hoina bhanera tauko halāyo. To u lai na diyera aru lāi diyo ; sabi chiz bāntdio u lai diyena. Tab usko didi le tithāyo " Bhāi bhāi " bhanera bhanio " pāri ko ko ho tio manchha, tio lāi pani de khāna lai " bhandakheri : " dinchhu, khānna bhanchha na pattāyo bhani, āja dekhis, didi " bhani bhanio. To bāntna gāyo, usko sāmne gāyo ; jo āgāri gari thyo use gari garera " gorash ko bhitra mā chhuti māngne timi ho ki ? " bhandakheri, tauko halāyo, m hoina bhanera. "Hir didi khānna banchha" bhani bhanio. Tab āphna didi le pāni barhna jānchhu bhani dhākar ko pen mā gāgro ko tala bhāt hālio ko thyo; tab ui bokera pāni jāna lāgia ko thyo. Usko bhāi āyo—"Ne timi āja jāna hunna, timro gara gaunro katio." Usko bhāi le dhākar khosio pāni mā āphi gāyo; to āile para gayera yahān kehi lāyo ko chha ki bhani herio, tab bhāt khāne chiz dekhio. Tab-han, bhāi tāinle ishāra gario ko rahechhas; pāni jāne bato ko tala māthi holas bhanera dhunga le hirkāunę gāyo; ek thāun mā basio ko rahechha, dhunga lāgio; tio dhunga lāgera mario. Tab pāni bāta ghar mā gāyo. "Lo, binaju, timro garo gaunro kati dio āja bātā" bhanera, usko sāla ghar ma gāyo. Sāta pandra din mā to herna āyo usko sāla le. Usko binaju besgari moto bhāyo ko thyo. Ab bātā thik hola bhanidio. Aune mā khub rāmro gari basithyo.

---

2. Yota lognia thyo, yota shwāshni thyo tisko. Lognia māl mades mā gāyo ghiu ko bhāri bokera. Shwāshni ghar mā basio, Tio swāshni le kya gario-kapal korera tiko lagāyera, pheri bāto mā basio taba yota manchha āyo; u le bhanio iti rāmro manchha kina bāto mā basio? bhandakheri. "Maile bhanio u le dinna, u le dio, m māndena; is sabab le m bāto mā basio." "Tapāin le kati bhanio" u le bhanio bhandakheri; "dheri bhandena, pachās rupeya bhanchhu." U le bhanio "tio pachās rupeya m dinchhu," tab dio pachās rupeya. "Aba kaile āunla" bhanio. "Parsi ānu" bhanio shwāshnile. "Achchha" bhanera u gāyo. Pher ārko din mā usi hālat mā shwāshni āyo bāto mā ui thāun mā. Tab ārko manchha ui din mā āyo aile thulo manwāla. U le bhanio "Ahā iti rāmro manchha kina isto mā basio ko chhas?" "Mero bhanio ko dinna, u le dio ko māndena, ye sabab le m basio ko chhu" "Achchha, kati ho t" bhanera bhanio manchha le bhandakheri—"assi rupeya ho" shwāshni le bhanio. "Achchha, m dinchhu assi rupeya" bhanera assi rupeya dio. "Kaile āunlā" bhanio tio le. "Bholi sānj ko ānu" shwāshni le bhanio. Pheri tio manchha pani gāyo. Rāt pario shwāshni le assi rupeya bokera ghar mā āyo. Pheri ārko din mā uste hālat sita basne gāyo. Āyo ārko manchha jhan thulo manwāla; pheri u le

bhanio " Kina isto basis, saphai ko manchha māilo dāilo mā kina basio." Tab u le bhanio " Maile bhanio ko ule dinna, u le dio ko m māndena " " Kati ho t" bhanio ; shwāshni le bhanio " Ek sau rupeya chhu " sau rupeya dio. Kaile āunla, bhanera—" bharai sānj mā ānu." Pheri shwāshni ghar mā gāyo, dhāl ra bhāt pakāyo u le. Yota lota mā setu rang dālio, yota mā hario, yota mā pahilo, yota mā rāto, lota mā rākhi rākhio ko thyo Jo pāila āyo " ghar bhitra chhas " bhanera bhanio. " Ghar bhitra chhu " bhanera bhanio shwāshni le. " Bhāt pākio kāyera jāunla." shwāshni le bhanio " nohānu parchha ; timi bas m nohaidinchhu." Tab lognia basio ; pheri shwāshni le khanāidio ek pati rāto ek pati khanāidio setu, ek pati khanāidio pahilo, ek pati khanāidio hario. Nohāidiyera āgo tāpnu parchha bhanio-pheri lognia āgo thāpne gāyo ; āgo tāpdakheri rang sukhio-jilimili dekhne pa lāgio. Tab pheri ārko manchha āyo—" T ghar bhitra chhas " bhanio. U le sanka mānio ārko lognia rahechha dar lagera bhāgio, anāz hālne bhakāri mā pasio. Pheri dusra ādmi bhitra gāyo. U lāi pani bhanio " Lo, bhāt pākio, khāyera jāna parchha ; nohānu parchha ; uslāi pani nohaidio, jilimili ko rang dāldio. " Āgo apne parchha " bhanio ; pheri āgo tāpdekheri rang sukhio ; ue tpani jilira mili bhāyo ko thyo. Pheri tistra manchha āyo, jole dhere rupeya diyo ko thyo. Us bela mā shwāshni le dhoka lagāyo. " Ghar bhitra chhas ? " bhanio ; shwāshni le bolina tio bela mā. Pheri jo basio ko thyo dusra manchha uslāi pani dar lagera u pani bhāgio, dāilo kuna ma lukio. Tisra manchha le lāt le hānio dhoka mā, dhoka phukālio. " Yahān pa chha iski bhai tokne " bhanera bhakari lāi hirkāidiyo. Tab u duita niskio jili ra mili, dar mānera bhagio. Pheri tisra manchha le bhanio " tio bokshini rahechha, m lai pani khānchha " u pani bhāgio, tin jana gāyo. Usko lognia ghāt bazār ma gāyo ko thyo ghiu ko bhāri bokera ; ab u pheri āyo. " Kati lio rupeya, burha " bhanio shwāshni le. " Jānde ā- le karza khāndakheri thik bhāyo " bhanio. Tab shwāshni le bhanio " M ghari mā basera iti rupeya jorio." Tisto gari bhanio shwāshni le.

ENLISTMENT QUESTIONS IN GURKHALI.

Note.—These are literal translations only and would probably have to be explained at greater length to a raw recruit.

Questions 1, 2 and 4 see Useful Sentences, 1, 2, 3 and 4.

English.	Khas.	Magar.	Gurung.
3. What is your religion, etc.?	3. Tero jhāt kya ho ? Kya (Magar) ho ? etc.	3. Nāku hi jhāt āle ? Nāku hi Magar le ?	3. Kia jhat to mo? To mhe mo ?
5. Have you ever been imprisoned, etc.?	5. T kaile jhelkhāna mā gayis ki gayenas ?	5. Nāku sien jhelkhāna ang nunga ki mā nunga ?	5. Ki kāyan jhelkhāna yai ki āya ?
6. Do you now belong, etc.?	6. Taile kehi aru paltan mā jāgir khanchhas ?	6. Nāku inang jāgir jele phoko paltan ang ?	6. Ki jāgir cham ki ācha ?
7. Have you ever served, etc.?	7. T kaile pani kehi paltan mā jāgir khāyis ki khāyenas ? Pāri ko paltan mā pani khāyenas ?	7. Nāku sien jāgir jia ki mā jia ? Pārlag o paltan ang jia ki mājia ?	7. Ki kāyan jāgir chei ki ācha ? Kian jwe (paltan) jāgir chei ki ācha ?
8. Have you truly stated, etc.	8. Tero aile bhania ko bāt sāncho sāncho ho ? (Tero sabi jāgir pura battāyis ?)	8. Nākung inang dichu sāncho sāncho āle ?	8. Ki tokan biba sānche mo are ?

ENGLISH.	KHAS.	MAGAR.	GURUNG.
9. Are you willing to be enrolled, etc.?	9. Hāmro paltan mā ānu lai (bharti hunnu lai) rāzi chhas ?	9. Kānung paltan ang bharti chanki rāzi le ki māle ?	9. Yo paltan ra bharti toba rāzi mo birāzi mo ?
10. Willing to go wherever ordered, etc.? and allow no caste usages, etc.?	10. Jahān Sirkār le tā lai jānu ko hukm dinchha, yāta zamin ko bato hos, yāta pāni ko bāto hos, t jālas ? Aru jo hukm Sirkār le dinchha, usto garnu parla. T bhanna bhāinas ki na ; mero jhāt isto ho, m ye kām gardena. Testi bhannu paune bhāyenas. Yo duite bāt mā rāzi chhas ?	10. Kulang Sirkar hukm yāle holang nungki parsale yāta jagolām yāta di o lam ; aru su hukm Sirkāra yāle sui hukm mānne parle. Nāku mā dele ki na ! ngo jhat iranchu le, gnā issa kam mā zātle. Horānchu deki mā dinle. Hossa nis bāt ang rāzi le ?	10. Kana Sirkāra ji yābe hukma pimo yāl pardim. Zamin klo yāl pardilena yāl pardim ; khola kyya yāl pardilem. Sirkari hukma kagli pimo, chagli lāl pardim. Ki cha bila ta nge jhāta chagli mo, gna chu le ala. Cha bila ayu. Chu taha gniola rāzi mo āre ?
11. Permanently transferred, etc.?	11. Jo t kehi aru paltan mā jāna ko hukm paulas, t jālas ? M yo paltan lāi mātrai bharti bhāyo bhane bhayenas ; is ma rāzi chhas ?	11. Jo nāku hukm dinle phoko paltan ang nungā deniking, nungki parsale. Ngā issa paltan mātrai bharti chāna dena mā dele ; hossang rāzi le?	11. Ki kābe paltanri yābe hukma tamo yal pardim. Gnā chu paltanri bharti tāi aru klo ri āta ; cha bila ayu. Chu taha rāzi mo āre ?

12. Vaccinated, etc.	12. Tero hāth khopāunu lāi rāzi chhas ?	12. Nākung hut khopdike rāzi le ?	12. Ki yo khopobe razi mo āre ?
13. Conditions of service, etc.	13. Hamro paltan mā chār baras rahnu parla. Chār baras samma aphnu nām katne bhāyenas. Chār baras pura bhāyera tab āphnu khushi le tero nām kātisaklas. Siwai larāi ko bela bhāya yāta larāi hunnu lai kehi khabar chha, testo bela mā nām kātnu paune bhāyenas. Aru jo tero kampani mā manchheharu kamti bhāyo, tab pani nām kātnu paune bhāyenas. Aru nām kātnu bhanda paile dui mahina mā khabar dinu chainchha m nām kātchhu bhanera. Ye sabai bāt mā rāzi chhas ?	13. Kānung paltan ang buli baras rungki parsale. Buli barasara mino ārmin chiāke mā dinle. Buli baras pura chaniking mino kushi ārmin chiāke hegle. So larāi chanche belang yāta larāi chanki khabar le hossa belang armin chiāke mā dinle. Aru jo nākung kampani ang bharmi thore le, tab pani ārmin chiāke mā dinle. Jo armin chiāke guile nis mahina agāri khabar yaki parsale gnā ārmin chiāk deniking Issa pata bāt ang rāzi le ?	13. Ngio paltanare plidi til pardim. Plidi samma āphi mi tol āyu. Plidi pura tā bakya āpni khushi mi tol yum. Larāi wākht taji ki larāi khabar kābe wākhta mi tol āyu Kia kampaniri mhi kamti tāi bisya mi tol ayu. Aru mi tol bhanda mahina ngiola bidige khabar pāl pardim. Chu jama tahari rāzi mo āre.

COURT MARTIAL QUESTIONS IN GURKHALI

ENGLISH.	GURKHALI.
1. Do you object to be tried by me as President, or by any of the officers whose names you have heard read over ?	1. (Literally). Timi lai mā Kort ko President bhāyo ko aru koi Afsar Sāhibharu ko nām paria ko sunio wārdat ko fasila garne mā kehi uzar chha ? (Explanatory if not understood). Mā Kort ko President bhāyo ko chhu. Ini sāhibharu junko nām maile aile paria, Kort mā basne sāhibharu, chhan. Timi sabi lai rāzi chhau ki chhenau ?
2. What is your objection to (Captain X) ?	2. (Captain X Sāhib) ko bāra mā timro kya uzar chha ?
3. Do you object to (Lt. Z) as interpreter ?	3. Timi (Lt. Z Sāhib) do bhāshe huna mā rāzi chhau ki chhenau ?
4. Accused No. , (Rfn.) 1/13th G.R., is charged with in that he, at A on etc.	4. Sazawār No. , (Rfn.) 1/13th G.R. ko māthi kasur lagāi gayo jasma usle A mā tārikh , etc.
5. Are you guilty or not guilty of the (first) charge against you which you have heard read ?	5. Timi (pailo) kasur mā, jo timi le paria ko sunio aru jo timro māthi lagāya ko chha, kasurwar chhau ki chhenau ?
6. (On plea of guilty) Do you wish to make anystatement in mitigation of punishment ?	6. Timi le kasur gario ko mā kehi bāyān garnu chha (ki isto bhayo ko thio bhanera to mālai dherai saza na hawas) ?

ENGLISH.	GURKHALI.
7. (On plea of guilty) Do you wish to call witnesses as to character ?	7. Timi āphnu chāl chalan ko {bāra / nimte} ma koi gawāhi (bolaunu) māngda chhau ?
8. Do you wish to cross-examine this witness ?	8. Timi ye gawāhi ko kehi kura kātna māngchhau? (This means, Do you find fault with any statement of his ?) Do you wish to question him ? would be :—Timi ye gawāhi sitha kehi sawāl (or kura) sodhna māngchhau ?
9. Do you intend to call any witnesses in your defence ?	9. Timi āphno bachao ko lagi koi gawāhi (bolaunu) mang-chhau ?
10. Is he a witness as to character only ?	10. Tyo gawāhi chāl chalan ko wāste mātre ho ?
11. Have you anything to say in your defence ?	11. Timi āphnu bachao ko lagi kehi bhannu chha ?
12. Do you wish to address the Court ?	12. Timi kehi kura kort sang bhannu māng chhau ?

USEFUL

English.	Khaskura.
1. What is your name ?	1. Timro nām kya ho ?
2. What is your father's name ?	2. Timro bābu ko nām kya ho ?
3. Where is your home ?	3. Timro ghăr kahān ho ?
4. What is your village ?	4. Timro gāun [ko nām] kya ho ?
5. How old are you ?	5. Timi kati bărăs bhāyau ?
6. Who enlisted you ?	6. Timilāi ko le bhărti gărio ?
7. How did he persuade you ?	7. Ule timilāi kăsari phăkayo? Ule timilāi kya kya bhănera phăkayo ?
8. Is your *father* alive ?	8. Timro *bābu* jiundai chha ki mărio ?
9. How many *brothers* have you ?	9. Timro *dāju bhāi* kăti chhăn ?
10. Are you married ?	10. Timi biāh găriau ki [gărinaun] ?
11. How many children have you ?	11. Timro chhoro chhori kăti chhān ?
12. Where are you going to ?	12. Timi kătă jānchhau ?
13. Where have you come from ?	13. Timi kahān bātā ayau ?
14. Which is the way to *Bombay ?*	14. *Bombay* jāne bāto ko ho ?
15. Come here ! Go away !	15. Yeta au (or Aijau) ! Jau !
16. What is the price of this ?	16. Yesko dām kăti chhă ?
17. Do you know how to *dance?*	17. Timi *nāchnu* jānda chhau ?
18. Can you *sing ?*	18. Timi *gānu* (or *git jhignu*) săkchhau ?
19. Sit down ! Stand up !	19. Bas ! Uth ! (or Thāro ho !)
20. Don't move ! Don't talk !	20. Na hil ! Na bhăn !
21. Have you eaten *bhat* or not ?	21. Timi *bhāt* kāyan ki khāyenau ?
22. Are you hungry ?	22. Timi lāi bhukh lăgio ?
23. Are you tired ?	23. Timi thākiau ?
24. What's the matter ?	24. Kya bhāyo ?
25. Does your *head* ache ?	25. Timro *kăpāl* dukhchha ?
26 Lift up your feet !	26. Timro khutta uthau !

SENTENCES.

MAGARKURA.	GURUNGKURA.
1. Nākung āmin hi ālé ?	1. Ki mhī to mo ?
2. Nākung bua o āmin hi ālé?	2. Ki āba mhi to mo ?
3. Nākung im kulăk lé ?	3. Ki thi kănă mo ?
4. Nākung lānga [o amin] hi alé ?	4. Ki masa to mo ?
5. Nāku kūrik bărăs chhana ?	5. Ki kăti bărăs tai ?
6. Nākuke su bhărti zāta ?	6. Ki kāwe bhărti lai ?
7. Hossa nākuke kuncho hūma ?	7. Chă ki lai kaimiu whai ?
Hoosa nākuke hi hi déniking hūma ?	Chă ki lai to to bīmoro whai ?
8. Nākung *bua* le ki sia ?	8. Ki *āba* sobăn mo si ?
9. Nākung *dāze bhuye* kūrik lé ?	9. Kia *dāze bhāya* kăti mo ?
10. Nāku biah zāta ki mā zāta?	10. Ki biah lai āla ?
11. Nākung jūjāko kurik lé ?	11. Ki păsipăsi kăti mo ?
12. Nāku kulăk nungle (or ănle) ?	12. Ki kănă yāmo ?
13. Nāku kulăki ra ?	13. Ki kănă piti koi ?
14. *Bombay* nungki lām su ălé ? or (kulăk lé).	14. *Bombay* yāge kiyā kāb chh (or mo).
15. Ilăk rāna ; āna (or nungo).	15. Chui ko ; yăd.
16. Issa dām kurik lé ?	16. Chu sé kăti mo ?
17. Nāku *shiaki* wārlé ki mā wārlé ?	17. Ki *shiem* rām ără ?
18. Nāku *lingki* (or *ling doki*) heglé ?	18. Ki *gwee preel* kām ākān ?
19. Mūni ! So ! (or Soni).	19. Tid ! Réd !
20. Nā whéka ! Nā déni (or Nā cheka).	20. Ā lăd ! Ā bid !
21. Nāku *cho* jia ki mā jia ?	21. Ki *koin* ché āchă ?
22. Nāku tukré sia ?	22. Ki po cre ăcré ?
23. Nāku munga ?	23. Ki nārai ānară ?
24. Hi chhāna ?	24. To tai ?
25. Nākung *tālu* bīkle ?	25. Kia *kără* nāmo ?
26. Nākung hil sotāko ?	26. Kia păle tăd !

	English.		Khaskura.
27.	Is it going to rain? Dunno!	27.	Pāni āla ki? Kunni!
28.	I am going now. When are you going?	28.	M āile jānchhu. Timi kāile jāula?
29.	What are you doing? Are you hurt?	29.	Timi kya gărnu lăgya ko chhau? Timi lăi chort lăgio ki?
30.	Who are those two men?	30.	Uni dŭite mănchhe ko ho?
31.	Is it a boy or a girl?	31.	Chhoro ho ki chhori?
32.	Go after your work is done.	32.	Timro kām săkio păchhi jau.
33.	Bring that; take away this Give it to me.	33.	Tio liau; yeslai lejau. M lăi de.
34.	What work is there *tomorrow morning?*	34.	*Bholibhyāna* kya kām chha?
35.	It is hot to-day.	35.	Āja ghām (or niāna) bhāyo.
36.	Hold the *rifle* firmly.	36.	*Rufal* bălio sămăt (sămău).
37.	What crops do you grow at your home?	37.	Timro ghăr mā kya kya khêti ropchha?
38.	How many days do you reach your home in?	38.	Timro ghăr mā kati din mā pugchha?
39.	What did you do on the way from A?	39.	A bāta āndăkheri timi kia kia găriau?
40.	Put on your coat. Take off your clothes.	40.	Kot lăgau. Lūga jhig.
41.	What is the time?	41.	Kati băjio (Kati baje chhă)?
42.	Go to hospital and say you are ill.	42.	Hospităl mā gayera m bimār chhu bhănera bhăn.
43.	I am thirsty. It was cold yesterday.	43.	M lai tirka lāgio. Hiju jāru bhāyo ko thyo.
44.		44.	
45.		45.	
46.		46.	
47.		47.	
48.		48.	
49.		49.	
50.		50.	

An expression often used by Gurungs is adding " mle " to the here," they would say " Chui kom le." This is also used when

Note.—The words *italicized* are the translation of the words translations. Words in square brackets may be added to make

MAGARKURA.	GURUNGKURA.
27 Nămăs āré ki mā āré? Chena.	27. Nā um ki āyu? Tosi!
28. Gnā chāhn nungle. Nāku sien ānunge?	28. Gna tokăn yāmo. Ki kāyan yām?
29. Nāku hi zātle? Nākuke chort lésa ki?	29. Ki to lă? Ki lai chort lédi ālédi?
30. Hossa nis bhŭrmi sū alé?	30. Chă mhi niōla kāwe mo?
31. Lenză mīja lé ki māja lé?	31. Chāme mo ki chā mo?
32. Nākung kām zātnīkīng ănă.	32. Kia ké kaimoro yād.
33. Hossa rāko; issa ālo. Gnā ke yo (yāni).	33. Chă pāi; chu bhoyād. Gna lai pin.
34. *Pihin goṙak* hi kām lé?	34. *Păna năkă* to ké mo?
35. Chining kān mole.	35. Tiën nīlé pré mo.
36. *Rufal* shiemo jimna (go.)	36. *Rufal* clénlé kat.
37. Nākung īm ăng hi kheti khāsle?	37. Kia thi ră to to plūm?
38. Nākung īm ăng kurik din tāle (tākle)?	38 Ki thī ră kăti din ră phem.
39. A lākin rā nāku hi hi zātā.	39. A inle kaimora to to ké lai?
40. Nākung kot bīlni. Bărin dōni.	40. Kia kot kéd. Khwai plid?
41. Kūrik ngā	41. Kăti gniyé?
42. Hospitāl ăng nungniking ngā chāhmole déni.	42 Hospitāl yāmoro ngā nai bīd.
43. Ngā lāi tirko. Tisini jum molia.	43 Ngā lai kiu pi. Tela kundi.
44.	44.
45.	45
46.	46.
47.	47.
48.	48.
49.	49.
50.	50.

end of a sentence. *E.g.*, instead of saying "Chui ko" for "Come talking in Khaskura. "Ayo" would become "Ayom le."

italicized in English. The words in brackets are alternative the sense clearer.

No. 1. GURKHALI SONG.

"Resami Nāni."

"I am much indebted to Mr. Reid the Bandmaster of my battalion, for the trouble and care he has taken in arranging this music."

March time (𝅗𝅥=120).

No. 2. GURKHALI SONG.

"Jāndā Jāndā Lahuria."

March time (♩= 120).

Nau - tu na, mā bā - to bi - ra - yo.
ff
1. Kā - ti khā-ne Su - pā - ri lai
2. Jan - chhu bha-ne San - go - ti lai
D.S.
Pho - ṛi Khā - ne hoi - na.
Cho - ṛi Jā - ne bhaye - na.
D.S.

No. 3. GURKHALI SONG.

"MĀSĀNI."

START SLOW (♩=80), GRADUALLY FASTER, FINISH ALLEGRO (♩=132).

No. 4. **GURKHALI SONG.**

"KHIALI."

MODERETTO (♩= 112).

No. 5. GURKHALI SONG.

"SALI JIU."

Jin, Ne-pal - - a - i kas - - - - - to
Jiu, dharam - - a - i sas - - - - - to
chha, Ne - pal- ai kas - - to chha.
chha, dhar - ma - i sas - - to chha.

No. 6. GURKHALI SONG.

"KRISHNA CHALLITRA."

ANDANTE (♩.=66)

la - - gio Ho Lan-ka pa - ti
Ped.
Ra - - waue le. Eh, ho
Ped.
ki-ta ha-ri la - gi - yo, Ba-su-ki de-wa

le Eh, ho ki-ta ha-ri
Rall last time Rall and only.
D.C.
la gi-yo Ba-su-ki de-wa-le.
D.C.
D.C.

No. 7. GURKHALI SONG.

"Sohani Barai" (Lali Maya).

Allegretto (♩=96).

No. 8. GURKHALI SONG.

"JHAMRIA."

MARCH TIME.

No. 9. GURKHALI SONG.

"Narain Jhāmria."

Tempo de March (♩=120).

Mäi - ta la - gio Jnl - fi kia - le ko - - - ru
dan - lat thi - o Joi bi na ma - ri - - - o
CHORUS.
dharma le deo - re. Pi - ra - - thi launla hai ki
dh. rma le deo - re.
ff
D.C.
Simbal dă li ba - - - si dharma le deo - re.
D.C
ff

No. 10. **GURKHALI SONG.**

"KARELI JHĀMRIA."

ALLEGRETTO (♩=96).

Jhia - ma mā-yā lo. Bha - lya la - gio
p 1st f 2nd
Iu - ria chil le Po - thi la - gio Siyāl le.
D.S.
Gorkha li lai u - pai la gio, Sar-kar-a ko rail le.
D.S.
ff
D.S.

No. 11. GURKHALI SONG.

"Jāonā Bhānije."

Andantino (𝅗𝅥 = 80).

He Jan-na ma-a-mai, ma-tä
ff
mf
Jän-na mä-a-mai he Pä-isu me-ro
mf
D.S.
1st & 3rd times.
2nd time.
du-khi än-chha Jän-nä ma-a-mai. mai. Eh,
D.S.
p
p
D.S.

No. 12. GURKHALI SONG.

"Āshish."

Andantino (♩. = 80)

bar - hio. Dhan - a - ra darbe

Ga - ie - - got - ha bar - hio ho.
f

No. 13. GURKHALI SONG.

"Sainlā Dāi."

Tempo de March (♩. = 120).

Chip-lo bā-to Gai ko bā-chho larkio,
Ha jar si-ta bhet na hunda man to me-ro
Fine.
1st time.
2nd time.
Last time.
Dharkio.
Dharkia, Sain, Dharkio.
Fine.

No. 14. GURKHALI SONG.

"RAMAYAN."

ANDANTE (♩=60).

pa-ā - - - chi Hā - mu ā ye
Ghar - a - ko rakh wa - le Bā . mn
ā - - ye Ghara - ko rakh wa le.
D.C.
D.C.
D.C.